Body Matters

Body Matters:
Essays on the Sociology of the Body

Edited by

Sue Scott and David Morgan

Taylor & Francis
Taylor & Francis Group

LONDON AND NEW YORK

First published 1993
By The Falmer Press
Reprinted 1996
Reprinted 2004
By Taylor & Francis
11 New Fetter Lane, London EC4P 4EE

Transferred to Digital Printing 2004

**A Catalogue Record for this book is available from the British
Library**

ISBN 1 85000 942 2
ISBN 1 85000 943 0 pbk

**Library of Congress Cataloging-in-Publication Data
are available on request**

Typeset in 9.5/11pt Bembo
by Graphicraft Typesetters Ltd., Hong Kong

Printed and bound by Antony Rowe Ltd, Eastbourne

Contents

Contents

Acknowledgments

Many thanks to Jacinta Evans at Falmer for her long-suffering patience and support. We should also like to thank all those who participated in the original symposium out of which this collection developed and Sarah Dimmelow and Pat Robinson for typing sections of the final manuscript.

Introduction

If this volume were to have a sub-title it might appropriately be 'Directions through Diversity', a phrase which reflects the diversity of existing developments in what has come to be called 'the sociology of the body' *and* the diversity of the substantive topics and empirical researches covered by the essays in this volume. Such a sub-title would also indicate, as do the papers collected here, the potential of the sociology of the body for indicating directions in which sociology and social theory might move in the future. The coherence of this collection lies in its focus on the embodiment of social actors, and the relationship between this embodiment and the problems of both everyday life *and* of sociological theorizing.

While the substantive topics represented here range through dance, men and masculinity, marital and sexual counselling, prostitution, body-building, representations of lesbianism and the management of a child's body, clear links and common threads are to be found running through these chapters. One such theme is to do with the social construction of the body, the various ways in which the different aspects of the body are given new and varied significances, thus undermining or calling into question what might conventionally be understood as natural. Another theme is to do with the social control and regulation of the body, with the complex interplays between societal regulation and individual self-surveillance. These themes will be found, in different mixes, running through all these papers. But they are clearly two interrelated and interdependent processes. To construct some bodily feature or process, to describe it in a certain way or to lay social emphasis on some aspect of the body is, in some measure, to exercise control or constraint. This is most obvious, for example, in cases of the gendered body or the healthy body. Similarly, to regulate or to exercise control over the body or bodies is to see these bodies in a particular way and to privilege certain understandings or constructions as against others. Bureaucratic control of bodies in large organizations, for example, also implicitly states the kind of bodily representations and presentations that are appropriate.

Other, more specific, themes may also be found running through these chapters. These are to do with, for example, gender and sexuality, health and illness, nature and culture. It seemed to us that there was little point in attempting to group these papers under rather artificial or forced headings. Rather, each paper may be seen as throwing light on all or most of these themes in different combinations thus, implicitly, throwing light on issues raised in some other paper or papers. The aim of this collection, therefore, is not to present a comprehensive 'sociology of the body' (indeed, we have some reservations about the over-development of such a specialized area), but rather to show how sociological research in a wide range of sub-areas might be informed by, and contribute to, a more embodied sociology as a whole. It is unlikely that any of the writers represented in this collection would describe themselves as 'sociologists of the body'; they come from and continue to work in a range of different specialisms. Nevertheless, there was a growing feeling among the contributors that we had much to learn from each other and that these overlaps in interest in concern were not artificial or forced.

In 'Bodies in a Social Landscape', the editors develop some of these themes, highlighting the growth of interest in bodily matters within sociology and other disciplines, and outlining some of the main influences: feminism, the sociology of health and illness and cultural studies. Particular emphasis is given to the contributions from feminism and from the sociology of health and illness and the ways in which these have called into question conventional distinctions between biology and culture. Further attention is given to issues of theory, especially to the way in which mainstream sociological theory might be enhanced by a more embodied approach, and, conversely, how existing themes in sociological theory might illuminate newer concerns with the sociology of the body.

The first substantive paper in the book, 'With My Body I Thee Worship', serves as a particularly apt illustration of the way in which a well-established area within sociology may be enhanced by a more bodily-aware treatment. Despite the words from the Marriage Service which give the paper its title, sociological treatments of marriage have been remarkably disembodied. We have had much about marriage as a relationship and, increasingly, about the economic aspects of marital life, but relatively little about sexuality and the body within marriage. Yet, as Clark argues, sexuality has become a major element in the way in which the marital relationship is constructed and understood. Drawing upon his work on Relate, he shows how particular discourses around sexuality become woven into understandings of marriage as a relationship and of marital problems.

Clark's paper shows clearly that Foucault has been one of the major influences in the developing sociology of the body. Foucault's concerns were very much to do with control and discipline and these themes are very much to the fore in considering the life and work of a modern dancer. This is the subject of Sherlock's paper, where she shows that a particular art form, conventionally understood in terms of timeless aesthetic categories, can be seen as reflecting, displaying and deploying social meanings at all kinds of levels and in all kinds of ways. The dancer's body, which we are encouraged to appreciate in terms of values such as grace, control and discipline, may also be seen as the site of a host of social processes and cultural influences. These include not merely what the particular dance is supposed to represent or may be read as representing terms of gender, nationality or ethnicity but also the routine understandings of high culture, the place of dance within these and the backstage experiences and careers of the dancers and choreographers involved in such productions. Yet, further, Sherlock's paper argues that dance is not simply to be seen at the receiving end of social and cultural processes but as an active role in shaping wider social processes and perceptions.

There are clear affinities between Sherlock's paper and the work of Mansfield and McCann on female body builders. For example, in the case of dance, the male performer is often seen as deviant, as someone whose gender and sexuality is open to question. In the case of body building women, issues of femininity are at stake. Both deal with sub-worlds, centrally concerned with the body and its deployment, with their specialized languages and understandings, and their own, often competing and contradictory, understandings of what is correct or natural. Both deal with aspects of public presentation and representation in a context of social change. Both papers clearly demonstrate the contribution that recent developments in theory may make to the study of embodied social situations and the way in which such analyses may themselves enhance cultural theory. Mansfield and McCann show how this apparently most embodied of activities is yet open to critical exploration, highlighting the ironies and paradoxes which many have come to identify with the post-modern condition.

Themes of gender are also very much to the fore in Morgan's paper dealing with men, masculinities and bodies. In much recent discussion, the focus has been on women and women's bodies and this might lead to the superficial conclusion that men are less embodied than women. However, Morgan argues that themes of embodiment and disembodiment work and combine in different ways for women and men and that this itself is enough to call into question many well-established oppositions such as those between nature and culture, body and mind, public and private and so on. Morgan argues for an exploration of the different sites where men's embodiment might seem particularly appropriate and for an examination of the complex ways in which gender, bodies and power work through different masculinities. While some sites are constructed as being more embodied than others, themes of embodiment run through all aspects of men's lives.

Gender, power and sexuality are obviously very much to the fore in Edwards' discussion of prostitution. As the popular expression 'the oldest profession' suggests, prostitution is often very prone to ahistorical analyses focusing upon assumptions about men's sexuality and male 'needs'. But, as Edwards argues in the course of critical survey of some of the theories of female prostitution, it is precisely these understandings of needs, desires and sexualities which must be subjected to historically based analysis. Issues of power, male power, are clearly centrally involved but this should not be seen as the straightforward cultural manifestation of a biologically based urge. Further, power is never total or absolute and in her survey of prostitute women, Edwards shows the various ways in which these women preserve a sense of self and personal identity in the context of such a clear site of patriarchal power. Here, paradoxically, what may conventionally be described as 'perversions' may be less damaging to a woman's sense of self than so-called 'straight' sex.

Different aspects of sexuality and gender are covered in Waterhouse's treatment of the lesbian body. In a cultural analysis and a development of the, by now familiar, theme of the way in which lesbianism has been socially and historically constructed, Waterhouse considers the various ways in which the lesbian body has been presented or misrepresented in heterosexist writing and images. As with several of the other papers, Waterhouse reminds us that constructions and deployments of the body are not simply to be viewed as the product of culture or history. Persons defined or defining themselves as lesbians are actively involved in shaping, challenging or negotiating with these constructions. In these processes, issues of the body and its deployment are very much to the fore.

The final paper illustrates another facet of the recent developments of an embodied sociology; their potentiality for illuminating aspects of the routine or the commonplace in everyday life. In her paper, Murcott links issues of the body with another relatively recent area of detailed sociological enquiry, that dealing with food and eating, linked on this occasion with the management of children and their bodies. In particular, the focus is on the process of defecation. As any parent knows, such considerations loom large in the everyday routines of child-rearing, although we would scarcely know this from reading works on the sociology of the family. We are also returning very much to issues of control, for in this most intimate area of bodily management aspects of societal control and individual self meet on the site of the human body.

This collection is the outcome of a continuous, and possibly long drawn-out, process. Following an original idea, emerging out of several discussions between the joint editors, a workshop was organized to which several of the present contributors were invited. Outlines were circulated in advance and formed the basis of a discussion which included suggestions for the fuller, paper-length, versions. During the intervening period some of the contributors to the original discussion dropped out and others joined the project. The list of topics covered also varied to some extent from what was originally proposed. At the same time, original contributions were rewritten and, where necessary, updated in order to take account of new developments. The symposium in September 1988 was, therefore, only a part of the process of preparing this volume just as this volume should be seen as only a part of the continuing set of exchanges between research and theory around the sociology of the body. The fact that this final book is not quite the one we started out with is not, therefore, a matter for regret. Rather it is a reflection of the vitality and the fluidity of this growing area of concern and we hope that the readers will share in the excitement we felt then, and continue to feel now, of looking at new themes and at old and familiar themes in new ways.

Sue Scott
David Morgan
Manchester May 1992.

Chapter 1

Bodies in a Social Landscape

D.H.J. Morgan and Sue Scott

When we first planned this essay we began in the conventional manner, namely noting the relative absence of work on the body within sociology. In the short period of time between this very early draft and the present version, matters have changed dramatically. The body is very much on the sociological agenda, and references to it are increasingly appearing in a variety of areas. Two main questions, therefore, present themselves for consideration:

(i) Why was there an apparent absence of sociological interest in the body until very recently?

(ii) Why has there been this recent development of interest in the subject, an interest by no means confined to sociological writings but to be found across a wide spectrum of social science disciplines?

There would seem to be little need, at this stage, to document the earlier relative lack of a sociological treatment of bodily matters, or indeed of a sociology informed by bodily considerations. We do not need a detailed analysis of the contents of text books or learned journals to make the point that overt references to the body or the sociology of the body were, certainly prior to the publication of Turner's influential book (Turner, 1984), very infrequent indeed. Whether there were covert or more submerged sociologies of the body is a more complex matter and one to which we shall be returning later in this chapter.

In attempting to account for this relative lack of interest in the body within sociology until fairly recently, several possible answers suggest themselves or have already been suggested. It may be noted, in passing, that this absence has been shared by a variety of other topics, touching on some fundamental human activities and attributes including sexuality, violence, the emotions and war. Here too, prior absences have to some extent been rectified. Interestingly, these other relatively neglected areas also have strong bodily connotations and there may be similar reasons for the relatively infrequent treatments of these issues within sociology. We may note, for example, that much sociological research is located within universities or polytechnics, institutions traditionally associated with the cultivation of the mind and with the deployment of reason. We may also note a kind of Puritan legacy which, even now, places some inhibitions on writing or lecturing about sexuality, defecation, nudity and bodily display or decay, for example. Certainly the subject of sociology, still seen by some as needing to establish its credentials as a serious discipline, might exhibit some wariness in whole-heartedly embracing topics too readily open to the fabricated outrage of some sections of the popular press.

However, there would seem to be two deeper, and interrelated, reasons for the relative neglect of bodily matters within sociology. The first is to do with the spectre of sociobiology. Much sociology, in attempting to establish its credentials, begins with a kind of distancing exercise, a statement of what it is *not* about. Classically, Durkheim's *Suicide* provides the model here. *Homo Sociologicus* is clearly distinguished from alternative versions relying upon biological processes, instincts and all other forms of reductionism or essentialism. A central example, to be discussed at length later in this chapter, would be the conventionally understood distinction between sex and gender where the former is taken to refer to biological differences, while the latter, the real subject matter of the discipline it is claimed, signifies socially or culturally constructed, accentuated or recognized differences. At a first glance, the body would seem to fall very much on the biological side of the biology/culture divide, such that any mention of the body might carry with it connotations of some kind of essentialism.

It is, however, one of the objects of this chapter and indeed of the volume as a whole, to cast a critical light on the biology/culture distinction. This discussion will be taken further at a later stage in this chapter, but, for the time being, it is argued that we are seeking to question this distinction and associated distinctions such as those between gender and sex, and to make the biological an object of sociological enquiry and theorizing, as topic rather than resource. This is not, therefore, to open the door to biological reductionism but rather to develop frameworks of understanding that call into question all forms of reductionism.

There is one final possible reason, again one which will be dealt with at greater length later, and that is to do with the particular rational and modern project that has characterized the mainstream of sociology from its earliest days. Rationalities have tended to open up distinctions between the ordered, the controlled and the abstract on the one hand, and the disordered, the uncontrolled and the concrete on the other, with the relegation of the body and bodily matters to the latter, implicitly discredited, set of categories. The project of modernity, closely associated with these rationalities, also seeks to emphasize the triumph of culture over nature. Bodily matters either become subservient to, or objects for, rational modernity, or linger as a source of embarrassment or awkwardness in the wings of a modern social order.

In the light of these, and doubtless other, reasons for the apparent absence of any treatment of bodily matters within sociology, how has the change come about? There can be little doubt that there has been a remarkable growth of interest in these topics in the space of a few years. This is not the place to provide complete bibliographic documentation but extensive references are provided in the two theoretical surveys by Frank (Frank, 1990, 1991) and in the conclusion of the three volumes with a historical and comparative emphasis (edited by Feher, 1989, with Naddaff and Tazi). A recent annual conference of the British Sociological Association, dealing with the topic of *Health and Society* (Scott *et al.*, 1992) included a large number of papers directly or indirectly dealing with bodily matters and containing extensive references to Armstrong, Foucault, Turner and others. A conference on a similar topic in 1976 produced few, if any, references to the body as a topic for sociological analysis. A couple of quotations may perhaps give the flavour of the present situation:

> Bodies are in, in academic as well as in popular culture. (Frank, 1990: 131)

> Everything is related to the body, as if it had just been discovered after being long forgotten; body image, body language, body-consciousness, liberation of the body are the passwords. (Starobinski, 1989:353)

Much of the credit for this growth of interest in the body, at least in English-speaking countries, must go to Bryan Turner. Although by no means the first in the field, Turner's *The Body and Society* (1984) may be viewed as setting the agenda for a wide range of research and theoretical work. It has certainly formed an important point of departure for this present volume, although our book should not be taken as providing an extended exegesis or critique of Turner's work. We have, for example, found value in Turner's discussion of the distinctions between and the relations between being and having a body, and certainly the four R's of Reproduction, Representation, Regulation and Restraint have provided a useful set of considerations in informing both this chapter and individual papers. Another way in which Turner's work has been particularly stimulating is in his attempt to link two hitherto unconnected sub-areas, namely the sociology of religion and the sociology of health and illness.

Why then, has there been this dramatic growth of interest, one symbolized rather than caused by Turner's book? One answer might be to question the assumption that bodily matters have been so neglected in the past. Turner, for example, has argued that an interest in bodily matters has always formed a part of the classic tradition of social anthropology (Turner, 1991) so that part of the explanation may lie in the rivalry between two disciplines. More extensively, in the same article Turner has argued for a hidden history of the body in Western thought, beginning with Neitzsche. While such thinkers have, for the most part, remained on the fringes of sociological enquiry, this would seem to argue for an ignoring of bodily questions raised elsewhere rather than a straightforward failure to address such topics. Indeed, as will be suggested later on, bodily issues have their own history, partly secret but sometimes overt, within sociology itself, even where they may not necessarily be signalled as such. There are the more obvious thinkers such as Elias and Goffman, but it does not take a great deal of rewriting or reassessment to claim Durkheim for the sociology of the body. Some more extensive work may be required to recover bodily themes from Marx or Weber, but the task is not inherently absurd. Indeed, as we shall see later, Weber's discussion of bureaucracy and rationality inevitably raises questions of embodiment.

Hence, perhaps the question should be reformulated to ask why has there been a growth of *explicitly* bodily-orientated sociology in recent years? It is possible to provide lists of reasons and influences. Frank, for example, gives pride of place to the development of various feminist theories and critiques mentioning, secondly, the massive and widespread influence of Michel Foucault. The third set of influences is, interestingly in the light of earlier comments, what he calls 'the contradictory impulses of modernity' (Frank, 1990:132). One aspect of modernity, the more positivist side, would tend to detach and remove the body as a solid and separate object. Another aspect of modernity, however, one that stresses fragmentation and constant flux, renders the body less stable, more mysterious. He sees the contradictory features of modernity (although others might find overlaps with post-modernity in the stress on flux and impermanence) as constituting a third set of influences being brought to bear on the growth of interest in the sociology of the body.

We would certainly agree in giving pride of place to a plurality of feminisms; their influence is discussed later in this chapter as well as being apparent in all of the individual papers to some degree or another. This is not simply a question of an identifiable set of topics that have been central concerns for feminists. Rather, it is the growing realization that a focus on the body presents a reformulation of the sociological project. A particularly strong version of this argument is provided by Game:

> My concern has been to argue that the body provides the basis for a different conception of knowledge: we know with our bodies. In this regard, the authentics of experience might be reclaimed; if there is any truth, it is the truth of the body. (Game, 1991:192)

In place of Frank's emphasis upon modernism, we should give greater emphasis to post-modernism, realizing that the boundaries between the two are hotly contested and often highly ambiguous. Turner certainly sees some affinities between the concerns of post-modernism and the sociology of the body and he is not alone in this (Turner, 1991). We may see affinities between the two developments, and the same set of impulses that conclude that the human body is too serious or too complex a matter to be left on the dissecting table may also conclude that the central narratives which separate mind and body and the social and physical sciences should be seriously called into question.

In listing the various influences we should also wish to give some weight to practical or policy concerns. Developments within sociology are rarely purely a matter of intellectual history, as indeed any sociology of knowledge would be quick to point out. In one sense, of course, the feminisms mentioned earlier provide a convergence of political, practical and theoretical concerns. But we also have in mind other practical considerations which, when taken together, may be seen as providing powerful stimuli both for a study of the body more informed by sociological concerns together with a sociology more directly involved at all levels in bodily matters. The current concern with AIDS provides one of the most obvious examples, one starkly highlighting issues of control, regulation, the interplays between religion, morality and sexuality and so on. Similarly, the various discourses around pornography have taken the debate beyond straightforward positions to do with censorship versus freedom of expression into issues of representation and control of the body. The burgeoning field of medical ethics may be seen as calling for a more rigorously founded sociology of the body. And finally, and quite differently, we may point to issues raised in recent international sporting events (especially in the 1988 Olympic Games) where debates around the use or alleged use of drugs highlighted concerns to do with the construction and understanding of normal or natural bodies, as well as with the body in sport being the site of interplays between commercialism and commodification, nationalism, gender and individualism. While these might on the surface seem to be very different public issues, it can be seen that a sociology of the body might provide some of the connections as well as separately informing the particular issues under scrutiny.

At this stage it is only possible to list, in some order of priority, some of the influences that have contributed to this significant shift of emphasis in recent years; the detailed sociology of this particular branch of knowledge will no doubt appear later. However, it is probably enough to say that many sociologists feel that there is a need for something in this area, a need not simply prompted by the practical concerns cited above, but also as a consequence of problems encountered in the routine business of doing sociology. Frank has argued that the direction of growth should be more in the direction of a bodily informed sociology as a whole and less in the direction of a new sociology of the body (Frank, 1990:160–1) and this is an argument with which we have some sympathy. Whatever the direction, it would seem clear that the body is here to stay for some time to come.

In his review article dealing with the topic, Frank suggests four broad headings: the medicalized body, the sexual body, the disciplined body and the talking body (Frank, 1990; for a different listing, see Frank, 1991). Even such a skeletal list indicates something of the range of issues with which we shall be concerned and certainly all these variations on the bodily theme appear in this present collection. In the rest of this introduction, we do not straightforwardly follow Frank but rather deal with sociology and biology; health, illness and the body; feminism and the body and issues of sociological theory.

Sociology and Biology

For all sociology's tendency to criticize reductionist explanations, sociologists have tended to let biology off rather lightly and much sociology operates with either an explicit or implicit acceptance of a biological base which is somehow outside the remit of sociological analysis. Sociology then, has tended to work with an additive conception, extra emphasis is placed on the social, and the importance of biology is minimized but a social/natural dichotomy is maintained. We would suggest that by not challenging biological understandings directly, sociology has left them intact rather than displaying them as cultural constructions, and that sociology's past failure to lay claim to the body has effectively left the way open for the increasing influence of sociobiology, which takes ideological understandings of the natural inevitability of certain bodily processes and practices and presents them back to us cocooned in scientific language. We would agree with Connell that 'bodies grow, work, flourish and decay in social situations that produce bodily effects' (1987:86) and consider that these processes are relatively under-theorized.

Even sociologists and, perhaps more importantly, feminists who argue against biological determinism and reductionism in relation to gender, tend to accept anatomical differences between females and males as the bottom-line. We

5

want to argue for a sociology of the body, informed by historical analysis, which will call even basic assumptions about anatomy into question. Sociology as a critical discipline has opened up for analysis many taken-for-granted and ideological assumptions, and there seems to be no reason to exempt anatomy (see Armstrong, 1983) from this process.

Clearly there are observable differences between most male and female bodies (although the existence of hermaphrodites and transsexuals calls even this assumption into question — see Foucault, 1980; Garfinkel, 1967) and it would seem that these differences have remained fairly constant over time (it is difficult to ascertain to what extent artistic representations are a result of actual variation rather than the result of cultural preferences and proscriptions). However, the modern period has seen changes in the interpretation of these differences which have undoubtedly had widespread repercussions. For example, there is evidence that, prior to the eighteenth century, males and females were understood as having basically the same genitalia, the major difference being that the female's were located inside and the male's outside the body.

> . . . though they of different sexes be,
> Yet on the whole they are the same as we,
> For those that have the strictest searcher's been,
> Find women are but men turned outside in.
>
> (Anon)

De Graaf who 'discovered' the ovaries in 1672 refers to them by the same word as that used for the male testes at the time, orchis, and as late as 1819, the London Medical Dictionary states: 'Ovaria: formerly called the female testicles; but now supposed to be the receptacles of ova or the female seed' (Gallagher and Laquer, 1987). What we see occurring here is a shift, from a vertical ordering of male and female bodies, with the female seen as an inferior version of the male, to a horizontal ordering based on opposition as well as inequality. Gallagher and Laquer argue that this shift owed more to ideology than to 'discoveries' about anatomy, as difference had always been an available basis for categorization due to female ability to give birth.

If we are to develop a better understanding of the social place of the body and of the ways in which we experience ourselves as embodied, then we must begin to understand biology as historically and culturally located. The body is not simply a set of facts which are gradually being uncovered by biomedical science. Obviously the body is made up of parts, but the perceived relative importance of these parts and their relationship to the whole is culturally defined. Even *Gray's Anatomy* needs to be understood as a cultural artefact (Armstrong, 1983), as a topic to be studied rather than more straightforwardly as a resource.

What sociology must do is to open up the biological/natural package and insert history and culture, in order to develop an understanding of the relationship between the social and biological as one of practical relevance rather than causation (Connell, 1987) and to illustrate the ways in which this relationship varies with age, class, gender and ethnicity. Indeed, a sociology of the body may be a significant point of departure for transcending or blurring the conventional opposition between nature and culture.

Health, Illness and the Body

The relationship between sociology and medicine can perhaps best be understood as a symbiotic one, both disciplines stemming from the need for modern societies to control both populations and individuals (Foucault, 1973; Turner, 1987). As Armstrong (1983) points out, sociology has in fact contributed to medicine's panoptic range; witness the critique of doctor-patient communication by sociologists which has encouraged medical practitioners to move closer to the social work model and to see their task as being to deal with the whole person rather than a set of symptoms (Silverman, 1987). Sociology has then been critical of medicine and medical practice, but has rarely, if at all, questioned medicine's right to exist as a distinct field of knowledge. Sociology has criticized over-medicalization, but rarely medicine itself. Medicine has in fact provided a rich seam for sociological research.

Medical sociology had, then, tended to accept medical understandings of the body, and it is only relatively recently that arguments have developed which suggest that these understandings should be seen as positions to be integrated rather than the absolute truth of our physical selves. In fact, medical sociology has had surprisingly little to say directly about the body. There have latterly been moves to illustrate how signs and symptoms are socially and historically constructed, for example in cases such as hysteria and anorexia. It is important, however, not to see such illnesses as simply instances of delusion or false consciousness, as 'all in the mind', but to extend our analysis to focus on the body as a site where sickness and health are played out. For example, our understanding of symptoms will depend on our understanding of how bodies work, which in turn will depend on what counts as adequate knowledge.

Theoretical issues relating to dualism and the body will be explored later in this chapter, but it is important at this point to explore the mind/body dichotomy as it relates to health and illness. The relative importance of mind and body varies historically and culturally. For example, prior to the nineteenth century in Europe there was no clear conception of mental illness; such symptoms were either the result of sin or possession, the product of physical excesses or imbalances, or simply the result of birth defects (congenital idiocy). Hysteria in women was thought to be the result of the womb moving around the body and getting too close to the brain, an understanding that persisted well into the nineteenth century. The stress then was either on the spiritual dimension or increasingly, on physiological defects having some effect on the mind. With the rise of psychiatry as a distinct discipline and the development of psychoanalysis, the mind became an important province in its own right as a producer of symptoms and illness. This has not, however, been a smooth transition. Psychiatry has, within the medical profession, been viewed as a poor relation to the scientific rigour of physical medicine. Physical illness has been seen as more 'real' than mental illness, which, although rarely seen as resulting from sin, tends to be seen as indulgence, escape from responsibility, weakness of character, etc.

An interesting example of the tensions around mind and body in relation to health is that of stress, or more particularly, executive stress. The OED defines it as a disease suffered by managers. Mental and emotional symptoms tend to be seen as acceptable and important when experienced by middle class men as a result of hard work and heavy responsibilities in the public sphere, whereas they

7

are (or certainly were until recently) taken as signs of intrinsic feminine weakness when presented by women who work hard and shoulder heavy responsibilities in the private sphere. In such men, stress is seen to result in physical, bodily symptoms and in premature invalidity and death, as a result of heart disease, for example. Whereas the physical illnesses suffered by housewives and mothers are often seen as stemming from female neurosis. Thus the ways in which the mind and body are understood are gendered as well as being culturally and historically variable.

In recent years there has been pressure on medicine from various sources, but perhaps most notably from the women's and community health movements, to move away from dualist conceptions towards a more holistic understanding and treatment of illness and its prevention. There is also an increasing tendency to stress the social and behavioural bases of an ever-widening range of ailments, smoking and lung cancer and cholesterol and heart diseases being the most well known examples. This coupled with a political climate which stresses the role of individual responsibility in relation to health has led to a discourse of blame. AIDS is of course the most extreme current example. In a more subtle way, discussions of a cancer personality place the blame/responsibility with the individual. Thus it is not what happens or even what we do to our bodies which produces ill health, but the sort of people we are, and the self is located in the mind. This particular way of conceptualizing illness has the effect of providing false security to those who don't fit this personality profile: our bodies won't let us down so long as we maintain the right state of mind. In such cases, the mind determines in the last instance what happens to the body, and dualism is restored.

Another example of the way in which the mind is privileged relates to the role of knowledge as power over the body. Health movements and pressure groups since the Sixties have attacked the power of the medical profession and demanded that people have greater access to knowledge in order to have more control over their bodies and consequently their health. This may seem laudable, while not without its problems. Recent developments which play on these demands also reinforce both mind/body and individualism/society dichotomies. For example, there has of late been a proliferation of telephone health information services (e.g. HealthCall) which offer knowledge (albeit watered-down medical knowledge) as a means of anxiety reduction. This process to a large extent begins and ends with the mind, as a little knowledge, rather than being dangerous, is presented as a form of protection. But, as health educators know only too well (Wellings, 1988), it is a very long way from the acceptance of information to behavioural change. Knowledge without action is not in itself power.

We would suggest that the sociology of health and illness and medicine itself needs to examine this changing and contradictory relationship between mind and body, and to move away from a holism which consists of glueing together social and biological factors towards a genuine holism which reconceptualizes the mind/body, biological/social divisions and permits the body a social status.

As has already been pointed out, health and illness are not simply a matter of biological changes which affect individual bodies, but are crucially social matters. Bodies are bearers of class, gender and a host of other social meanings which contribute to different health outcomes. For example, levels of morbidity are much higher for working-class than for middle-class bodies. The rate per 1000 (1988 figures) of chronically sick professional men was 80, whereas for male unskilled manual workers it was 234. For women in these groups the rates were 86 and 299 respectively. For males between 16 and 64 the death rate from ischaemic heart disease was 88 in social classes I and III (and this is supposedly an executive disease) and for bronchitis the rates were 36 and 188 respectively.

It is widely known that even death is gendered, the average life expectancy for women in the United Kingdom is 76, for men 70. However, women in all age groups experience greater morbidity than men. It is clear that bodies receive, rather than simply confer, gender. Women are, for example, more likely to suffer disability from strokes, rheumatoid arthritis, diabetes and varicose veins, illnesses which would appear to bear no relation to physiological differences, quite apart from reproductive problems which only affect women. It is also the case that women are on the one hand more likely than men to be labelled as frail and sickly, but on the other more likely to be labelled as suffering from psychogenic disorders, if they present to doctors with, for example, cystitis, PMT, dysmenhorrea or menopausal problems. It is assumed that women cannot be trusted to speak accurately about their bodies.

The development of the Women's Health Movement out of the second wave of feminism was in large part a result of women feeling that doctors could not be trusted, and beginning to engage in a struggle to gain control of their own bodies. However, much of this struggle, while radical in its intent, has been couched in the language of liberal individualism: rights, choice, freedom etc. and this has led towards potentially contradictory outcomes. For example, a woman's right to choose in relation to abortion or fertility treatment in the West needs to be set alongside compulsory sterilization and the use of Depo Provera without informed consent in the Third World. It is this notion of choice which has also led to the development of alternative 'feminist' health care in Britain for those who can afford it. This is not to suggest that the Women's Health Movement has been a reactionary force. In fact, in the main it has been feminists working in this area who have begun to counter liberal notions of choice. We simply want to point out some of the contradictions, and to stress the need for a sociology of the body which attempts to go beyond them.

The Women's Health Movement has played an important role in the battle against medical definitions of women as 'walking wombs', but there has been a strongly essentialist strand in the tendency to argue against allopathy on the grounds that it disrupts women's natural needs and rhythms (Kitzinger, 1978). For example, by defining childbirth as a natural event, rendered problematic only by medical intervention, the changing social meanings attached to birth tend to be ignored. This conflation of the biological and the 'natural' needs to be unpacked systematically. Interestingly, medical discourse has begun to make this separation in a way which is far from unproblematic. The biological events surrounding menstruation are being redefined by some sociobiologists as unnatural, as a twentieth century phenomena which results in gynaecological problems. Of course, what lies behind this separation is an even more essentialist notion of women's natural state, constant pregnancy and lactation as in an idealized past: the cure, medical intervention to create the correct biology with hormones. Nature is seen as something which we have damaged and disrupted and which we now need to simulate.

An important contemporary debate about the deployment and control of bodies has, of course, developed in the context of AIDS and HIV infection. With the rise of a 'moral panic' about the spread of this disease, which to a large extent had its roots in homophobia, the issue of what consenting bodies should do in private became once more a highly public issue. With the acceptance that this is not simply a disease of so-called high risk groups but one to which all who engage in certain high risk practices may become vulnerable, the focus has shifted to some extent towards a questioning of the appropriateness of bodily practices previously considered to lie at the heart of natural/normal sexuality. These discussions of safer sex have raised issues around what it is appropriate for bodies to do with/to other bodies in the context of sexual encounters. 'Unnatural' barriers must be erected and practices that have been taken for granted must be questioned. However, the body in its sexual mode is supposed to be a source of pleasure/power, not a source of disease and danger, and this contradiction lies at the heart of the problem which faces health educators trying to get their messages across. AIDS, and the discourse which has grown up around it, gives us a clear example of the necessity for a good sociology of health and illness to take thorough account of the body in a state of change, flux and interaction with other bodies, and as a site of contradictions in relation to both collective and individual strategies of health care.

Feminism and the Body

Bodies are intimately connected with power, and while brute strength is no longer generally necessary to the maintenance of social position it is still commonly used as a means of controlling women in both the private and public arena. Feminism has been the most significant force in raising consciousness about the oppression of women and in particular about the use of power and force by men, the State and state agencies to control women's bodies. Feminism has documented the control and exploitation of women's bodies via domestic violence, rape and sexual abuse, advertising and pornography, medical interventions, exploitation and harassment at work, etc. Feminist work has provided detailed documentary evidence of the working out of different social expectations about what male and female bodies can and can't do and where they are entitled to be. Women attempting to use the out-field of a village cricket ground for hockey in the winter (Imray and Middleton, 1983) were clearly a case of 'matter out of place' (Douglas, 1970) as they would be in male clubs (Rogers, 1988) and in many pubs (Hey, 1986).

As has already been noted in the context of women's health, a major feminist demand had been that women should have the right to control their own bodies, but this is not without its contradictions. Notions such as 'choice' need to be understood as ideological constructs with a particular history. Also greater choice does not necessarily result in greater freedom in a simple and direct sense, for example greater access to more reliable contraception has undoubtedly made it easier for women to avoid pregnancy. However, it can be argued that the availability of contraception has locked women further into male defined sexual practices (Pollock, 1985). Thus, women may have gained control of their bodies in relation to pregnancy only to have become increasingly defined as sexual objects.

Having stressed the importance of feminism in shaping and developing our understanding of the body, it is necessary to point out that feminism is neither static over time nor is it unified as a theoretical and political discourse, although dividing feminism too rigidly into socialist, radical and liberal typologies is not without its problems (Jaggar, 1983). However, it has been the strand usually called radical feminism which has paid most attention to the control of women's bodies.

Some of the early second wave radical feminists tended to reinforce the nature/culture dichotomy, by stressing the ways in which biology trapped women, and taking an extremely pessimistic view of the likelihood of men being able to change (many radical feminists remain pessimistic about men relinquishing their power, but this is more likely to be explained in terms of unwillingness, rather than inability). Firestone (1971), for example, saw technology as women's escape route from the trap of reproduction, a position which appears particularly problematic in the context of later feminist debates about new reproductive technologies. Such technology tends to be viewed as another potential weapon in medicine's armoury of social control rather than as a liberating force, although the extent to which this is felt to be the case is a matter of debate (Stanworth, 1987; Corea, 1985; Duelli-Klein 1985; Arditti *et al.*, 1984).

It is a common feminist complaint that society defines women in terms of their biological potentiality rather than as social beings, particularly in relation to motherhood. Simply because most women are biologically able to produce babies, all women are defined as potential, actual or failed mothers. It is often argued that what we are experiencing here is an ideological lag and that now women do have some choice about motherhood because of reliable contraception, social ideas will soon catch up and render these choices acceptable. This is an interesting example in terms of the development of a sociology of the body which takes seriously the historical relationship between individual bodies and bodies as populations, particularly in the context of pro-natalist ideologies, anxiety about Europe's falling birth rate (debate in the European Parliament, January 1989) and demands for more women in male-dominated jobs. Clearly, the expectation that female bodies will be in two places at once continues.

Most feminists operate with some notion of male power at both a structural and an interpersonal level, and although some find the concept of patriarchy problematic or even unacceptable (Barrett, 1980; Wilson, 1983) it still continues to be the most commonly used term. Turner (1984) argues that with the development of liberal democracy and the growth of capitalism, the material basis of patriarchy has been eroded and that what women in the West now experience by way of oppression is an ideological backlash, the death throes of an outmoded system of control, which he calls patrism. Feminists can readily point out the contradictions inherent in a legal system within a liberal democracy which continues to reinforce feudal notions of ownership. For instance it is, or has been until very recently, illegal for a man to use a woman's body against her will unless he happens to be her husband. However, it is still the case that a married women (in the UK) needs her husband's permission if she wishes to be sterilized, whereas a married man can make a unilateral decision to have a vasectomy.

While much feminist work over the last twenty years has drawn attention to ways in which women's bodies are exploited and managed under patriarchy these discussions have rarely taken embodiment as their starting point. However since we first began the process of editing this book there has been a veritable explosion of feminist work on 'the body' (Gatens, 1988; Martin, 1989; Sawicki, 1991) and now these theoretical developments are being utilized in the context of work on specific aspects of women's embodiment (Bordo, 1990; Holland *et al.*, 1992a, 1992b). Clearly the continuation of the debate about the basis of social differentiation between male and female bodies and the control of women's bodies by 'men' should be a major focus of a sociology of the body.

The Body and Sociological Theory

We have noted that the sociological tradition had apparently been indifferent, even hostile, to bodily matters. Apart from the reasons already suggested, one source of this hostility might derive from the particular understanding and place of theory within institutionalized sociology. By this we mean those tendencies whereby theorizing is both seen as occupying a privileged status within the discipline and is also understood in terms of its levels of abstraction and its distance from everyday experience, even where such experience may be the object of the theorizing process. That such theorizing has traditionally been carried out by grand-*masters* of the craft is also a matter of some significance. When such a tradition takes account of bodies it will do so in such a way as to maintain a distance from embodied experience.

Linked to this, as has already been noted, is a particular understanding or emphasis on rationality as being a key element within the theorizing process. Here we are less concerned with particular theoretical models which explicitly signal a concern with modes of rationality such as exchange theory or rational choice theory. We are more concerned with the fact that almost any model building, whatever its overall theoretical orientation, involves some kind of invocation of rationality. Much of this may be inevitable, even desirable. But, again, we can see that the body, with its apparent close associations with nature and the emotions, can only be admitted into such processes of theorizing through a kind of disembodying process.

In Weber's writings, rationality is simultaneously a historically situated topic to be explored and analyzed and an essential component in the process of carrying out such an analysis, or indeed of any other analysis. For all his recognition of tradition and the emotions, it would seem that rationality had a central and valued place in his work as a whole. As Bologh argues, for Weber rationality is linked to freedom of choice; conversely the emotional or the traditional are linked to a lack of such freedoms (Bologh, 1990:122). Bologh explicitly makes the link here with questions of the body both in terms, perhaps, of Weber's own autobiography and in terms of the central concerns in his mode of analysis:

> It seems to me that Weber's typology is a denial of community and body, embeddedness and embodiedness, perhaps a matter of fear and loathing. (Bologh, 1990:132)

The body, then, if not irrational is non-rational. It can become an object of theory only through being disembodied. Theory remains a central and rational enterprise. Theory may admit the body but the theorist remains disembodied.

It may be argued further that one strand in this particular model of rationality was the proliferation of those dichotomies and oppositions that constitute a major feature of much sociological writing. Two major clusters of such dichotomies are of particular relevance here. In the first place, there is the fundamental one for the project of rational social enquiry, that between mind and body and all the linked oppositions such as those between culture and nature. While these oppositions here have their own significances, they often derive added significance through their interplay; thus the body becomes especially associated with nature. Further power and solidity is given to these oppositions through their gendered connotations, a point made in several feminist critiques. The second cluster of oppositions, perhaps less obviously connected to the issues to hand, are those to do with the individual and society. These are related to other distinctions such as those between agency and structure or between methodological individualism and holism and may be seen as a variation of the part/whole distinction.

Turning to the first cluster of distinctions around the mind/body opposition, it hardly needs noting that we are dealing with distinctions that have a long philosophical pedigree which we shall not attempt to unravel here. However, it is likely that this distinction, or some variation, has had its part to play in determining the legitimate sphere of the social and the human sciences. The location of sociology amongst the *geistestwissenshaften* would almost guarantee that the mind/body opposition would not so much become part of the sociological debate but would, in a sense, become obliterated through the embracing of the former at the expense of the latter.

In general, the strategy for tackling this and similar oppositions is to treat them as topics for further detailed and critical examination rather than as everyday resources to be drawn upon in a more or less routine manner. Thus it should be possible to recommend a sociology of science or a sociology of knowledge whereby we examine the history and consequences of these distinctions both for, say, biology and medicine and for sociology. Indeed, such a project may already be seen as part of the Foucaultian legacy. Moving away from narrowly defined scientific knowledge, we may concern ourselves with everyday knowledge. Following Durkheim's lead in *The Elementary Forms of the Religious Life* (1976) we may seek to explore the social construction of some of our fundamental categories of being and understanding, the role these play in everyday social life and their various consequences. Thus when a westerner says 'It's all in the mind', what is actually being said? We could be concerned here with popular understandings rather than with philosophical controversy. It is possible, for example, that there has been a shift in the status of the mind in this popular sociomedical sense during the last century or so. In the past, to say that a certain medical condition was in the mind, or of mental origin, was to claim that it had a lower order of reality or seriousness. Undoubtedly, this understanding still exists. However, with the rise of psychoanalysis and with more recent understandings of stress, the idea of the mind has gained in status and has become a legitimate sphere for professional or medical intervention. The distinction remains, but its location and significance may have shifted noticeably.

Closely associated with the mind/body distinction is, as we have argued, the distinction between nature or biology and culture. This has already been discussed in various parts of this chapter and it is simply necessary here to stress the main argument, namely that the way to challenge various socio-biological forms of reductionism is not so much to insist upon the cultural as it tends to reproduce the original dichotomy. Rather it is to take biology/culture and nature/culture as topics for investigation in their own right; to explore what distinctions are made in different cultures, where the lines are drawn (if they are drawn at all) and what the consequences of such distinctions might be. A simple example might be the common condemnation of various forms of hooliganism as 'animal' behaviour. What understandings of the 'animal' are being used here and what distinctions between animality and civilization are being deployed? Some forms of nature are clearly seen in some other sense as being 'unnatural'.

Turning to our second clustering of oppositions around the individual/society distinction, two general points may be made. The first is to emphasize that the individual, the self, the agent must be understood in embodied terms. As Giddens argues:

> Bodily discipline is intrinsic to the competent social agent . . .

> . . . routine control of the body is integral to the very nature both of agency and of being accepted (trusted) by others as competent. (Giddens, 1991:57)

These quotations should not be interpreted in too restricted a way. While 'discipline' and 'control' have particular connotations in a modern rational society, all societies and all social situations make their own particular demands upon the deployment of the body such that bodily performance is consistent with the requirements of time and place. Social competence as expressed in bodily demeanour is always that which is appropriate to the particular demands of the context, whether it be marching on the parade ground, expressing grief or speaking in tongues. Further, such bodily considerations are not something which may be simply added to standard interactionist accounts of self and others but are an integral part of such accounts.

A second general point is to stress that bodily considerations do not simply apply to the individual side of the individual/society division. Conventionally, of course, people are often encouraged to think in this way. Our sense of separate individuals is powerfully reinforced by our locating these individuals within separate bodies. On the other hand, to see whole societies in bodily forms is to deploy certain modes of metaphorical discourse which are largely discredited. Indeed, it may be sociology's traditional preoccupation with 'Society' or other collective entities that may provide yet further reason for the relative neglect of bodies within the discipline.

However, it has been one of the merits of Turner's refocusing of attention onto bodily matters that we are no longer confined to an individualistic understanding of bodies. This is not just a question of bodily understandings being socially shaped. It is also the fact that social orders have always been concerned with bodies and their control and surveillance and that, in certain ways at least, these concerns have increased in modern societies. Thus modern societies may be concerned with population policies, issues of public health and the control of epidemics, the mapping and counting of populations and the threats presented by those defined as aliens or outsiders.

There is, indeed, something fluid and indeterminate in the interplay between individual and societal representations and concerns with bodies. An example may be provided in the ways in which 'the problem of refugees' is constructed in modern societies. Refugees are clearly constructed at a societal level; their likely numbers are calculated and their very identity as a problem exists with reference to nation states and national boundaries. Yet, especially through modern means of communication, they appear to us as individualized bodies, bodies of a different colour or culture, bodies in need of food or medical care, bodies suffering pain or deprivation. Attempts are made to distinguish between genuine or political refugees on the one hand and economic refugees on the other, a distinction based upon ideal typifications of different sets of individual life experiences, motivations and aspirations. Yet, once again, those individual faces fall back into the collective, the social problem revolving around distinctions between 'them' and 'us'. This is not simply a question of the individual face being lost in the crowd but rather a constant moving in and out of focus between the individual and the collective, between individual identifiable bodies and the body politic.

The challenge to the rationalities developed within the sociological tradition, to the assumptions about the place of theory and the nature of theorizing, and to the dichotomies and oppositions that have developed in these contexts have come largely from various strands of feminism, sometimes in uneasy alliance with post-modernism (Nicholson, 1990). These challenges, although often presenting their own difficulties and complexities, have been particularly favourable to the development of a critical understanding of the body in society. Feminism, as we have seen, has had central concerns with bodily matters, and the identification of some of the main traditions of sociological thought with masculinist hegemonies has also allowed, through the critique of this tradition, a more 'body friendly' sociology. Post-modernism, with its critical demolition of some dominant modes of thought and its celebration of diversity and fluidity has, in its own way, been generally friendly to approaches to the body which transcend the nature/culture divide. To repeat, these developments have not been unproblematic. Feminism, as we have seen, may sometimes resurrect new forms of essentialism while post-modern theorizing may all too readily become a highly cerebral, and ultimately disembodied, activity. However, there is no doubt that there are convergences between the developments in feminist thought, post-modern theory and the development of a critical sociology of the body.

We may illustrate the possible significance of a more embodied sociology through the consideration of some well-rehearsed themes within the discipline. In the first place, let us consider the extensive volume of theorizing and research around the theme of bureaucracy and bureaucratization, stemming from Weber's ideal type. At a first glance this work would seem to have nothing to do with the body. However, this apparent absence may be a matter of considerable significance. The ideal type, and many of its elaborations in subsequent research, does not appear to admit the body, which is deemed to be formally irrelevant to the model. Patterns of bureaucratic recruitment, the conduct of our everyday bureaucratic life and the way in which this is structured by systems of rules and a clearly defined hierarchy represent a radical denial of the body. *Formally*, the bureaucracy is indifferent to shapes and sizes of bodies, and issues of health and disability only arise where these are deemed relevant to the successful performance of the tasks to hand.

Substantively, in practice matters may be very different. Bureaucracies, it need hardly be emphasized, are gendered, and male and female bodies are not randomly distributed throughout bureaucratic offices and hierarchies. The practice of locating 'attractive' women at reception or frontstage areas of bureaucracies is a clear illustration of the interplay between gender, bodies and power within formally rational organizations. We also know, despite formal rules in some cases, that the colour of bodies is also often a matter of some significance. Age and certain forms of disability or stigma may also constitute deviations from formal rationalities.

Even in terms of the formal model, bureaucracies may be found to be embodied after all. Bodies are interchangeable within and between functionally equivalent offices. Bodies within organizational hierarchies are controlled and disciplined, their movements clearly defined in terms of time and space. While some attention has been given to the elaboration of some bureaucratic *personality*, relatively little attention has been given to the bureaucratic body, its reproduction and the ways in which certain modes of bodily posture and deportment derive from and give solidity to organizational offices. Conversely, the issue of sexual harassment at work is clearly a bodily matter, dealing with the interplay of gender and power within formal hierarchies, but this understanding has only been recently linked to discussions of the nature and structure of formal organizations (Hearn *et al.*, 1989). Who sits where, when and how, and the assumption and the use of rights to stand or move have often provided the substance of popular or scientific studies of body language, but it is rare that these studies have been incorporated into wider studies of bureaucratic rationality. It is, perhaps, significant that lower participants in bureaucratically organized hierarchies such as the military are often referred to as bodies or just 'bods'.

There are several points that may be made about this illustration. In the first place, merely to raise these issues is to illustrate both how traditionally, sociological work has been disembodied and how it might be enriching to bring bodies back in. In the second place, it points to a two-way interchange between general sociological theory and the study of the body. Just as many classical themes may derive further life from being informed by a developing sociology of the body, so too may studies of the body be informed by some classical issues to do with, say, rationalization, the contrast with traditionalism and so on. Finally, it is a fact worth stressing that the rationale of most, if not all, state (and other) bureaucracies, is to do with the surveillance and control of bodies:

> There is no law that is not inscribed on bodies. Every law has a hold on the body. (De Certeau, 1984:139)

This may be a dramatic way of making the point, yet one which provides a forceful reminder as to what bureaucracies are *about*. While generally and popularly understood in terms of abstractions or the inanimate — paper work, red tape, etc. — bureaucracies are embodied systems dealing ultimately with the control of bodies in time and space.

We may also consider the case of social stratification. Again this would appear to be at some distance from bodily concerns, at least in the ways in which the subject has been classically understood. Certainly, if stratification is understood to refer to positions rather than to persons, then issues of the body would seem to be ruled out of court at the outset. Yet such an approach is not to be identified with the whole of stratification theory; rather it relates to one approach of understanding *class* in Marxist terms. And even here, an emphasis upon position can only be a point of departure, for structural positions are readily seen to have consequences for individuals, and embodied individuals at that.

Certainly, the consequences of systems of structured inequalities, whether these be in terms of class, gender or ethnicity, can be easily understood in bodily terms. More striking, of course, are inequalities in terms of health and health-care provision which can have direct and observable bodily consequences. Moreover, such consequences in terms of health may constitute major mechanisms by which structured inequalities are reproduced over time. In many cases, then, there is no need to invoke questionable concepts such as 'the culture of poverty', 'transmitted deprivation' or 'the underclass' in order to understand continuities in social inequality over time and across generations; the nexus of physical living conditions, working conditions, health and access to health-care may provide at least a sufficient point of departure for the understanding of the reproduction of social inequalities.

There are some other features of stratification as an embodied social phenomena which are worthy of further investigation. For a start, bodily considerations may be a source of stratification either in their own right or, most likely, in combination with other dimensions. Lucien Chardon, the hero of Balzac's *Lost Illusions*, relies upon his grace and his ability to cut a dashing figure in fine clothes, thus being able to carry off the dubious identity of Lucien de Rubempré as a consequence. Movie stars and fashion models may rise to accompany princes and bankers. Physical attractiveness is an important dimension of stratification in small groups and interpersonal relationships. Similar observations may be made about physical strength and athletic skill, again important bases of individual mobility and of interpersonal prestige.

Secondly, the representation of hierarchy and inequality may be directly physical. The lower orders may be portrayed as having bowed heads and shuffling gaits. Men, and sometimes women, of consequence stand erect and move purposefully and confidently through public space. The identity of the fop or the dandy is impossible to imagine without seeing it in physical, bodily terms. Images of class struggle, in contrast, give a sense of the class for itself, and the most direct and worldwide way of representing this is through images of physical strength, the working man's muscles or clenched fists. Against this iconography of mass class interest, the rulers become portrayed as fragmented, obese or effete. From the other side, the olfactory dimensions of class representation and social distance are well known in popular speech and social imagery and are beginning to receive their due recognition by social research (Corbin, 1986; Duroche, 1990).

These examples could be multiplied both for the specific topic of social stratification and for many other familiar themes and text-book chapter headings within sociology. While it cannot be argued that all this adds up to a subterranean sociology of the body, it does indicate that bodily matters are not at too great a distance from well-established sociological themes and that their consideration could give rise to a multitude of research projects.

Before concluding this section, however, it might be worthwhile to consider two other themes that have arrived relatively recently on the sociological scene and which may be seen as having some affinities with the sociology of the body.

These are growing interests to do with issues of space and time (Adams, 1990; Giddens, 1991; Young, 1988). While these interests have, generally speaking, developed separately it may be argued that they have something in common. At the most basic level, body, space and time all represent fundamental categories of being and of ordering social relations, perhaps categories so obvious that social scientists have, with some striking exceptions in each case, failed to notice them. Much the same could have been said about gender until some years ago. They all have a certain quality of elusiveness, a sense of 'now you see it, now you don't' and perhaps for this reason have been somewhat resistant to social analysis. It is worth noting, again, that the exception here may be social anthropology where a tradition of looking at social wholes or collectivities of persons defined as 'others' may have rendered what is generally opaque in our own society more transparent to the eyes of the stranger.

That bodies exist in time and space would seem hardly worth saying until we remember the difficulties that temporal and spatial considerations had in gaining a systematic hearing within sociology. Clearly, any talk of bodies must take account of space and time as a matter of course. One possible difficulty here is that the three terms, body, space and time, add up to a large number of abstractions with the consequences of distancing and alienation from experience that we have noted in connection with some other theoretical enterprises. Yet time, space and bodies are not just abstractions; they refer to the immediacies of everyday, lived experience. This is not, clearly, a question of any crude anti-theoretical stance but rather a plea for the working through of these complexities in the context of particular case studies.

At this stage the rich possibilities of this kind of work can only be indicated and indeed plenty of examples are already to hand in the literature, requiring only a modest amount of re-analysis. In the area of medical sociology, for example, experiental accounts of illnesses or disabilities almost invariably raise questions to do with time and space. The inevitable question of the hospitalized patient, 'when do I go home?' neatly encapsulates the interplays between time, space and the body (Davis, 1963; Roth, 1963; Zola, 1982). The sociology of the street (another underdeveloped area) clearly deals with bodies in urban time and space, their differential rights of access and presence, issues of threats and danger, solidarity and separateness. These issues and priorities shift between day and night as studies of traffic wardens (Richman, 1983) or feminist accounts of the 'Reclaim the Night' movement demonstrate. One final but beautiful example of bodies in time and space is provided by the account of the different ways in which men and women moved about the streets of Marienthal when it was hit by unemployment in the 1930s (Jahoda *et al.*, 1972). As with so much sociological enquiry, the work is already there; it just requires re-reading in a slightly different way.

It is this emphasis upon the importance of working through case material that we would wish to stress in this present volume. We assume that the case for a more bodily-informed sociology has already been made, here to some extent, but certainly elsewhere. The task now is to open up the interplay between theory and research that characterizes the best use of case study material. It is for this reason that we tend towards preferring a more bodily-informed sociology than a sociology of the body, while recognizing that the latter has developed and will continue to develop and that sociology gains from the development of specialisms as well as through interactions of specialisms.

However, it is possible to imagine a volume in the near future beginning with the words: 'In recent years, sociology has become too much obsessed with the body and the emotions'. In other words, there are possible dangers with this emphasis which we should begin to face at this stage. Some of these are relatively obvious: the dangers inherent in the faddish or the fashionable; the dangers of the development of esoteric cults working out ever more complex combinations of post-modernism, feminism and the body; the possible dangers of new essentialisms or bodily pessimisms. There is, however, one danger that is worth stressing a little more. The body, and its close companion, the emotions, are after all the very matter of everyday experience. In dealing with the body and the emotions we are dealing with that which is closest to us, as researchers or as readers, with our very sense of being in the world. Yet, in our attempts to study the body to make it accessible as an object of enquiry we are likely to achieve that distancing from experience which has characterized much sociological enquiry, distancing through language, through technique, through the sociological gaze itself. Once again, the body both solid and elusive at the same time, has slipped through our fingers or, to change the metaphor, has evaded our gaze. While these problems are true with all fields of sociological enquiry (one only has to consider similar debates within the sociology of religion) it is likely that bodily matters raise them with a greater urgency.

At this stage, it is probably enough to put these problems on to the agenda and to encourage debates around issues which are not simply to do with method or epistemology but also to do with the ethics and politics of research. In so doing we may perhaps remember that the pleasures and dangers of research may not be all that distant from the pleasures and dangers of the body itself:

Because we are embodied beings, all sociable relations have an erotic dimension (the body and senses are affected); all sociable relations are erotic relations. We all find the actual presence or some trace . . . of another more or less pleasurable, more or less affective. (Bologh, 1990:218)

References

ADAMS, B. (1990) *Time and Social Theory*, Oxford, Polity.

ARDITTI, R., DUELLI-KLEIN, R. and MINDEN, S. (Eds) (1984) *Test Tube Women: What Future for Motherhood?* London, Pandora.

ARMSTRONG, D. (1983) *The Political Anatomy of the Body*, Cambridge, Cambridge University Press.

BARRETT, M. (1980) *Women's Oppression Today*, London, Verso.

BOLOGH, R. (1990) *Love or Greatness? Max Weber and Masculine Thinking: a Feminist Enquiry*, London, Unwin Hyman.

BORDO, S. (1990) 'Material girl: The effacements of postmodern culture', *Michigan Quarterly Review*, Fall, pp. 653–676.

CONNELL, R. (1987) *Gender and Power*, Oxford, Polity.

DE CERTEAU, M. (1984) *The Practice of Everyday Life*, Berkeley, University of California Press.

CORBIN, A. (1986) *The Foul and the Fragrant: Odor and the French Social Imagination*, Leamington Spa, Berg.

COREA, G. (1985) *Man-Made Woman: How New Reproductive Technologies Affect Women*, Hutchinson.

DAVIS, F. (1963) *Passage Through Crisis: Polio Victims and their Families*, Indianapolis, Bobbs-Merrill.

DOUGLAS, M. (1970) *Purity and Danger: An Analysis of the Concepts of Pollution and Taboo*, Harmondsworth, Penguin.

DURKHEIM, E. (1970) *Suicide*, London, Routledge and Kegan Paul.

DURKHEIM, E. (1976) *The Elementary Forms of The Religious Life*, London, Allen and Unwin.

DUROCHE, L. (1990) 'Male perception as a social construct', in HEARN, J. and MORGAN, D. (Eds) *Men, Masculinities and Social Theory*, London, Unwin Hyman, pp. 170–185.

FEHER, M. (Ed.) with NADDAFF, N. and TAZI, N. (1989) 'Fragments for a History of the Human Body', Parts 1, 2 & 3, *Zone*, Vols 3–5, New York, Urzone.

FIRESTONE, S. (1971) *The Dialectic of Sex*, London, Jonathan Cape.

FOUCAULT, M. (1973) *The Birth of the Clinic*, London, Tavistock,

FOUCAULT, M. (1980) *The History of Sexuality*, (Vol. 1) Harmondsworth, Penguin.

FRANK, A.W. (1990) 'Bringing Bodies Back in: A decade review', *Theory Culture and Society*, 7(1), pp. 131–162.

FRANK, A.W. (1991) For a Sociology of the Body: An analytical review', in FEATHERSTONE, M., HEPWORTH, M. and TURNER, B.S. (Eds) *The Body: Social process and Cultural theory*, London, Sage, pp. 36–102.

GALLAGHER, C. and LAQUER, T. (1987) *The Making of the Modern Body*, Berkeley, University of California Press.

GAME, A. (1991) *Undoing the Social: Towards a Deconstructive Sociology*, Milton Keynes, Oxford University Press.

GARFINKEL, H. (1967) *Studies in Ethnomethodology*, New Jersey, Prentice Hall.

GATENS, M. (1988) 'Towards a Feminist Philosophy of the Body', in B. CAIN, E.A. GROSZ and M. DE LEPERVANCHE (Eds) *Crossing Boundaries: Feminisms and the Critique of Knowledge*, Sidney, Allen and Unwin.

GIDDENS, A. (1991) *Modernity and Self Identity*, Oxford, Polity.

HEARN, J. *et al* (1989) *The Sexuality of Organization*, London, Sage.

HEY, V. (1986) *Patriarchy and Pub Culture*, London, Tavistock.

HOLLAND, J., RAMAZONAGLU, C., SHARPE, S. and THOMSON, R. (1992a) 'Power and Desire: The embodiment of female sexuality', paper presented at the First International Conference on 'Girls and girlhood: transitions and dilemmas.' June 1992, Amsterdam.

HOLLAND, J., RAMAZANOGLU, C., SCOTT, S. and THOMSON, R. (1992b) 'Desire, Risk and Control: The Body as a site of Contestation', in L. DOYAL and T. WILTON (Eds) *AIDS: Setting a Feminist Agenda*, Basingstoke, Falmer (in press)

IMRAY, L. and MIDDLETON, A. (1983) 'Public and Private: Marking the Boundaries', in Garmarnikow, E. *et al.* (Eds) *The Public and the Private*, Aldershot, Gower.

JAGGAR, A. (1983) *Feminist Politics and Human Nature*, Brighton, Harvester Wheatsheaf.

JAHODA, M., LAZARSFELD, P. and ZEISAL, M. (1972) *Marienthal: The Sociography of an Unemployed Community*, London, Tavistock.

KITZINGER, S. (1978) *The Experience of Childbirth*, Harmondsworth, Penguin.

MARTIN, E. (1989) *The Woman in the Body*, Milton Keynes, Open University Press.

NICHOLSON, L.J. (Ed.) (1990) *Feminism/Postmodernism*, London, Routledge.

POLLOCK, S. (1983) 'Women, Sexuality and Contraception', Unpublished PhD. thesis, University of Warwick.

RICHMAN, J. (1983) *Traffic Wardens: An Ethnography of Street Administration*, Manchester, Manchester University Press.

ROGERS, B. (1988) *Men Only: An Investigation of Men's Organizations*, London, Pandora.

ROTH, J. (1963) *Timetables: Structuring the Passage of Time in the Hospital Treatment and Other Careers*, Indianapolis, Bobbs-Merrill.

SAWACKI, J. (1991) *Discipling Foucault: Feminism, Power and the Body*, London, Routledge.

SCOTT, S., WILLIAMS, G., PLATT, S. and THOMAS, H. (Eds) (1992) *Public Risks and Private Dangers*, Aldershot, Avebury.

SILVERMAN, D. (1987) *Communication and Medical Practice*, London, Sage.

STANWORTH, M. (Ed.) (1987) *Reproductive Technologies: Gender, Motherhood and Medicine*, Oxford, Polity.

STAROBINSKI, J. (1989) 'The natural history of bodily sensation', in FEHER, M. (Ed.) Part 2, pp. 350–393, *op. cit.*

TURNER, B.S. (1987) *Medical Power and Social Knowledge*, London, Sage.

TURNER, B.S. (1984) *The Body and Society*, Oxford, Blackwell.

TURNER, B.S. (1991) 'Recent developments in the theory of the body', in M. FEATHERSTONE, M. HEPWORTH & B.S. TURNER (Eds) *The Body: Social Processes and Cultural Theory*, London, Sage.

WEBER, M. (1930) *The Protestant Ethic and the Spirit of Capitalism*, London, Allen and Unwin.

WELLINGS, K. (1988) 'Do we need to change sexual behaviour, should we and can we?' *Health, Education Journal*, **47**, 213, pp. 57–59.

WILSON, E. (1983) *What is to be done about Violence against Women?* Harmondsworth, Penguin.

YOUNG, M. (1988) *The Metronomic Society: Natural Rhythms and Human Timetables*, London, Thames and Hudson.

ZOLA, I.K. (1982) *Missing Pieces*, Philadelphia, University Press.

Chapter 2

'With My Body I Thee Worship': The Social Construction of Marital Sex Problems

David Clark

We are often reminded of the countless procedures which Christianity once employed to make us detest the body; but let us ponder all the ruses that were employed for centuries to make us love sex, to make the knowledge of it desirable and everything said about it precious. Let us consider the stratagems by which we were induced to apply all our skills to discovering its secrets, by which we were attached to the obligation to draw out its truth, and made guilty for having failed to recognize it for so long. These devices are what ought to make us wonder today. More-over, we need to consider the possibility that one day, perhaps in a different economy of bodies and pleasures, people will no longer quite understand how the ruses of sexuality, and the power that sustains its organisation, were able to subject us to that austere monarchy of sex, so that we became dedicated to the endless task of forcing its secret, of exacting the truest of confessions from a shadow. (Foucault, 1984:159)

The subject of this chapter, the history and development of 'marital' sex therapy, might easily be seen within commonsense versions to represent one of the ways in which, during the course of the twentieth century, a particular realm of interpersonal problems was liberated from the shrouds of secrecy, anxiety and repression. Some accounts of the development of sex therapy and the knowledge base which underpins it therefore emphasize a sea change from thinking about sexual activity as procreation, to seeing it as recreation, and give considerable prominence to the extent to which this new science is capable of increasing the sum of human happiness. In a recent self-help guide, Masters, Johnson and Kolodny, for example, make the following claim:

... we believe that learning about sexuality in an objective fashion will enable our readers to examine important sexual issues — some intensely personal, some social, some moral — and emerge with deeper insights into themselves and others. We also believe that sexual knowledge can lead to reasoned, responsible inter-personal sexual behaviour and can help make important personal decisions about sex. In short, learning about sexuality is an invaluable preparation for living. (Masters, Johnson and Kolodny, 1987:4)

As the quotation from Michel Foucault illustrates, however, there is also a darker interpretation to be made of these accounts, which emphasizes that a new and apparent openness about sexual matters may mask structures of power and knowledge, which combine to exert new and more closely delineated forms of social and psychological control. My task in this chapter will therefore be to offer a critique of the liberal perspective, by showing, firstly, that 'marital' sex therapy has from the outset had an explicit purpose in seeking to shore up and buttress both the institution and relationship of marriage and secondly, that sex therapy has contributed to a wider discourse in which the sexual behaviour of individual subjects has become the object of scientific enquiry, leading to an expansion in the surveillance of sexual attitudes and practices. Accordingly, whilst the notion of 'treating' sexual problems might appear on the one hand as an example of sexual emancipation, it may also be seen as further extension of sexual and bodily regulation by what Donzelot (1979) calls the 'psy' forces. I shall illustrate this argument by detailed reference to the growth of 'marital' sex therapy within one organization, the National Marriage Guidance Council (since 1988 known as Relate).[1]

Sexual Problems and Sex Therapy in Marriage Guidance

The Marriage Guidance movement in England first took shape in the 1930s in an amalgamation of doctors, clergy and others concerned about changes in marriage and family life. These founders of the movement were concerned about changing sexual relationships between men and women, the importance of birth control and the implications of divorce law reform for the stability of marriage. Two key strands were evident in the early days. On the one hand Herbert Gray, a Presbyterian minister, represented those who were attempting to rethink the spiritual aspects of sexual relationships and who, whilst rejecting the views of the sex radicals of the 1920s, sought to establish Christian teaching on a new and more positive basis. Dr. E.F. Griffith represented the other strand. Coming to the movement via an interest in birth control and eugenics, Griffith was eager to lift the taboos which surrounded questions of sex and marriage. The interests of both men were underpinned by a concern to preserve and foster healthy marriage and parenthood.

From the late 1930s Marriage Guidance therefore existed to promote marriage and family life in a context where moderate sexual reform was seen as a crucial determinant of the movement's success. Initially this focused around the importance of sex education prior to and during marriage. During World War Two and in the decade following, attention shifted to the need for a concerted effort to raise standards of sexual morality which had been affected adversely by wartime dislocation. In 1945 David Mace, the first ever paid secretary of the NMGC, produced evidence that one woman in six had abandoned the ideal of premarital chastity (Mace, 1945) and three years later, in his book *Marriage Crisis*, went on to summarize his concerns about both male and female sexual morality:

The First World War helped them to kick over the traces, and the Second finished off the breakaway. 'Do what you like' became the new code of sexual behaviour. (Mace, 1948a:49)

Mace also had other preoccupations — with the 'misuse' of birth control methods, both within marriage and outside it and was concerned too about the spread of venereal diseases. The NMGC strategy therefore involved the exploitation of national anxieties about the disintegration of the family in order to argue for chastity before and fidelity within marriage. In a context where women's needs in particular were seen as best served by traditional marital role divisions, attention focused on the improvement of sexual relationships in marriage. Mace argued that 'good sex adjustment for husband and wife means satisfying orgasm for both' and that simultaneous orgasm was a 'desirable ideal' (Mace, 1948b:123). It was stressed that sexual experimentation outside of marriage, however, carried greater perils for women; for whereas men sought bodily gratification, women wanted homes and security and found through maternity the fulfilment of a process of psychological maturation. As Jane Lewis points out: 'this interpretation of the meaning of sex fitted neatly with the late 1940s concern to encourage a higher birth rate and better quality mothering' in a climate where 'sexual fulfilment in marriage represented the best guarantor of sexual morality' (Lewis, 1990:250, 251).

From its inception, therefore, the NMGC was committed *inter alia* to the safeguarding of the family unit and permanent monogamous marriage, to education and guidance about marriage for young people, and to 'the provision of sympathetic and expert treatment for the prevention and cure of marital disharmony'.[2] Initially it existed primarily as a *campaigning* organization, which sought to use mass education and guidance as part of the larger aim of promoting marriage and family life. In the postwar years, however, as Marriage Guidance became operational in centres throughout the country, the early model, based on the broad principle of public health, quickly gave way to a curative model which drew its inspiration from medicine, psychiatry, counselling and psychotherapy. Attention focused more and more on direct work with individuals and couples, presenting with a range of 'problems'. Grants in aid were received from the Home Office to foster the development of selection and training programmes for volunteer counsellors, who offered their services to these 'clients' in local centres around the country.

The rise of counselling was also related to wider discourses about post-war social and economic reconstruction. Counselling was both supported by and itself helped to generate a belief that in the increasing affluence of the postwar success story, problems rooted in economic disadvantage had been largely supplanted by those which lay in the realm of interpersonal relations. As features of the new era, these personal and emotional problems, as they related to marriage, were thought amenable to innovative approaches, which the emergent ideologies and practices of counselling seemed suitably poised to exploit. Such discourses related in turn to the growing preoccupation with the marriage *relationship*. Sociologists began to interpret this preoccupation as a consequence of the increased *isolation* of the nuclear family from wider social networks. New ideals of 'companionate' marriage emerged in which the marital relationship was increasingly valued as a source of personal and sexual fulfilment and the site of central life interests.

Sexual fulfilment therefore came to be seen as one of several expectations of the marriage relationship, a measure against which overall levels of marital satisfaction could be judged. Montefiore expressed this from an Anglican perspective:

> . . . the act of sexual intercourse cannot properly be divorced from all other aspects of married love without injury to the persons concerned. Unless two people share their lives in a deeply personal way, their sharing of sex will be shallow and superficial. (Montefiore, 1963:75)

The following year, 1964, Berger and Kellner's famous essay, written from a secularized and humanistic standpoint, described marriage as 'a dramatic act in which two strangers come together and redefine themselves' and in which the dominant themes are 'romantic love, sexual fulfilment, self discovery and self realization through love and sexuality' (Berger and Kellner, 1964:5). Such discourses clearly helped to establish the preconditions for regarding 'sexual problems' within marriage as a subset of the wider category of *marital* problems and perhaps most importantly as a crucial set of difficulties around which others in the marriage might rotate. In due course Marriage Guidance was to single out this area for special attention.

As early as 1955, David Maclay, a psychiatrist writing in *Marriage Guidance* and working as a 'tutor' leading case discussions for counsellors, had raised the issue of dealing with psychosexual difficulties, and proposed that a number of counsellors should be chosen 'to improve their skill by extra study and by supervised work in this direction' (Maclay, 1955:4). Whilst the selection and training of counsellors to undertake the general 'remedial' work with couples was considerably developed and refined in the 1960s, it was not until the 1970s, however, that this proposal for a specialized service dealing with sexual problems was taken up. The initial stimulus came from Mace himself, on a return visit to Britain from the USA, whence he had removed in the mid-1950s. Subsequently NMGC was in the forefront of the development of sex therapy services in Britain. That sex therapy had become thinkable in this way was largely a product of the influence of William Masters and Virginia Johnson.

It was in 1966 that Masters and Johnson's milestone *Human Sexual Response* was first published. In this work they sought to isolate two basic physiological responses of the human body to sexual stimulation: vasocongestion and muscle tension, emphasizing the similarities, rather than the differences, in the sexual responses of men and women. On this basis they went on to describe a four-phase 'normal sexual response cycle', consisting of: excitement, plateau, orgasm and resolution, established by reference to the discrete anatomical and physiological changes which take place as sexual stimulation is established (Masters and Johnson, 1966). As Brown (1979) points out, this work broke new ground in sexology, being based on laboratory observations of human subjects. It was this anatomical-physiological model which in turn formed the foundation for Masters and Johnson's work on intervention in the field of sexual 'problems', which they outlined in their next work, *Human Sexual Inadequacy*. Here the authors made three critical observations:

> 1) Since sex tends to happen between two people, it is preferable for both to be seen together in therapy.

2) Since a male therapist is unlikely to appreciate fully the sexual experience of a woman, and vice versa, it is advisable to have male and female therapist present with the couple.
3) Since sexual arousal and response is a physiologically normal function, problems in sexual relationships (dysfunctions) might be approached through the processes of education rather than psychopathology. (Masters and Johnson, 1970)

Building on this, they went on to propose a fourteen-day rapid treatment programme for couples, working with co-therapists.

In late 1971 David Mace, on a visit to NMGC headquarters, showed a range of sexually explicit film material which was being developed in the USA for educational and research purposes (Brown, 1979:11). In the following year he published a short book with NMGC in which he outlined his ideas on sexual problems in marriage. The book, which is still in print, contained a fulsome dedication to Masters and Johnson. It also began to mark out sexual difficulties in marriage as a significant and autonomous area of psychosocial problems, claiming that 'about half of all married couples develop sexual problems of one kind or another' (Mace, 1972:v). Problems on such a scale called for skilled helpers, but Mace was forced to acknowledge the limited availability of services for couples experiencing sexual difficulties (Mace, 1972). Couples were therefore encouraged to monitor their own sexual satisfactions and dissatisfactions.

A marital sex problem is not the problem of one person. It is the joint problem of two persons, and can only be solved by changes in their relationship brought about by improved communication and cooperation. (Mace, 1972:vi)

Those within Marriage Guidance were not slow, however, to exploit the opportunities afforded by this growing debate on intervention in sexual problems. The same year two Marriage Guidance counsellors described their own self-tutored attempts at offering a sexual therapy service in their local setting (Harris and Usborne, 1972). Soon afterwards another local marriage guidance council invited Paul Brown, a clinical psychologist, to conduct a series of training sessions on the work of Masters and Johnson. Then NMGC'S own Head of Counselling worked as a co-therapist with Brown and subsequently recommended that sex therapy should be further investigated. In an atmosphere of considerable anxiety and caution, the Department of Health and Social Security was approached to support an experimental programme of sex therapy training and intervention, which would be directed and evaluated by Brown. The department was most concerned however that only married couples should be seen and so the initiative, when it received support, was named the Marital Sexual Dysfunction Project (Heisler, 1983).

Six women counsellors took part in the project in the first year, when they were trained by Brown: the following year they too took on trainees. The study concluded that counsellors could develop relevant knowledge and apply it with increasing accuracy to the diagnosis of sexual problems. It was also found that therapists working alone could be just as 'effective' as those working in pairs. The report estimated an annual incidence of cases of sexual dysfunction at around

50,000, of which some 14 per cent were referred.[3] Brown presented his final report in 1979; it was enthusiastically received and the organization went on to secure further DHSS funding for a project which would extend Marital Sex Therapy (MST) training and service provision to all areas, under the direction of a specially appointed NMGC officer. From the beginning of the 1980s, MST activities were founded from within NMGC's mainstream budget. By 1985 130 counsellors were doing this specialist work in sixty-eight MST 'clinics' (Tyndall, 1985:103). Tyndall, the NMGC's Chief Officer at the time MST was established, distinguished several features of the sex therapy programme. Couples had to be willing to attend together and were seen as 'very much their own therapists', being set 'homework' tasks. There was an extensive diagnostic stage to sex therapy, with comprehensive questions and answers and forms to be completed; the nature of the helping relationship was described as that of 'educator giving instruction'. Departing from the Masters and Johnson model, couples were seen weekly, often by therapists working alone (Tyndall, 1985:103–4). This style of working also represented a departure from counselling orthodoxies within NMGC.

A particular feature of this programme of sex therapy was the use of behavioural methods. As counselling programmes within the NMGC had been developed in the 1960s and 1970s, they had been associated primarily with the use of Rogerian, non-directive, techniques (Clark, 1991). These represented a distinct movement away from the 'expert' models of *guidance* which had been offered to clients in the 1940s and 1950s. A move to non-directiveness also involved to some extent the repudiation of medical models of diagnosis and intervention in favour of those which promoted 'unconditional positive regard' for the client and attempted to facilitate a process of self-exploration and disclosure. Sex therapy was, by contrast, much more task-oriented. Following an initial diagnosis of the 'problem', couples engaged in a contract to work for an agreed period of time, in a manner that subsequently allowed review and evaluation.

More generally, within a medical model which emphasized the inter-relationship between practice and research, sex therapy was soon to develop its own epidemiology of sexual dysfunction. This, coupled with a growing range of behaviour modification techniques, in turn established sex therapy's own special knowledge claims. The 'new' sex therapy, which followed Masters and Johnson, was a rejection of psychoanalytic approaches which saw sexual problems as the expression of intrapsychic conflict arising from traumatic early life experiences. In some ways, therefore, it sought to reassert a dualism, challenged by Freud, which would allow sexual problems to be seen more mechanistically, largely as bodily dysfunctions. In sex therapy, couples would be encouraged to monitor and regulate their sexual functioning by reference to a range of techniques and principles of bodily self-assessment.

The implications of the rise of sex therapy programmes within Marriage Guidance were twofold.

First, the programmes represented a continuation of the early preoccupation with sexual issues which characterized the founders of the movement; they should not therefore be seen as an attempt to promote the wider cause of sexual liberation. As Finch and Summerfield have observed about the postwar period: 'Marital stability was increasingly seen as dependent on both contraception and sexual pleasure' (1991:12). Indeed, the heightened attention given to the sexual aspects of marriage must be linked to a wider discourse which promoted concern with marriage as a Relationship (Morgan, 1985; Clark and Morgan, 1991). The marriage Relationship, in this strong sense, could be expected simultaneously to create and to fulfil a complex range of human needs and emotions. But such an edifice, the site of so many expectations, could also prove fragile and vulnerable. To function effectively it might need specialist help of various kinds. Marriage Guidance was not only important in defining the broad field of 'marital problems' (Clark and Morgan, 1991) and in creating sub-fields like marital sex problems; it also offered a source of skilled help and assistance with the very difficulties it had contrived to define. Its programme for couples experiencing sexual difficulties was significantly titled *Marital* Sex Therapy. It sought to focus on sex within the marriage relationship and on the ways in which, with technical help, marital sex could be improved. As we shall see, this took place within a framework which reinforced, rather than challenged, existing gendered assumptions about sexual relationships. The underlying purpose of this was the protection and strengthening of the marriage relationship, not least in a context where, during the 1970s, marriage was construed as being under threat from rising divorce rates (Burgoyne, Ormrod and Richards, 1987:14–18). To this extent Marriage Guidance was relatively absent from the wider debates in the 1960s and 1970s about the inherent problems which could exist within marriage as an *institution* predicated upon sexual exclusivity, preferring instead as Halmos put it: 'to correct the complainer and not the cause of the complaint' (Halmos, 1966:117). Within the discourse of MST, sex, rather than marriage, was seen as problematic.

Second, the introduction into the Marriage Guidance programme of ideas and practice in the field of sex therapy carried a certain price. Whereas the non-directive counselling approach, which became the recognized house style in the 1960s, had been based on an explicit rejection of organic models of marital psychopathology (Lewis, Clark and Morgan, 1992), medical models were now once again in evidence, as they had been in the early days of 'guidance'. Although Brown's original pilot study claimed that only two out of the first 108 cases seen involved sexual problems with a medical basis,[4] those who received specialist training in working with sexual problems became known as *therapists* and they frequently practised in medical settings, such as doctors' surgeries (Clark and Haldane, 1990). Their training and overall orientation made them far more comfortable than the typical non-directive marriage counsellor with an overall medical orientation that involved the 'diagnosis' and 'treatment' of problems.

The new freedom to offer 'help' to couples experiencing sexual problems would also bring with it other effects. As we shall see in the next section of this chapter, within the wider discourse of sex therapy, there existed possibilities for the development of classifications and taxonomies of sexual dysfunction. Firmly underpinned by a medical model of diagnosis and treatment, these provided a developing framework for sexual regulation in which the intimate worlds of bodies would be opened up to scientific scrutiny and therapeutic endeavour.

Medicalization, Surveillance and Regulation of Marital Sex Problems

One aspect of the use of the medical model in the sex therapy literature is the small place it accords to any discussion of sexuality within the nexus of interpersonal relationships. In this context marital sex therapy is seen as a sub-specialty within the field of sex therapy as a whole. Relatively little attention is given, therefore, to the conflicting meanings which may attach to sex, to cultural and historical variations in sexual attitudes and practices and to the important critiques which have emerged from the feminist and gay liberation movements (Weeks, 1989). Whilst some writers on sex therapy see the sexual relationship as 'the microcosm of the total relationship' (Bancroft, 1985:77) or argue that 'human sexual behaviour is highly variable, making it extremely difficult to be able to judge whether a particular response should be classified as *normal* or *dysfunctional*' (Cole and Dryden, 1988:3), in general this is a discourse which pays greater attention to the classification of sexual 'dysfunctions' and to arguments about their aetiology and treatment than to the social and cultural construction of sexuality and its problems.

This literature categorizes sexual practice within a framework which uncritically regards heterosexual penetrative intercourse as the exemplar of authentic sexual activity. Sexual 'dysfunction' is therefore codified into those conditions, whether experienced by men or women, which prevent heterosexual penetrative sex from satisfactorily taking place. Following Cole and Dryden (1988), the *nosology* of sexual dysfunction can be seen to have six major components:

1 *Impaired sexual desire*: a lack of sexual desire, found more commonly in women than men. It may be a problem confined to particular situations; it may relate to earlier life experiences (e.g. sexual abuse); or it may be seen as a function of 'low sex drive'.

2 *Erectile dysfunction*: is thought to be the commonest male sex disorder in the Western world. Again, it may be primary (life-long); secondary (subsequent to a period of 'normal' functioning); or situational. There is considerable debate about the extent to which it is an organic condition: some men who complain of the condition may also experience nocturnal penile tumescence (NPT), drawing into question an organic aetiology.

3 *Premature ejaculation*: is said to be the second most frequent presenting problem at sex dysfunction clinics and is described as a condition where a man reaches orgasm and ejaculates so quickly that neither he nor his partner is satisfied by the experience.

4 *Retarded ejaculation*: is thought to occur in only about 1 per cent of men, it describes a situation where the man finds it impossible to ejaculate or reach orgasm.

5 *Orgasmic dysfunction*: refers to the apparent 'failure' of one-third to one-half of all women to reach an orgasm in intercourse, without some form of 'additional' stimulation.

6 *Vaginismus and dyspareunia*: the former of these refers to constrictions in the lower third of the vagina which prevent the entry of the penis; the latter refers to pain or discomfort in the vagina (or the penis) once entry has taken place

Such a classification, in addition to exposing an apparently disproportionate concern with the sexual difficulties of men, clearly reveals the application of medical thinking to a particular field of 'problems'. Individual subjective experience is generalized and labelled and the resulting categorizations provide the therapist with a diagnostic map with which to identify the 'presenting' problem. In this context psychotherapeutic interventions may also be accompanied by other modalities, including surgery, hormone therapies and drug treatments. Central to this is the distinction between 'psychogenic' and 'organic' dysfunction (Friedman, 1988). The status of this distinction is what separates the activities of 'lay' and medical sex therapists, though it is recognized that these may often work in close liaison or even as co-therapists. Whether practised by doctors or not, the entry of sex therapy into the wider field of marital therapy and counselling has undoubtedly given greater prominence there to medical attitudes and practices which had previously been repudiated within a model drawing more heavily from humanistic psychology than medicine or psychiatry.

A recent chapter by Eddy Street and Jean Smith (1988), two clinical psychologists, illustrates this further. Using the concept of marriage as an 'open system', they show how the 'presenting' sexual dysfunction can be explored in the context of 'the core issues that affect the relationship at a particular point in time' (Street and Smith, 1988:205). The authors find it necessary, however, to rely on a deterministic model of 'developmental stages of marriage', where in 'the normal cycle of a couple's development' it is possible to identify particular phases and marital tasks (*ibid*:208). Characteristically, these are seen in individual/biographical/gendered terms, rather than within the broader framework of the life course, which would allow historical and personal time to be viewed in a dynamic interrelationship (Cohen, 1987; Harris, 1987; Morgan, 1985). For Street and Smith the stages of this 'normal' cycle are: courtship and marriage; young adulthood parenting; early mid-life; late mid-life; retirement; old age. Each of these is endowed with its own set of sexual tasks, for example in the first phase 'gaining knowledge of partner's sexuality' or in the last phase 'accepting [the] changing nature of sexual relationship in response to physical changes' (Street and Smith, 1988:209). It is clear that such a model has diagnostic import for the therapist in facilitating an assessment of the presenting problem in relation to some notion of the developmental phase of the marriage (for example, 'vaginismus' in the first phase or 'impaired sexual desire' in the last). It does this, however, within a somewhat over-determined framework of biological ageing that pays little attention to the disputed and socially constructed nature of such 'stages'. More crucially, within the wider promulgation of sex therapy discourse, it also creates potentialities for self-monitoring and self-diagnosis on the part of couples who may never participate in a therapeutic programme as such.

Richards and Elliot (1991) have recently reviewed some of the material on advice books relating to sex and marriage in Britain in the 1960s and 1970s. A strong theme which emerges from much of this material is that sex and the mutual orgasm are important parts of a marriage relationship in which the underscoring values are ones of closeness, openness and sharing. Although a wider appraisal of the burgeoning sexual advice literature published in recent decades goes well beyond the scope of this chapter, it is clear that such material is relevant to my central theme. Indeed some of it has been produced by practising sex therapists. Pearsall's (1987) *Super Marital Sex* is a recent example. In this work, drawing on clinical experience in the USA, the author maps out a broad agenda for overcoming the humdrum routines of the marital sex lives of his readers. *Super marital sex* is hailed as far more rewarding and exciting than sex outside marriage. As Pearsall puts it:

I am suggesting in super marital sex a new model for intimacy, a new course objective for our culture's sex education, a new priority, a choosing of intimacy. The AIDS crisis should not frighten us into fidelity. We should celebrate the potential of fidelity, its capacity for super sex where the super means whole, lasting, comforting, fulfilling. (Pearsall, 1987:8)

This particular application of sex therapy to the purpose of bolstering marriage includes a whole array of suggestions and 'practical' help. Readers are encouraged to test themselves for sexual 'wellness'; to 're-court' one another; and ultimately to convert their bedrooms into 'sex clinics' dedicated to marital sexual pleasure. With an eye to the demographic situation, there is a special final section on 'senior citizen sex education'. By such means sex therapy discourse has been extended into the domain of self-help and self-education. Here it contributes to a considerable literature in which individuals and couples are encouraged to assess their sexual satisfaction against measures and ratings composed by a variety of 'experts'. The 'sexual revolution' of the 1960s, which encouraged much of this writing, has thus contributed to a host of privatized mechanisms whereby sexual regulation within marriage is performed through exhortations to pleasure, rather than denial or abstinence. The particular burdens of this situation for women are clear. Within the ideal of companionate marriage, wives must not only be friends and confidantes to their husbands; they must also continue to shoulder inequitable burdens of childcare and domestic labour whilst themselves participating in increasing numbers in the paid labour market; and finally they must function as effective and lifelong lovers and sex-partners. In this sense sex therapy has exerted power and influence which extend well beyond the therapeutic setting, to promote wider discourses about sex and its regulation within marriage.

Conclusions

It is clear that within Western-Christian traditions, images of the body play a central role in the institution of marriage. Marriage has served to legitimize sexual access and the procreation of children. It binds bodies together in sickness and in health. Anxiety about sexual contact outside these marital bodies, either premarital or extra-marital, therefore has a long history. That it has been a dominant theme in public debates during the decades since World War Two (Lawson, 1988; Richards and Elliot, 1991) reflects wider concerns about the apparent fragility of 'modern marriage'. Available evidence suggests that sex before marriage has become normative sex outside marriage, the same authors report, is more commonplace but if anything, increasingly condemned (Richards and Elliot, 1991:42–3). At the same time there has been growing concern about the quality of sexual relationships *within* marriage, stimulated at first by debates about 'marriage hygiene' and the use of contraception, and later located in rhetoric about companionate marriage as a fulfilling partnership of 'equals'. My focus in this chapter has been upon the ways in which sexual relations in marriage have been problematized and the manner in which therapeutic responses have been articulated and delivered. But these should not be separated from more general considerations about the relationship between sex and marriage. The idealization of marital sex and its regulation are two elements within a continuous process.

One feature of this social construction of marital sex problems is the dynamic interplay between perceptions of body and mind. Within the Freudian tradition sexual problems are seen as manifestations of intrapsychic disturbance or psychopathology, treatable by psychoanalysis and involving processes of resistance, transference and countertransference. For behaviourists, sexual difficulties are the product of inadequate knowledge, poor technique or psychological blocks which create performance anxieties; these can be addressed through processes of behaviour modification or deconditioning, in which educational methods predominate over psychotherapeutic ones. Between these two positions, clinical medicine seeks to isolate the organic causes of sexual dysfunction, responding with drug treatments and surgical interventions. The sexual acts of marital bodies have thus become a site for major theoretical and professional disagreements. And whilst the *nosology* of sexual dysfunction represents a common vocabulary between the different approaches, there are major disputes about the cause and cure of such 'conditions' as 'premature ejaculation' or 'orgasmic dysfunction'.

Critics of Masters and Johnson, such as Shainess (1968), take the view that sex therapy in this form has served to mechanize sexual relations, removing them from their place within human relationships. Others however, such as Bancroft, have sought to integrate the Masters and Johnson method within an overall approach to couple/marital therapy. But as Bancroft also makes clear, the prerequisite for any intervention must always be the elimination or treatment of organic causes:

> It is often assumed that there should be a clear divide between sexual and marital problems and hence between sexual and marital therapy. But there are many instances when improvement in the sexual relationship will follow improvements in the non-sexual aspects of the relationship and vice versa. The main proviso is that the physical causes of sexual dysfunction are understood and dealt with when appropriate. (Bancroft, 1985:78)

Sex therapy therefore constructs a powerful triad of explanations for sexual 'dysfunction': technical, relational and organic. Sexual difficulties may lie in the domain of poor technique/understanding; they may reflect underlying problems in the relationship; or they may yet have some biomedical basis. Each explanation may provide a counterweight to the other, so that the 'outcome' of any one style of intervention may depend on that of another. Learning new 'skills' in sexual stimulation may be insufficient without an improvement in the couple relationship and neither may be sufficient to produce success if an underlying organic problem is not properly treated.

In this chapter, by exploring the development of the Marital Sex Therapy programme within the work of the National Marriage Guidance Council (now Relate) I have tried to illustrate something of the power of sex therapy discourse. The introduction of sex therapy into the work of the NMGC built upon an established concern with the welfare of marriage. Although in some ways sex therapy took the organization into new and uncharted territory, in other ways it kept it on familiar ground: the alleviation of sexual difficulties as a means to securing and enriching marriage. At the same time, through the promulgation of its literature on sexual problems and the expansion of a programme of sex therapy services, the organization was constructed as a source of expert knowledge and therapeutic skill in the field of sexual problems. NMGC simultaneously helped to define the nature of marital sex problems and then offered a service in response. More recently, through the influence of its specialist training programme for sex therapists, NMGC/Relate has been introducing sex therapy to increasing numbers of health care professionals.[5] Although its own service has been non-medical, sex therapy in NMGC/Relate has undoubtedly gained some of its influence from associations with the medical world. In a twenty-year period the organization has had a major role in the social construction of a discrete therapeutic zone. During this time, whether in the therapy room or through the encouragement of self-surveillance, the sexual activities of marital bodies have undoubtedly been exposed to a new and penetrating gaze.

Notes

1   The material presented in this chapter forms part of a larger study of the marital agencies, focusing on the history and development of the NMGC. This study was undertaken in collaboration with Jane Lewis and David Morgan and funded by the Economic and Social Research Council (grant number R000231060) and is reported more fully elsewhere (Lewis, Clark and Morgan, 1992). The study draws on a wide range of primary and secondary documentary materials, as well as interviews with key figures in the world of Marriage Guidance. I am grateful to all those who offered their time and expertise in the collection of this data, and particularly so to the headquarters staff of Relate, National Marriage Guidance.
2   General Principles of Marriage Guidance Councils, adopted 1943.
3   Brown, P.T. (1976) *Report to the Counselling Advisory Board of the NMGC of the Research Work of the Marital Sexual Dysfunction Project*. NMGC.
4   *Ibid.*
5   *Relate News*, No. 16, April 1991, p. 2.

References

BANCROFT, J. (1985) Marital sex therapy, in DRYDEN, W. (Ed.) *Marital Therapy in Britain*, Vol. 2, London, Harper and Row.

BERGER, P.L. and KELLNER, H. (1964) Marriage and the construction of reality, *Diogenes*, 1–23.

BROWN, P.T. (1979) Practical modifications of Masters' and Johnsons' approach to the treatment of sexual dysfunction, *Unpublished PhD Thesis*, University of Leicester.

BURGOYNE, J., ORMROD, R. and RICHARDS, M. (1987) *Divorce Matters*, Harmondsworth, Penguin.

CLARK, D. (1991) Guidance, counselling, therapy: responses to 'marital problems', 1950–90. *Sociological Review*, November pp. 165–298.

CLARK, D. and HALDANE, D. (1990) *Wedlocked? Research and intervention in marriage*, Cambridge, Polity.

CLARK, D. and MORGAN, D. (1991) The gaze of the counsellors? Discourses of intervention in marriage. Paper presented to British Sociological Association Annual Conference, Manchester, March 1991.

COHEN, G. (Ed.) (1987) *Social Change and the Life Course*, London, Tavistock.

COLE, M. and DRYDEN, W. (1988) Sexual dysfunction: an introduction, in COLE, M. and DRYDEN, W. (Eds) *Sex Therapy in Britain*, Milton Keynes, Open University Press.

DONZELOT, J. (1979) *The Policing of Families: Welfare versus the State*, London, Hutchinson.

FINCH, J. and SUMMERFIELD, P. (1991) Social reconstruction and the emergence of companionate marriage, 1945–59, in CLARK, D. (Ed.) *Marriage, Domestic Life and Social Change: Writings for Jacqueline Burgoyne (1944–88)*, London, Routledge and Kegan Paul.

FOUCAULT, M. (1984) *The History of Sexuality*, Volume 1, Harmondsworth, Penguin.

FRIEDMAN, D. (1988) Assessing the basis of sexual dysfunction: diagnostic procedures, in COLE, M. and DRYDEN, W. (Eds) *Sex Therapy in Britain*, Milton Keynes, Open University Press.

HALMOS, P. (1966) Counselling morality, *Marriage Guidance*, July, pp. 116–8.

HARRIS, C. (1987) The individual and society: a processual approach, in BRYMAN, A., BYTHEWAY, B., ALLATT, P. and KEIL, T. (Eds) *Rethinking the Life Cycle*, London, Macmillan.

HARRIS, J. and USBORNE, H. (1972) Sexual dysfunction, *NMGC Newsletter*, No. 58, p. 2.

HEISLER, J. (1983) *Sex Therapy in NMGC*, Rugby, National Marriage Guidance Council.

LAWSON, A. (1988) *Adultery: An analysis of love and betrayal*, Oxford, Blackwell.

LEWIS, J. (1990) Public institution and private relationship: Marriage and Marriage Guidance, 1920–68, *Twentieth Century British History*, Vol. 1, No. 3, pp. 233–263.

LEWIS, J., CLARK, D. and MORGAN, D. (1992) *Whom God Hath Joined Together: The work of Marriage Guidance 1920–90*, London, Tavistock/Routledge.

MACE, D. (1945) *The Outlook for Marriage,*, London, Marriage Guidance Council.

MACE, D. (1948a) *Marriage Crisis*, London, Delisle.

MACE, D. (1948b) *Marriage Counselling*, London, Churchill.

MACE, D. (1972) *Sexual Difficulties in Marriage*, Rugby, National Marriage Guidance Council.

MACLAY, D. (1955) First year impressions, *Marriage Guidance*, May, pp. 3–4.

MASTERS, W.H. and JOHNSON, V.E. (1966) *Human Sexual Response*, London, Churchill.

MASTERS, W.H. and JOHNSON, V.E. (1970) *Human Sexual Inadequacy*, London, Churchill.

MASTERS, W.H., JOHNSON, V.E. and KOLODNY, R.C. (1987) *Sex and Human Loving*, London, Macmillan.

MONTEFIORE, H.W. (1963) Personal relations before marriage, in MACKINNON, D.M., ROOT, H.E., MONTEFIORE, H.W. and BURNABY, J. (Eds) *God, Sex and War*, London, Fontana.

MORGAN, D.H.J. (1985) *The Family, Politics and Social Theory*, London, Routledge and Kegan Paul.

PEARSALL, P. (1987) *Super Marital Sex*, London, Ebury Press.

RICHARDS, M.P.M. and ELLIOT, B. JANE (1991) Sex and marriage in the 1960s and 1970s, in CLARK, D. (Ed.) *Marriage, Domestic Life and Social Change: Writings for Jacqueline Burgoyne (1944–88)*, London, Routledge.

SHAINESS, N. (1968) The problem of sex today, *American Journal of Psychiatry*, 124, 1076–1084.

STREET, E. and SMITH, J. (1988) 'From Sexual Problems to Marital Issues', in COLE, M. and DRYDEN, W. (Eds) *Sex Therapy in Britain*, Milton Keynes, Open University Press.

TYNDALL, N. (1985) The work and impact of the National Marriage Guidance Council, in DRYDEN, W. (Ed.) *Marital Therapy in Britain*, Vol. 1, London, Harper and Row.

WEEKS, J. (1989) *Sex, Politics and Society: The regulation of sexuality since 1800*, 2nd ed., London, Longman.

Chapter 3

Dance and the Culture of the Body

Joyce Sherlock

Breath-taking moments create the memorable in dance and lend themselves to explanations of dance ability rooted in the metaphysical. Thus, it is not surprising that such explanations are widely taken-for-granted in British theatre dance even though the milieu provides professional work. Dancers, choreographers, critics and audiences commonly share an idealist philosophy which implies that art is outside society and artists' achievements arise from natural talent. This belief is largely unchallenged in much dance study too, for few British studies which emphasize the cultural nature of dance have been undertaken. That the breath-taking moment depends on long and arduous training to become part of the cultural memory of a company is rarely noted. Nor is it considered in movement observation and dance notation, widely employed as starting points for study. Developed to precisely record bodily movements, they perpetuate what has happened in most dance teaching, namely that style has become separated from cultural knowledge so that dance movements are rarely recognized as bearers of cultural values. Concern with step precision and personal skill has perpetuated naturalistic attitudes towards the body overlooking the reality of its social construction and the transformation of the cherished values of a social group into movement imagery. However, once dance movements are read as signifying such cultural values and the responses of different social groups towards them, it is then possible to reveal dimensions of the British way of life mediated through dance.

Contemporary British studies of dance which emphasize the cultural pay oblique attention to the way it and the body relate in dance. Some, featuring dance as part of the way of life of highly visible youth sub-cultures, focus on the 'awkward question' of youth as it has manifest itself to the media and the authorities since the late 1950s. Richard Johnson (1983) referred to 'awkward questions' as aspects of British culture which arouse conflict between social groups. One group's moral objection to the behaviour of another, such as generational conflict resulting from the music, dance and style of youth culture is the stuff of 'awkward questions'. For example, Geoff Mungham (1976) showed how the Mecca Dance Hall was an integral part of the lives of working-class young people in the 1970s. John Fiske and John Hartley (1978) read television's 'Come Dancing' as a text to show how the format of commentary, camera shots and competition, embody codes of meaning. These reaffirmed the ideology of social harmony and acceptable social stratification, the illusion of legitimate spaces for glamour in the otherwise modest lives of hairdressers and clerks. The glamorous image underlined the woman's commodified sexuality. Dick Hebdige (1979) examined the 'awkward question' of the punk sub-culture being regarded as an outrage by the moral majority in Britain.

Alternatively, a case-study of Ballet Rambert[1] and Christopher Bruce's 'Ghost Dances' (Joyce Sherlock, 1988) addressed the 'awkward question' of general philistinism towards 'high-art' by exposing the cultural nature of dance and the cultivation of the body. It demonstrated how dancers are made by dance institutions, and that meaning attributed to a dance is affected by the body language and audiences' perceptions of bodily propriety. Thus, a professional dance company was considered as part of a sub-culture of the hegemonic group in society. Cultural and ideological aspects of the history and contemporary situation of the company were emphasized against promotional histories and critics' appraisals. Juxtaposing the latter with working class audiences' views of 'Ghost Dances' exemplified the cultural and class-specific location of the company in 1983 and the similarities and differences with the 1930s when the company was first successful. Treated culturally and ideologically, the creation of a dance and consideration of whose interests were served indicated important affiliations with contemporary culture, countering individualist notions of a social meritocracy and cultured individuals with good taste. Theoretical aspects of the study, namely culture, social class and visual ideology (Hadjinicolaou, 1978) and extrapolations relating to gender and ethnicity, form the main basis of illustration in the chapter. Theoretical points applied to wider examples are introduced at this stage to clarify the background to a cultural production way of thinking.

Theory, Dance and Culture

The few sociological and cultural studies of dance in Britain have focused mainly on 'social dance' (Rust, 1969) and popular culture. Cultural production theory recognizes that these, treated differently, as cultural forms, reveal unique histories and traditions belonging to particular social groups, passed on and changed by successive generations. The focus on a theatre dance company by Sherlock (1988) demonstrates that theatre dance forms are also cultural forms. Such a treatment enables all forms of dance to be recognized as existing within society and that theatre dance, rather than being regarded as asocial and aesthetic, as high-culture, has its own particular orientation towards key social attitudes which can be identified as related to British history. It also shows that the apparent gap which exists between the 'individualism' of modern dance (in all its forms) and socio-cultural explanations could be related to the commonsensical way in which there is a tendency to treat individuals as separate bodies in our culture, rather than recognizing that we are socially constructed and culturally produced. Juxtaposing art and working-class culture and treating theatre dance as related to a sub-culture of dominant middle-class values, enables consideration of these to be approached afresh.

Hebdige's (1979) study is helpful in showing how two different meanings of culture coexist uneasily in appraisals of post-war British working-class life (e.g. Richard Hoggart, 1957). Juxtaposing the arts and working-class culture is highly relevant to an understanding of the contemporary social period as Tony Dunn's (1986) quotation from Louis Menand (1982) shows:

> Before the 1960s criticism of popular culture was sociological and criticism of high culture was moral and aesthetic. From then on popular culture was so all-pervading in the USA that cultural critics had to do something about it. The alternatives emerged as to treat all culture as commodity, or to treat all culture as art. (Dunn cites Menand but does not give source)

Hebdige (1979), who considered the grounds for calling punk culture art, shows how two basic definitions of culture emerged from different traditions, though not necessarily congruent with them. The traditions relate firstly to Matthew Arnold's (1932) view of the cultured person where culture is defined as a standard of aesthetic excellence based on the classical Greek ideals of proportion, harmony and unity: in layman's terms, high-culture. The second tradition relates to Karl Marx's and Frederick Engels' social analysis and a definition of culture deriving from anthropological study, where most definitions of culture have been modifications of E.B.Tylor's:

> complex whole which includes knowledge, belief, art, morals, law, custom, and any other capabilities and habits as acquired by man as a member of society. (Mitchell, 1968:47)

This conceptualization tends to distinguish the cultural from the biological or natural as something which is learned.

The two approaches to the definition of culture are implicit in much dance study where theatre dance is treated as art or appreciated by the cultured individual as a standard of aesthetic excellence (e.g. Stokes, 1934). The anthropological definition is evident in studies drawing on that discipline, (Kurath, 1960; Royce, 1977; Hanna, 1979; Lange, 1980; Kaeliinohomoku, 1983), in Rust's (1969) and Thomas' (1986) sociological studies, and implicit in general writings which assume that dance has a function in society (Adshead, 1986; Banes, 1986). Conflict conceptualizations of culture in dance study are scarce; apart from the cultural studies already mentioned, there are studies by Blacking (1979) and proposals for conflict approaches from Brinson (1983) and Dyer (1983). The significance of an anthropological conceptualization set in a capitalist class-framework, questions the idea of culture as implicitly capable only of presenting a patronizing, sentimental or inauthentic view of the working class. It legitimizes as meaningful to the group, their views and statements about cultural objects. Allied with a view of social relations derived from a capitalist mode of production, 'awkward questions' can be readdressed within the framework of conflictual social relations between interest groups. These can be weighed against an idealist ideology of social harmony, aesthetic taste and cultural transcendence.

Social Class, Cultural Production and Dance Audiences

Pierre Bourdieu (1984) has demonstrated that cultural preferences have strong class relationships influenced by social access, class background and ideological factors. At different levels of the social hierarchy one is more likely to be introduced to some cultural activities than others, even in highly technological Western societies dominated by what have been termed mass and consumer cultures. As far as audiences are concerned, John Myerscough's (1988) study confirmed that access to the arts in Britain is largely urban, centring around London and the South East. Although London residents form the minority of London's overall art audience, they are in the majority at the Royal Opera House (62 per cent). Females predominate in London's theatre and concert audiences (56 per cent) in London. Consistently across the rest of the country 10 per cent of the population attend concerts, ballet, opera and pop concerts. The higher figures for the South East may be because of the presence of higher proportions of upper and lower middle-class occupational groups, for the arts reach twice as many people in the top three occupational groups as in the bottom three. In Glasgow 11 per cent of the upper three occupational groups attend ballet, which is exceptionally high. Myerscough recognizes that very active minorities of enthusiasts clock up large proportions of total attendances for dance (hence the phenomenon of the balletomane; Marwick, 1971), concerts and opera.

Thus, ballet has a minority appeal for a select group of mainly professional and semi-professionals, predominantly female. Myerscough's findings are supported by Rosemary Deem's (1987) research into female leisure. Furthermore, my research bears witness to the inaccessibility to working-class occupational groups of a theatre dance which commanded full houses. It also revealed the middle-class nature of dancers' social backgrounds which supports the theory of cultural production rather than the biological one of natural talent. Thus, the theory suggests that features of one's social background such as class and gender have a broad socializing effect on the individual in relation to becoming part of a dance audience, becoming a professional dancer and colluding with cultural perceptions of bodily image. The harmonious connotations of multiculturalism, prevalent in current dance ideology, need closer examination, for equality of opportunity may be less than a reality precisely because of social class and ethnic cultural differences.

The Cultural Production of a Professional Dancer

Turning to Sherlock's (1988) case-study to illustrate further this way of thinking, observed working practices and personal interviews with Rambert dancers revealed that social class, dance-training, body-type, selection procedures, working relationships, ethnicity, physical above intellectual requirements and the commodification of the body, were significant cultural features in explaining success. Dancers came mainly from middle-class backgrounds where there was an interest in the arts, and not surprisingly, all of the female dancers and most of the males had had considerable classical ballet training, although not from the age of two as is commonly thought. The type of body required to present the correct image on stage means that the look of the dancer is paramount. This was encouraged in daily ballet classes and a requirement stated by the choreographer, Christopher Bruce. He worked with the classical style, and dancers needed to be trained accordingly to work with him. He personally wielded considerable power in the company at the time in suggesting who should be recruited. It is important in choreographing that a dancer and choreographer should be able to work compatibly. Selection procedures for classical ballet dancers to train at the highest level are extremely stringent and training is centred around London. Physical slimness, height, flexibility, beauty and stamina are some of the qualities which are prerequisites and vary from one culture to another even within the ballet world. If we take height, to be a tall female in London means being above 5'6" high, and this will exclude a candidate from serious consideration. In New York it will not. Being black may still be a disadvantage in some British companies, but not in New York. The Royal Ballet was, until recently, all white, perhaps because of the needs of the repertoire, perhaps because of the paucity of black ballet-trained dancers in Britain; perhaps, as later reference in the chapter to Bharata Natyam dance suggests, because of cultural incompatibility. Whatever the reason, the visual ideology, that is the cultural values that can be read off the image the dancer projects (Hadjinicolaou, 1978), will read not-too-tall, slim and mostly white. Although not totally the case in the company studied where thirteen of the sixteen dancers were white, the one West Indian female was educated in Trinidad, a West Indian male was Dutch and the single Asian male was brought up in Singapore. In view of stereotypes about blacks' propensity to rhythmic movement, it is telling that the ascribed abilities of black Britons were not visible in this type of dance in 1983, although there have been changes since then.

Dancers were unfamiliar with dance history, and felt that their secondary education, once a member of a company school, was token, leaving them feeling inadequate intellectually. Several said how the demanding touring schedule burnt them out so that few saw other dance companies perform or followed the other arts seriously. The mind/body split was articulated further in the emphasis on the technical training of the body to the detriment of the emotional as well as the intellectual dimensions of a person's being. One choreographer believed this limited the range of expressive potential in role interpretations by some dancers. On the other hand, many were intent upon 'self-development'. For some females this involved an interest in feminist literature. For one male at least it meant being openly homosexual. Although not evident from the research except in the case of two older dancers (aged between 30 and 35 — the youngest dancer in the company was 20) there have been examples of extremes of dislocation between dancers' actual lives and their stage performances.[2] Such cases highlight that control of the body is not simply a matter of the discipline exercised by the school or the dance directors, but is influenced by wider ideological notions of bodies, movements and good dancing. One female dancer who knew Lynne Seymour well also knew how exceptional she had been to combine having children with a long dance career. The dancer interviewed was deciding when to give up dancing in order to have a child. One of the limitations of combining the two is the lack of provision for maternity leave. Another is that the pregnant woman's shape is not an acceptable image. Unsocial hours and constant touring schedules made any personal life very difficult for many of the dancers, whether male or female. The eldest male dancer saw himself as being a pawn in the company's game: being encouraged to move into teaching before he was ready to give up his dancing career.

As an observer, the term 'balletomane' began to take on a new connotation for my appreciation of performances. As a result of the interviews, the performances of the dancers, whom I had not known previously, ceased to be purely visual as I recognized them as people with thoughts, aspirations, feelings and lives of their own. However, they clearly subjected themselves to a process of training to make their bodies capable of the demands of the performance style. The process is one of 'cultivation', both active and passive: being selected, being nurtured and nurturing one's movement towards a desired image which means moving in the way expected.

Culturally Producing a Dance Interpretation: Social Class and Gender

Switching the focus from the viewed body of the dancer to the cultural location of the viewer, another aspect of the cultural production thesis draws on evidence which indicates that our perceptions are shaped by our cultural experience. One of the dances most popular with Ballet Rambert audiences in the 1980s, 'Ghost Dances', was dedicated by its choreographer, Christopher Bruce, to 'the innocent people of South America who from the time of the Spanish conquests have been continuously devastated by political oppression'.[1a] Viewed by groups of shop stewards, vehicle maintenance engineers and hairdressers, its appeal was less convincing. I found that the shop stewards protested that they did not understand it and yet were pleased they had watched the superb dancing. Analysis of discussion shows that a high degree of meaning was evident, but created in terms of their social group's view of society, taking the part of the oppressed group in the dance and making a parallel of it with their perception of the situation of the working class. From this stance they thought that the struggle between the oppressors and oppressed would be meaningful to the actual South American people to whom it was dedicated. Vehicle maintenance engineers 'thought it was pathetic', 'didn't know how to judge it' and thought the people of South America would have 'about as much clue as I had about it', which it was claimed was none. The all-male group responded mockingly to the dance but spent most of the discussion revealing the importance of their own music and dance culture in their lives, to which only one of the group did not contribute. Theatres were considered 'posh', but the cinema was popular. The group could not, or would not, attempt to interpret the dance which the choreographer considered access-ible. They were not interested in a cultural form which was not their own. A group of all-female, bar one, hairdressing students responded to the dance in four main ways: that it was good and clever, different, and boring. The responses rested on the degree to which a story-line could be followed, and this was not achieved by many in the group. Views on what the people of South America might think of it varied around them not understanding it, not being interested in it and thinking it rubbish. It was observed that it was not taken from South American dance style, which would contribute to the unfamiliarity. Although some girls had had ballet and modern dance lessons, most preferred Madonna. References to the weirdness of the dancers, how they were considered 'poncey', and that homosexuals would like to watch them, suggested their view of gender conventions and bodily propriety amongst the hairdressing group.

This opportunity to let subjects speak for themselves and to probe an under-standing of the logic underlying behaviour interpreted in everyday parlance as 'philistine', 'uncouth' or 'snobby' by others, reveal entrenched attitudes towards social class in Britain. Movement styles and aesthetic appreciation are strongly associated with cultural expression and can be read as ideological. Thus, art can be conceptualized other than aesthetically or stylistically, as a cultural activity promoted by a powerful social group who value it. The ideological significance of the body is that the particular body image is symbolic of a way of life and its reception draws together those who idealize it, and alienates those unfamiliar with it. Transposing Hadjinicolaou's (1978) term 'visual ideology' from the visual arts context can enable the 'look' of dance to be examined through body image and style of movement being recognized as containing codes of meaning related to cultural practices and dominant ways of thinking.

Comparative Cultural Production

Kaeliinihomoku (1983) reviewed a range of dance writings for their lack of anthropological knowledge and their ethnocentrism, with regard to the superiority of ballet as a dance form developed by Caucasians speaking Indo-European languages and sharing a common European tradition. Their work embodied an 'us and them' attitude towards our own and other cultures. Also implied was the social production of the ballet aesthetic in relation to 'our' aesthetic values embodied in the particular 'look' which ballet has. Patronization towards other cultures, Kaeliinihomoku claimed, derives from the linguistic difficulties of English-speaking writers finding ways of evaluating dance without recourse to Western standards of judgment. However, the critique does not recognize that English culture is heterogeneous, and reference to 'our' culture comes under question. Ballet is not regarded as 'ours' by every social group in England. It is considered an élite activity and is shown to be class-related, revealing that the 'us and them' phenomenon exists within as well as between cultures (Hoggart, 1957).

An example of 'us and them' between cultures arises from a series of lectures on an Asian dance residency given by Shobana Jeyasingh where she demonstrated how aesthetic value in dance is cultural.[3] Elegance in British dance is associated with tallness, slimness, extended and pointed limbs. In India the squat, similar to the demi-plié ballet position, is considered elegant, accompanied by the flexed foot. The very word squat in English is derogatory. Jeyasingh also revealed much about social stratification in British society from her own experience. From a position of status as a dancer of Bharata Natyam (derived from courtly traditions in India), she is not only without status in a solo dance form in Britain where ballet, large companies and large theatres denote status, but she is also an immigrant, a brown-skinned person who has no clear place in the social system except at the bottom. In dance performance one can avoid confrontation with this fact for the audience is distanced, and take their personal likes and dislikes away. In dance residencies, the children who enjoy the sessions most are often Anglo-Saxon girls who have had some ballet lessons and who understand the formality of technique. Bangladeshi children often expect to be taught Bhangra, a popular form of dance, and are disappointed that the Asian dance taught is not their perception of Asian dance. 'Asian' as a label conceals vast differences in religion and culture. Asian immigrants from urban and rural areas will display varying degrees of Westernization and education. What Jeyasingh's observations imply is that there can be more affinities between Asian and Western courtly forms of dance than within ethnic cultural groups. The cultural may be unifying across nations when similar status groups are involved, and conflicting within nations where different cultural groups and statuses are considered.

Cultural Globalization in T.V. Dance

Broadening the theme, dance is entertainment, art and cultural heritage but has the appearance of being apart from the main business of industrial production and consumption in a capitalist society. With world-wide availability of telecommunications this is no longer tenable. Dancing, although not considered as secure and lucrative a career (Sherlock, 1988) as, for example, medicine or law, nevertheless has a highly structured system literally shaping the body into tightly defined proportions. Whatever form of dance one is talking about, it needs to be learned, and the degree of proficiency, usually associated with skill, is also associated with body image. Observed practices of a dance company produced evidence that social processes perpetuate a correct image of the body, and in selecting out those bodies least appropriate, reproduce bodies suitable in shape and abilities to the form of dance. However, different dance forms produce different images, but all of these relate to contemporary culture (in ways mediated by each cultural tradition) because of the predominance of contemporary ways of thinking which require a polished product, standardized and clearly formed. This is a dilemma Jeyasingh considers: whether Bharata Natyam should keep its integrity as a solo dance for small spaces and forgo status in Britain, or adapt to a Western large scale. What Jean Baudrillard (1985) called the 'ecstacy of communication' is a powerful influence on this dilemma, symbolic of cultural power.

Frederic Jameson's (1984) reference to postmodern culture, consistent with such conceptualizations as high-tech communications culture, consumer and mass culture, refers to the global dominance of contemporary culture and its Western origins and ideology. Through the example of television it can be argued that dominant images of the body suggest cultural superiority. Such an analysis acknowledges the variety of dance forms currently available but addresses the cultural status attached to some, more than others, as recognized through the social processes of format, presentation and financial support. From a British perspective it is a belated sign of the recognition of the significance of Asian dance in Britain, that government funding for dance residencies is now available. This signifies to some degree that the culture of a minority group is now being accepted. It does not mean a change in the power base, however, for not all dance forms are being labelled 'cultural'. And the power base is no longer the British middle-class, but the multinational corporation.

Jameson (1984) identifies a schizophrenic feeling engendered by an inability to locate oneself politically in the 'new world space', directing attention to the fact that global capitalist communications culture presents itself as the object of aspiration world-wide. Jameson is arguing that we have lost a feeling of political control over the direction of the predominant culture and its ideology of secular materialism displayed through the moving pictures of bodies on television.

Dance features strongly in the medium of television. If one examines whether images of dancers transmitted through the Western media have a particular visual ideology, there are aspects of the 'look' of Kathkali, when televised, which make it clearly non-Western and a speciality for Asian series or black programmes. Its visual ideology may be related to the values and practices of only a part of a culture whose way of life is unknown and strange to others, but it is presented within the format of the television spectacular, and merely reinforces the fact that predominant body images in dance on television, transmitted world-wide, in pop-show extravaganzas and fast moving routines are Western. The success of Western culture and Western bodies is their familiarity to non-Western cultural groups. Trends towards this becoming the universal aesthetic will diminish the richness of cultural diversity. Telecommunications perpetuate the separation of high-art and popular culture while overlaying on both the logic of technical rationality.

The immense variety in the images of the body that dance presents on television can be shown also to draw attention to the social body. Thus Indian dance is above all exotic to the Western eye. In Bharata Natyam and Kathkali the musical accompaniment, constant sounding of bells attached to the ankles, use of the wrists, feet, bodily posture and facial expression, and allusion to gods and superstitions strange to the Western ear, are Asian. There is bright spangled colour, jewels in the nose, vivid enhancement of the eyes and lips. Rhythm is persistant, mime is ingenious.

If space allowed, one could extrapolate upon such themes as tap dancing and the irresponsible image of the negro in 'Cotton Club', the carefree charm of youth in Gene Kelly and Fred Astaire films, the inaccessibility of the classical ballerina: all culturally produced and signifying. Fiske and Hartley (1978) show through the example of 'Come Dancing' that the programme is a means of reinforcing ideologies of competition. They emphasize the closeness of the television message between dancing and sport by demonstrating that 'Match of the Day' is no more football than 'Come Dancing' is dancing: both are a 'second-stage structure of reality' (p. 142) which means that the structure of the television programme has selected out from the original event material which suits the construction of the television show. The formality of the ballroom dancing competition is reformed in such a way that what the television producers interpret as the culturally central motifs of the live event become prominent; in this case, competition.

The televising of 'serious' dance such as ballet and contemporary dance is a second-stage structure of reality also in the way that aspects of the coming performance are explained in the introduction to the programme. The theatre audience dines on smoked salmon sandwiches and chilled white wine before the show, as a matter of course. Their being knowledgeable is taken for granted. Television producers cannot rely on a knowledgeable mass audience. They are aware of the unfamiliarity of the dance form. The television screen is substituted for the proscenium arch and makes for an uneasy transition of the dances. The perception that dances do not speak for themselves reveals an overt attempt to woo an audience. Implicit in this is the idea that this is 'culture' (an example of an aesthetic standard of excellence) which will require some concentration. Entertainment becomes education. On the other hand the format of the light entertainment show and the form of stage dance, which has evolved to suit it, fits more neatly the perceived requirements of a mass audience. This form of dance has adapted and changed from a form of stage dance to enhance the television spectacular. The soap opera ingredients in the film 'Fame' enabled its adaptation to precisely that, as a weekly complete story with opportunities for dance performances. Twyla Tharp's 'Catherine Wheel' was an innovative attempt to confront the medium of television and computer choreography.

Gender

One area heavily structured is gender. Fiske and Hartley (1978) observed women's glamour objectified in 'Come Dancing'. The professional Latin American and Jive competition final was televised on the programme in 1989 and there was a clear presentation of both the male and female as sex-objects. The winning couple's performance of the Jive bore little relation to its original style in terms of the rawness of the music, of the dress and the age of the dancers. The 1989 style of music, dress and dancing for the contest were 'musak' and simulachra (Jameson, 1984). This means their historical reference was emptied out of meaning.

Although the male led, male dominance was not overt. Both partners expressed sexual passion in the physical energy of their interpretation. This was a mature couple. The *passa d'oble* of the bull-fighter and the bull had become reconstructed in the jive. The dance no longer spoke of the social body of Harlem or even the 1950s American high school, but of a romanticized South American vista. The tanned bodies of the white Scottish and Northern English couple, their sleeked back dark hair and figure-hugging clothing were kitsch: a 1980s veneer had streamlined past representations and reflections. Male and female both presented themselves as sexually empowered and to be surveyed (Berger, 1972), and the glamour was revealingly offset in interviews focusing on the degree of hard work needed to achieve their goal. This was the pay-off of 1980s enterprise. From former routine jobs, success was achieved on television.

The status attached to the art forms of ballet and contemporary dance is maintained partly by suppression of the effort required. But the body images of light entertainment dance competitions and the high-art dances are very similar: tall, slim, very supple and athletic, scantily clad, streamlined, efficient, economical, nothing superfluous, not emotional, rehearsed rather than improvised, formal and polished, gender-specific, often white or Afro-Caribbean, less often Italian or Asian. These characteristics can be identified also in jet and car design: clear, unambiguously and lusciously functional, expressive of the now global cultural obsession with efficiency, speed, commodification, technology, depersonalization and image creating. There is something sinister and true in Baudrillard's (1985) observation that the car is no longer possessed so much for driving as for image and status. The body in contemporary dance culture is equally commodified.

Nevertheless, Sherlock's (1988) audience research suggested resistance to dance forms perceived as culturally alien by working-class occupational groups in Britain. John Wyver (1986) argues that although we live in a mass culture we do not simply submit to it. Images, narratives and formulations of desire are taken and re-worked and re-used as they are matched against real experience in the real world. The popular culture of television he says, quoting Raymond Williams'

'*Towards 2,000*', is thus reformulated into individual resistance. But this view takes no account of power. There is another approach to resistance and that is the long tradition of subversion within the arts which Alan Sinfield (1988) referred to. He pointed out how the arts generally are labelled effeminate and associated with gay men (tolerated in the dance sphere in a homophobic society). The arts were also being starved of financial aid in the 1980s under Thatcherism. He identified gay men, high-art and left-culturism as a bloc which Thatcherism opposed. Convincingly, he argued that the arts illustrate what Thatcherism labelled as bad, but that they are a repository for many subversive needs in society. Of all the arts, dance is probably the one most associated with gay men and the effete. The male ballet dancer is read as displaying 'unhealthy', 'weird' and homosexual connotations.

During the period of cut-backs in the arts the 'gender issue' has become legitimized in the form of female rights. With an awareness of traditional English attitudes, in the 1970s there was a strong resistance by several dancers and small companies to the entrenched dominance of mainstream ideology in dance in Britain.[4] One aspect of this ideology was the narrowness of the image of woman-hood exemplified by the ballerina and associations with upper-class ideology. Experiments with perceptions of masculinity were also undertaken. One dance, 'Bleeding Fairies', had cultural connotations about males, females and religion: the sacred and the profane in our culture. There is the reference to the body of Christ, and ambiguity about the body, dance and Christianity. There is the reference to the ambiguity of the status of the male dancer. The image on the front of a New Dance journal of a Giselle-like figure of a ballerina speaking the words of the title in a comic-like balloon, refers to the fairy image of women in ballet who in real life menstruate. These artists considered theatre dance to be élitist and wished to bring dance to a wider audience, outside conventional theatre settings. There was a desire to demystify dance, to explore avenues which allowed dancers to use everyday movement, and to avoid the hatred and alienation from the body which they claimed ballet training brought about. In spite of optimism about the popularity of such enterprises (Murray, 1979), there is little evidence of theatre dance audiences being extended (Myerscough, 1988) by such events, apart from perhaps interest amongst other artists. In the 1980s their experimental ideas were being absorbed by the establishment companies without any change in the power base. The large companies were having to depend more and more on business sponsorship than on government subsidy. They have to be economically viable. However, there are several examples of ongoing work by females contributing to fulfilling their demands in dance (Adair, 1992).

Jeff Hearn (1987) observes that the questioning of what it is to be a women brought about by modern feminism has prompted questioning about what it is to be a man. As examples of attempts to redefine masculinity Hearn draws attention to

the development of unisex or bisexual images, and the frequently apolitical blurring of gender roles in pop culture as in the Boy George, Marilyn, Sigue Sigue Sputnik, and other members of the 'gender bender' phenomenon. Men also seem urged by both the leaders of pop fashion and commercial advertisers to change their clothes, wear skirts, make-up and jewellery. Men's images and masculinity are fragmented, softened, subtly altered by reference and allusion. Men occasionally appear in advertisements as sensual, caring, even effeminate; the 'new man' phenomenon, a true creation of the media, is promoted in magazines and television, particularly in America but now also in Britain, Australia and elsewhere; and sportsmen and trade unionists weep in public in times (and perhaps as signs) of victory and defeat. Increasingly, though not for the first time, masculinity is in 'crisis'. (Hearn, 1987:5)

Here examples of social changes for men are listed as the loss of interest in the traditional male 'breadwinner role', increased divorce, rising unemployment and 'men's liberation'. The return of style for males, and the image which mass culture encourages, even if it is in conflict with traditional British ideas of 'manliness', is unlikely to embrace the elevation of the traditional image of the male ballet dancer as a popular hero. Superman's tights do not detract from his mission, for he denotes the all American male in flights of 'daring-do'. The ballet dancer denotes an expressivity for males which is uncomfortable in Britain, even though male and female bodies in another dance context in the 1980s became objects of power to be surveyed.

Resistance to gender stereotyping occurs but, in the broadening of legitimate masculine and feminine roles, the hegemony of a type of masculinity for the male, close to a traditional one of efficiency, toughness, rationality, unemotional involvement and practicality has become predominant behaviour for males and females alike. Radical opposition has extended the choice of possibilities, but has also become mainstream insofar as the ideas are compatible with consumer culture. There is evidence that the masses have as little interest as ever in the cherished forms of dance of the hegemonic group, and that their attitudes towards gender roles are traditional. But this does not mean that the resistance inherent in élite dance should not continue. The values of the style may be associated with a cultural life-style which no longer has the political power that it once had, but which has certain affiliations with global capitalist communications. Those who value it need openly to promote it, rather than mystify it as something special, and it may be that women in particular should strive to make it speak for their interests (Sherlock, 1990). What is special to different cultural groups needs to be promoted as precisely that by the protagonists, as resistance to the infringement of civil rights and personal liberties, instead of being presented as apart from politics and culture. In Britain's attempts to keep pace with global telecommunications technology, the valued manifestations of cultures and subcultures other than technical rational culture are subversive tendencies, struggling to avoid co-option into the system and to maintain control and freedom. A study of dance may show how bodies represent and encode such struggles, and help us to understand those dancers attempting to articulate the struggles in their work.

Notes

1   In 1982, when the study began, Ballet Rambert was still the company name. This was changed in 1987 to The Rambert Dance Company.
1a   Programme Notes for 'Ghost Dances'.

2   The well-publicized example was in the USA: Gelsey Kirkland's autobiography 'Dancing on my Grave' (1987) recounting her attempts through plastic surgery to make herself George Balanchine's favourite and, later, her cocaine addiction overlooked by New York City Ballet so that she could continue to perform and dazzle their audiences. The company was aware that her life was at serious risk from her addiction which she continued with partly to maintain the level of performance needed, but they made no attempt to intervene or curtail her performance. She presents herself as a commodified object of delight whose personal anguish was of no consequence to her employers.

3   An Asian Dance Residency took place between January and March 1989 at Bedford College of Higher Education, Bedford. Shobana Jeyasingh was one of the Indian Classical dance performers, and a lecturer on the residency.

4   See the journal '*New Dance*' since 1976 for writings on dancers included under this experimental umbrella in the 1970s, in Britain. Such writers were Jacky Lansley, Fergus Early and members of the X6 company. Themes were critical of the ideology of the dance establishment, training and repertoire. Gender and contemporary themes were prominent and devices related to the American post-modern dancers (see Banes, 1980, 1986).

References

ADAIR, C. (1992) *Women and Dance*, Macmillan.

ADSHEAD, J. (Ed.) (1986) *Choreography: Principles and Practice*, Study of Dance Conference 4, University of Surrey.

ARNOLD, M. (1932) *Culture and Anarchy*, Cambridge, Cambridge University Press.

BANES, S. (1980) *Terpsichore in Sneakers: Postmodern Culture*, Boston, Houghton Mifflin Company.

BANES, S. (1986) 'American (Postmodern) Choreography in the 1980s', in ADSHEAD, J. *op cit.*, pp. 107–116.

BAUDRILLARD, J. (1985) 'The Ecstasy of Communication' in FOSTER, H. (Ed.) *Postmodern Culture*, London, Pluto Press, pp. 126–134.

BERGER, J. (1972) *Ways of Seeing*, Harmondsworth, Penguin.

BLACKING, J. (1979) 'The Study of Man as Music Maker', in BLACKING, J. and KAELIINIHOMOKU, J.W., *The Performing Arts: Music and Dance*, The Hague, Mouton.

BOURDIEU, P. (1984) *Distinction. A Social Critique of the Judgment of Taste*, Cambridge, Massachusetts, Harvard University Press.

BRINSON, P. (1983) 'Scholastic Tasks of a Sociology of Dance', *The Journal of the Society for Dance Research*. Vol. 1, No. 1, pp. 100–107, Spring and Vol. 1, No. 2, pp. 57–68 Autumn.

DEEM, R. (1987) 'Sport in the Context of Women's Leisure', *Women's Studies International Forum*, Vol. 10, No. 4, pp. 443–451.

DYER, R. (1983) Unpublished Paper: Dance Conference, Surrey University.

DUNN, T. (1986) 'The Evolution of Cultural Studies', in PUNTER, D. (1986) (Ed.) *Introduction to Contemporary Cultural Studies*, Harlow, Longman Group Ltd.

FISKE, J. and HARTLEY, J. (1978) *Reading Television*, London, Methuen.

HADJINICOLAOU, N. (1978) *Art History and Class Struggle*, London, Pluto Press.

HANNA, J.L. (1979) *To Dance is Human: a Theory of Non-Verbal Communication*, Austin, University of Texas Press.

HEARN, J. (1987) *The Gender of Oppression: Men, Masculinity and the Critique of Marxism*, Brighton, Wheatsheaf.

HEBDIGE, R. (1979) *Subculture: the Meaning of Style*, London, Methuen.

HOGGART, R. (1957) *The Uses of Literacy: Aspects of Working Class Life with Special References to Publications and Entertainments*, London, Chatto and Windus.

JAMESON, F. (1984), 'Postmodernism, or the Cultural Logic of Late Capitalism', *New Left Review*, July/Aug., 146, pp. 53–92.

JOHNSON, R. (1983) *What is Cultural Studies Anyway?* Stencilled Occasional Paper, General Series: SP No. 74, Centre for Contemporary Cultural Studies, The University of Birmingham, P.O. Box 363, Birmingham B15 2TT.

KAELIINIHOMOKU, J. (1983) 'An Anthropologist Looks at Ballet as a Form of Ethnic Dance', in COPELAND, R. and COHEN, M. (Eds) (1983) *What is Dance? Readings in Theory and Criticism*, Oxford, Oxford University Press, pp. 533–549.

KIRKLAND, G. and KIRKLAND, L. (1987) *Dancing on My Grave: An Autobiography*, London, Hamish Hamilton.

KURATH, G. (1960) 'Panorama of Dance Ethnology', *Current Anthropology*, Vol. 1, (3), pp. 233–254.

LANGE, R. (1980) 'The Development of Anthropological Dance Research', *Dance Studies*, Vol. 4. Centre for Dance Studies, Jersey, Channel Islands.

MARWICK, A. (1971) *The Explosion of British Society 1914–1970*, London, Macmillan.

MITCHELL, D. (1968) *A Dictionary of Sociology*, London, Routledge and Kegan Paul.

MUNGHAM, G. and PEARSON, G. (Eds) (1976) *Working Class Youth Culture*, London, Routledge and Kegan Paul.

MURRAY, J. (1979) *Dance Now*, Harmondsworth, Penguin Books.

MYERSCOUGH, J. (1988) *The Economic Importance of the Arts*, London, Policy Studies Institute.

ROYCE, A.P. (1977) *The Anthropology of Dance*, Bloomington, London, Indiana University Press.

RUST, F. (1969) *Dance in Society*, London, Routledge and Kegan Paul.

SHERLOCK, J. (1988) 'The Cultural Production of Dance in Britain with Particular Reference to Ballet Rambert and Christopher Bruce's "Ghost Dances"', Unpublished Ph.D. thesis, Laban Centre for Movement and Dance at Goldsmith's College, University of London.

SHERLOCK, J. (1990) *Culture, Ideology, Gender and Dance*, Paper presented at the XIIth World Congress of Sociology, Madrid.

SINFIELD, A. (1988) *Changing Concepts of the Arts*, Unpublished plenary paper to the Leisure Studies Association International Conference: Leisure, Labour and Lifestyles, Sussex University, 4–8 July.

STOKES, A. (1934) *Tonight the Ballet*, London, Faber and Faber.

THOMAS, H. (1986) *Movement, Modernism and Contemporary Culture: Issues for a Critical Sociology of Dance*, Unpublished Ph.D. thesis, University of London.

WYVER, J. (1986) 'Television and Postmodernism', in I.C.A. Documents 4 & 5, *Postmodernism*, Institute of Contemporary Arts, London.

Chapter 4

Pumping Irony:
The Muscular and the Feminine

Alan Mansfield and Barbara McGinn

The law endlessly writes itself on bodies. It engraves itself on parchments made with the skin of its subjects. (de Certau, 1988:7)

A vascular woman may turn the average pencil-neck off. (Ross, Sept. 1990:45)

The Hard-core GYM and the Disciplined Body

Posing: The Art of Hardcore Physical Display. . .

Rip Up: Your Secret Blueprint for the Ultimate Ripped Physique — A new three-way programme for razor sharp rip-up techniques for that cut-to-the-ribbons look . . . brutal iron-pumping routines. . .

Savage Sets: The Ultimate Pre-Exhaust Pump Out — Your guide to the savage-cut look you've always wanted . . . It digs down deep into muscle fiber, pulverises layers that have never been stressed before and shocks the most stubborn, lazy areas of your body. (Kennedy, Summer 1990: 47)

'Awesome Arnie' is the archetypal image of the bodybuilder. 'The Titan of Testosterone', 'the Deltoid Destroyer', 'the Pectoral Prince', 'the Pied Piper of Pump', Arnold Schwarzenegger is, in Dylan Jones' words 'Rambo one step on: a little more irony, a little more vicious realism, a little more muscle' (Jones, 1990). What the imagery surrounding Schwarzenegger and his films makes clear is that muscularity and masculinity can be, and often are, conflated. The lexicon and imagery of the Robert Kennedy books cited above would not be out of place on one of the posters for a Schwarzenegger film, or indeed any of the other violent macho movies of Hollywood's current crop. The perhaps surprising thing, however, is that these books are all publications directed specifically towards women. Although couched in quite violent and brutal language they are all from the '*Female Bodybuilders' Bookshelf*'.

The picture of the bodybuilder Sandy Riddell on the front cover of *Ironman*, October 1990, displays much of the contradiction and irony of this mismatch between bookshelf and language, between the feminine and the masculine. Sandy

Riddell is an encapsulation of the contradictions and ironies we seek to address here. The iron-MAN on the front cover of the magazine is a WOMAN. Sandy Riddell is one of the world's top female bodybuilders. It is in the public controversies over what is an acceptable body for a woman bodybuilder, and the ways in which the challenge of muscularity in women has been received and coped with by society ('made safe' as we shall argue below) that our interest lies. The discourses of bodybuilding are, unsurprisingly, gendered discourses.

> Since Adam and Eve the roles of the sexes have been set . . . when man first stepped on the moon he broke all barriers of possibilities, when women first stepped into the gym they must have broken all barriers of social acceptability. (*Bodybuilders Monthly*, May 1989:57–58)

We have chosen the title Pumping Irony for this paper both to signal a strategy we intend to pursue ourselves (we intend to pump some of the ironies in order to see what they might reveal) and as a description at least in some part, of what women engaged in bodybuilding are about. We are extremely conscious of the ironies present in the conjunction of considerations of gender (specifically femininity) and muscularity, and of bodybuilding and a built, that is, socially and discursively constructed body.[1] Our exercise then, should be considered a small part of what Feher describes as a

> history of BODYBUILDING, of the different modes of construction of the human body . . . a history . . . apprehended through relations of power. (Feher, 1987:159)

There is an explicit politic to our inquiry into the transmogrification of the flesh. At some level our paper is part of a larger inquiry concerned with the way in which gender structures the social world. We are concerned at some level with the relation between masculinity and violence. No account of bodybuilding, particularly one concerned to speak of women, could ignore the connection between musclepower and manpower. More specifically, however, what we want to focus on in this paper is the number of levels in which the experience of women bodybuilders and women's bodybuilding reflects the irony of the connections between powerful muscularity and (potentially) violent masculinity. What we are examining then is the socialization of women into the world of bodybuilding, seeing, in common with other sociologists, socialization as a process of 'making safe'.

Bodybuilding as we would wish to use the term applies to something more specific than simply using weights in a gym, and it is important at this point to explain just what is being talked about when the term 'bodybuilder' is used. We do not want to discuss powerlifters and weightlifters (those who train to competitively lift maximum amount of weight, and whose physiques are developed as a by-product of this activity), not because they are uninteresting but simply because their inclusion would dissipate the focus of the paper.[2] Nor are we looking specifically at those people who use gyms and health clubs for what they might describe as keeping fit or 'body toning', although it is clear that these discourses are important and do intersect with those of bodybuilding.[3] The bodybuilder can be described as a person who deliberately cultivates an increase in mass and strength of the skeletal muscles (hypertrophy) by means of the lifting and pushing of weight.[4] The aim is to produce a body which fulfils certain criteria in terms of muscular size, shape, definition and tone. Success in achieving these aims on the part of an individual athlete is measured by means of physique contest ranging from the professional competitions such as Ms Olympia, to those held in local gyms. This is not to suggest that all bodybuilders by definition enter competitions, because most do not, but simply to point out that a definitional structure exists in the sport which powerfully influences what happens in the gym. It is interesting to note that whilst there are many men who bodybuild seriously without any idea of ever competing, it seems that there is a much higher proportion of women bodybuilders who see competition as an important part of the activity. This suggests that there is a significant difference in the meaning that bodybuilding has for men and for women.[5]

Another distinction may usefully be made here, and that is between what has been called the 'chromed-up health spa' (Francis, 1989:23) and the 'hardcore' gym. Certainly over the last ten to fifteen years there has been a rapid expansion and growth of health clubs commonly associated with meeting the exercise needs of middle class professionals. Bodybuilders are actively discouraged from using this type of institution by the deliberate exclusion of certain aspects of the technology necessary to carry out the activity from the facilities on offer. It is often the case that the weights available are simply not heavy enough to meet the needs of a bodybuilder. The ambience created by bodybuilding is not one which is valued by health clubs.[6] A gym, on the other hand, whilst of course not being used exclusively by muscle 'freaks', can best be described for our purposes as being situated within a discourse which makes the 'outlandish' body possible.

The work of Foucault is important to our enterprise for a number of reasons, centrally because of his theorization of discourse and the body. In his investigation of the formation of the contemporary social sciences Foucault's work provides a political somatics of what he termed the biopolitical realm and a series of what may be referred to as technologies of the self. Bodies are constituted by what he terms power/knowledge relations, this latter coupling emphasizing the way in which power and knowledge are inextricably linked. His studies of institutional architectonics, significantly those of medicine and penal institutions, provide a re-theorization of the body. Unlike earlier Marxist analyses, Foucault's work centres on the body and not on ideology. It is Foucault who reminds us that the body is not an inert ahistorical given but an object of psychical and physical inscription.

> The body perceived in this way is not a reality to be uncovered in a positivistic description of an organism . . . it is instead a reality constantly produced, an effect of techniques promoting specific gestures and postures. (Feher, 1987:159)

Bev Francis comments on 'posing', the display of muscle structure in competitions. Her discussions here illustrate the degree of bodily specificity of the discourse of bodybuilding and are extraordinarily reminiscent of Foucault in *Discipline and Punish*.

Side Chest Pose.

... Your feet should be set parallel, with your side facing towards the judges. Your feet can vary from about 3 to 8 inches apart. Keeping the foot away from the judges flat on the floor, rise up on the other toe, while simultaneously bending your leg about 20 degrees. Tense both calves in this position...

With your torso erect, bend the arm towards the judges at about a 90 degree angle, palm facing either directly upwards or more towards the midline of your body. The hand position primarily affects the appearance of your forearm in the pose. Reach across your abdomen with your free hand and either clasp hands or grasp the waist of your arm towards the judges; your grasping hand should be facing the floor. Pull the judges' side shoulder a bit back, the other one a bit forward. Tense all of the chest, shoulder and arm muscles, pressing your flexed arm against your side to flatten it out and make it appear a bit thicker. Experiment with various degrees of arm bend and hand rotation. Look towards the judges when you have the pose composed. (Francis, 1989:142)

Francis comments on another aspect of this inscription process. For bodybuilders, nutrition is as important as training with weights. It provides fuel for muscle growth and is also a means of manipulating muscle to fat ratios to produced the 'ripped to shreds' look necessary for competition, where body fat is reduced to an absolute minimum to reveal maximum muscle definition (cuts) and detail (striations). Francis gives an eleven-point guide to general nutritional principles for the bodybuilder (Francis, 1989:82–85). Eating, like training, for the bodybuilder is a constant process of self-monitoring, tied always to a search for new and improved practices. 'Bodybuilding nutrition is a highly complex subject, which continues to grow more complex each year as new information is discovered' (Francis, 1989:85). As with training sessions, bodybuilders are encouraged not only to scientifically manage what they eat (with all its associated structures of denial, restraint and commitment) but to chart and record their nutritional intake—in order to monitor, measure and improve their bodily self-production.

The ironic figure of the bodybuilder makes manifestly obvious, that if one was looking for an example of a 'technology of the self' which shows the constructed nature of the human body there is no starker instance than body sculpture. Female bodybuilders, we argue, stand in a special relationship to the discourse of bodybuilding. Available discourses enable and constrain the possibilities of social action and are crucial in the formation of identities. Although, for example, there are many and varied strategies for representing women bodybuilders in bodybuilding magazines we have yet not come across any women labelled as 'bad-ass talking' women — although several (often black) men have been described thus. We have only rarely seen 'Beef' or 'Beefcake' labels on women, although men have often been described thus. When audiences at bodybuilding competitions — who are always very vocal — call out 'Beef, Beef' at women contestants as they do at the men, this is felt as strongly ironic.[7] The resonance of a particular advertisement for vitamin pills is also salient: 'Don't piss good money down the drain' (*Bodybuilding Monthly*, June 1989). Operating, as our opening quotes from the *Female Bodybuilder's Library* also shows, within such a markedly 'masculine' sphere makes the woman bodybuilder a doubly ironic figure.

Foucault's model of the panopticon and what we might call a model of 'urban disciplining' can be used to elaborate a contemporary testing of the body in the gym. Here the gym, and working out with weights, becomes a form of panoptic anthropometric disciplining. In a section of his book on the politics of style entitled '*Hard Bodies*', Ewen gives us the story of Raymond H.

> Three times a week after work Raymond goes to work in his local health club to the mirrored walls of the Nautilus room where he attaches himself to a series of specialised machines designed to work his hips, buttocks, thighs, calves, back, shoulders, chest, upper arms, forearms, abdomen and neck. (Ewen, 1988:189)[8]

For Foucault, the notion of the soldier as a social-type gave way to a notion of the soldier as the end product of a series of specific disciplined practices. Foucault compares earlier notions of the soldier as someone born with certain attributes with a more recent understanding of the 'soldier' as someone that was/could be produced by military training. This was a result of two separate but connected notions of human potential arising in the Enlightenment. The first is related to the way in which science and reason could emancipate humanity from the repressive and reactionary hierarchies of the past. The second was a much more instrumental conception of humanity where secular science and reason provided tools for understanding and therefore managing human beings. The new conception of the trainable body, or as we might put it, the echoes of Foucault's marching legions, are present in the 1980s practices of yuppie body maintenance, in Raymond H's visits to the Nautilus room, and 1990s conceptions of New Age muscle.

Bordo, writing primarily about dieting and notes some interesting connections between the slender body and the muscled body. Her argument is basically that the anorexic body and the muscled body are on a continuum, and although superficially very different images, are united against 'a common platoon of enemies: the soft, the loose; unsolid, excess flesh' (Bordo, 1990:90). Both dieting and bodybuilding are seen as powerful panoptic technologies producing self monitoring 'docile' bodies. Bordo argues

> increasingly, the size and shape of the body has come to operate as a marker of personal, internal order (or disorder) — as a symbol for the state of the soul. (Bordo, 1990:94)

She also notes, however, something of the gendered nature of these normalizing practices. She argues, in relation to bulimia and anorexia, that a focus on the pathology of these phenomena obscures the function of the technologies of diet and body management as a central means in the production of gender. As she concludes, 'no BODY can escape either the imprint of culture or its gendered meanings' (Bordo, 1990:109 — our emphasis). Bordo's argument is generally very convincing: there certainly are a number of connections to be made, notably in the way the body is objectified in both the discourses of dieting and those of bodybuilding.

Bodybuilding is about developing individual body parts into a symmetrical, well balanced whole, but is important to note that although symmetry and proportion, that is, the way muscles and muscle groupings relate to each other, are crucial things for the bodybuilder's body, the discourse of bodybuilding produces a structure of fragmentation and objectification of the body. Basic and isolation exercises allow the bodybuilder to experience individual muscles and groups of muscles. Carol Mock, for example, talks about training her arms: 'I loved training my arms. Watching my biceps and triceps literally explode, really turned me on' (Bradford, Summer 1990:28). Robin Parker talks about training her calves: 'I think that calves are an outrageously sexy body part. I have been able to put a lot more size on them in the past year. I love to train them and I love to watch them grow' (Nixon, Summer 1990:27). One of the problems, however, is that Bordo's work is weaker and less specific in relation to bodybuilding. This becomes clear in her discussion of the changed meanings in the muscled body where she talks about muscles 'developed to extremes' (Bordo, 1990:94) and in her difficulty in explaining the obvious pleasure in their bodies experienced by the women quoted above.

The failure to specify whether one is talking about the users of health spas or gyms has led to a great deal of confusion when discussing women's bodybuilding, and generally in relation to issues of women, the body, and social power. Contrary to what some writers, even in bodybuilding magazines, would suggest, there is a great deal of difference between two kinds of female hard body image. The currency of body maintenance techniques and the proliferation of health clubs is part of an acceptable hard body image such as that of Madonna, Elle McPherson (better known 'simply as Elle the Body' [*Cleo*, November 1990: 104])or indeed the woman in the advertisement for The Joy of Cooking which Bordo (1990:108) mistakenly suggest is that of a bodybuilder. There is, however, another hard body image which appears to be potentially more threatening: the image of the female bodybuilder, an image which goes far beyond that of the 'more athletic woman of today.' This image is clearly not safe enough for consumption yet, even (or should it be especially) in the market of fitness products. It is interesting to note that Reebok refused to sponsor a women's bodybuilding contest because 'they only liked the way three or four of the girls looked', whilst being happy to attach their corporate image to the UK National Aerobic Championships 1990 (*Musclemag*, July 1990:104). Much of the second part of our paper is devoted to a discussion of the ways in which the bodybuilding community, which would include contests, judges, sponsors, bodybuilding magazines, regulating bodies, and women and men bodybuilders themselves, make safe the figure of the woman bodybuilder. Women body-builders themselves could be said to be at the forefront of this process, being more aware than anyone of what their bodies mean. This process of making safe for social, cultural and economic consumption should be understood as a process which occurs in may different ways on may different levels.

Pumping Iron Too!

Women's bodybuilding in its current manifestation dates from the late 1970s when women (particularly in the USA) began to push for a place for women in the sport which radically changed the *status quo*. Prior to this time, the only contests available to women were little more than 'bathing beauty' contests, albeit organized by bodybuilding organizations. The other place for women in the sport, the gym itself, also had to be 'taken' and the last ten years have seen unprecedented numbers of women working out with weights in gyms which were previously exclusively male. We should also mention at this juncture that there are, of course, other significant sites of this struggle, more generally, the mass media and the public sphere and more particularly, for our purposes here, in bodybuilding magazines. There are women's bodybuilding magazines, women's bodybuilding is covered in 'men's bodybuilding magazines (that is, those directed at men, and those directed at 'bodybuilders'). Further, other magazines occasionally deal with women's bodybuilding.[10] A discussion of magazine representation raises many issues to do with the commercial organization of publishing, histories and conventions of representation and so forth. We cannot in this article focus in sufficient detail on these matters, but we do make some comments about the relation between such matters and the issues we are concerned with. Representations of women's bodybuilding and women bodybuilders in magazines are very complex and contradictory, but it is precisely these contradictions which are evident in the judging of female bodybuilding competitions and in discussions of the ideal female bodybuilder's body. Constantly in the variety of discourse available, it is women bodybuilders, like others of their sex in other spheres, who carry manifestly the contradictions (and often penalties) of their gender. This is clear, for example, in the doubly transgressive nature of bodybuilding for women as opposed to men.

Increasing numbers of women have, however, been using weights and gyms, and a number of these women have become serious competitive bodybuilders. In an editorial in *Muscle and Fitness* Joe Weider ('the master-blaster, trainer of champions for over half a century') makes the point that women have invaded this traditionally masculine territory with 'their own form of muscular development'. He argues,

> It has given woman the opportunity to claim her equality. Her initial struggle for superiority has given way to pure love for her activity. And muscle becomes cut-glass through which we see the heightened qualities that make her so essential to our existence.

Weider concludes with the statement that

WOMEN'S BODYBUILDING IS ONE OF THE STRONGEST EXPRESSIONS TO COME OUT OF THE FEMINIST MOVEMENT. (Weider, July 1990:6)

One of the more well-known commentaries on women bodybuilders is, of course, the film *Pumping Iron II: The Women* which, as Annette Kuhn notes, was hailed by some as THE feminist film of the year. The narrative of the film concerns a bodybuilding championship held in 1984. The action, then, is set around who will win the contest, the 'shapely' Rachel McLish or the Australian power-lifter turned bodybuilder, Bev Francis. To cut a long story short, Carla Dunlap wins, and Bev Francis is placed well down the line in eighth position. All three of these women are muscular. What is important is that Bev Francis' position reflects the judges' point of view that she has muscles which are 'too masculine'. Francis clearly has more and bigger muscles than anyone else in the competition, and what is perhaps even more important, these muscles are also in different places from those of her competitors. Dunlap wins the competition because her body is judged to be somewhere between that of McLish and Francis. It is not our purpose to comment here on the film's resolution of the plot, something of a compromise as Kuhn suggests. It is, however, important to point out the wider parameters of the debate the film sets up as they are crucial to our aims in this paper.

In *Pumping Iron II* the contest, particularly between Francis and McLish, is also a contest over definitions of women's bodies and what they do or should look like. Most simply, then, this concerns what is the ideal shape or look for a female bodybuilder. More broadly, however, this involves questions of women's and men's bodies generally and how they differ from each other, but also the question of who controls these images, and the locations of their enactment and reproduction. It is the 'transgressive' nature of female bodybuilders, that is, women with pronounced musculature, cut-glass muscle as Joe Weider would have it, which becomes the focus. When does muscle on a woman become 'too much', that is 'masculine'? What is the relationship between muscularity and femininity, and how is this affected by the relationship between muscularity and masculinity? What happens when there is the 'threat'/possibility of muscularity equalling femininity? Our concern is to examine the ways in which this irony, these contradictions are negotiated. This involves an account of hegemonic struggle within the discourse and discursive practices of bodybuilding. Our account is thus put forward as an attempt to sketch out, albeit briefly, an account of power, resistance and social change. How will women's bodybuilding alter the sexual formation? How does the sexual formation manage or make safe women's bodybuilding? How can/do women bodybuilders resist or subvert this process?

Kuhn notes something of the difficulty of these questions, given the way in which the body figures as an

> irreducible sign of the natural, the given, the unquestionable, and its significance as a signifier of sexual difference . . . (however) . . . The concept of sexual difference is itself an ideological battleground: it holds together — or tries to — a range of discourses and meanings centring on biological sex, social gender, gender identity and sexual object choice. The encapsulation of all of these within the constructs of sexual difference is an historically grounded ideological project which works to set up a heterogeneous and variably determinate set of biological, physical, social, psychological and psychic constructs as a unitary, fixed and unproblematic attribute of human subjectivity. (Kuhn, 1988:16)

The consequence of this is that human beings get defined as either male or female and from these definitions flow a succession of others dependent upon this primary difference. The film *Pumping Iron II* (and in our analysis women's bodybuilding generally) highlights something of what is going on in this process. The irony is then that bodybuilding unavoidably suggests a purposive and active production of the body. The enormous amount of hard work over a long period needed to produce the sculpted body cannot be ignored. Women's bodybuilding raises unavoidably questions about both the naturalness of the body AND the meanings centred via the body upon sexual difference.

Kuhn notes that muscles already do of course carry a great deal of cultural meaning, most significantly in those meanings centred upon the givenness of sexual difference, where of course they are heavily coded as masculine. Any investigation of women bodybuilders then must also be investigation of bodybuilding *per se*. The matter is quite complex, being classed and raced as well as gendered, but some male bodybuilders can encounter a certain social approbation for their pumped highly vascular physiques. Even on men muscles are given and natural only up to a point. Of concern to us at the moment is the greater degree of social approbation incurred by muscular women and the vastly different points of transgression for men and women. We develop the point below, but for now we can note that if muscles are 'natural' and the body 'given', then there is a double transgression involved in female bodybuilding. As Kuhn concludes,

Thus when women enter the arena of bodybuilding, a twofold challenge to the natural order is posed. Not only is the naturalness of the body called into question by its inscription within a certain kind of performance: but when women have the muscles, the natural order of gender is under threat as well. (Kuhn, 1988:17)

Why can't a Woman be More Like a Man?

Women are women, men are men, there's a difference and thank God for the difference. (Ben Weider: *Pumping Iron II*)

Thank heavens for little girls, for little girls get bigger every day. (Maurice Chevalier, in the film *Gigi*)

The entry by women into what had been an almost exclusively masculine area was not, as we have indicated, achieved without a struggle. As Caroline Cheshire relates,

Back home I was finding that training facilities for women were few and far between, a long way from today's explosion of gyms and health studies. In fact, it was a real struggle to find places to train each week day. Finally at the eleventh hour, my luck changed . . . St. George's was a gym of the old school — old, damp, tough, rough and ready. After applying for membership for several months with little response I finally received a reply. It was positive. I had been accepted . . . But all was not over yet. The first day I walked in I was greeted by a petition. On the notice board was a list of names supporting the motion that women members should be debarred. Fortunately good sense prevailed and the petition died a death. (Cheshire, 1985:9)

It is interesting to note, however, that women, when first entering gyms, do not necessarily do so with the intention of becoming bodybuilders. It is important to realize that the choice for women between weights and aerobics and even more particularly between weight training and bodybuilding is not simply a choice between different ways of keeping fit. It is as much a choice between a perceived masculine or feminine process of altering the body image. When joining an unknown gym, a woman is often presented with training options and aims in a certain order. Aerobics, weight loss, body toning, general fitness. The last resort is bodybuilding ('you mean you want to build muscle?'). More commonly, those women who do bodybuilding 'progress' through these options. '. . . how many, I wonder, actually stepped into the gym knowing that they wouldn't settle for anything less than a 16" arm cold!!?' (*Bodybuilding Monthly*, May 1989:57) When Robin Parker, an habitué of Madison Avenue Muscle first entered the gym she

> only wanted to firm up, but when beautiful muscles appeared she took the next step and made bodybuilding a career move . . . typical of the progressive phases that women experience . . . she started with the notion of merely firming up . . . but then . . . she became enamoured of muscularity, no longer viewing it as the exclusive province of males . . . I had no great aspiration . . . it struck me as a very peculiar activity until my eye became accustomed to it. (*Female Bodybuilding*, Summer 1990:26)

Carol Mock, a top woman bodybuilder who was asked to compete in the 1989 Ms International section of the Arnold Classic in Columbus, Ohio and other prestigious competitions relates a similar story in getting involved with body-building.

> I first entered a gym when I was at Johnson and Johnson in Texas . . . I ate poorly and my stomach was starting to get soft and flabby. I couldn't allow myself to look like that. Not only would it be bad for business, but I had a certain amount of pride in my appearance. I couldn't let it happen. So I started training at this health club. I didn't even know what a pump was but sure knew I was getting a real intense one, every time I picked up a weight. (*Female Bodybuilding*, Summer 1990:28)

Mock continued her work in the gym and now describes her aim in bodybuilding thus: 'When I'm on stage I want my body to talk, I want it to almost sing with muscle, to stay in a person's mind like a familiar tune' (*Female Bodybuilding*, Summer 1990:28). The interview with Mock reveals a number of interesting things about women's bodybuilding, demonstrating a certain ambivalence in the discourse of bodybuilding for women, an ambivalence bolstered by the commodity structure of bodybuilding magazines. The magazine article giving her biography talks about her skills, dedication and achievement as a bodybuilder, but places these comments in a significantly gendered discourse. She is described for example as 'the caramel-coloured siren from Oakland, California who slithers and slinks into spellbinding poses of sinewy femininity' (p. 28). It is important to see such writing as typical of a certain kind of journalistic style, but a central argument of this essay is that such genre characteristics are importantly gendered and work to construct and maintain certain kinds of ideological schemas in relation to muscularity and gender difference. Moreover, in the discussion of Mock's arms, we can see that the contradictions manifested in the public arena and in the commodity culture of bodybuilding magazines have a personal impact for her:

My arms are my strongest body part . . . but they are a blessing and a curse . . . big arms can intimidate other women on stage, so that's good. What can be a problem is when my arms intimidate men who don't weight train. I have over 30 clients I personally train. I would probably have more male clients, but when some of them see me in a tank top I think they get a little embarrassed being trained by this little lady with big arms . . . men can have such sensitive egos. (*Female Bodybuilding*, Summer 1990:29)

— a statement at odds with the obvious pride with which Mock speaks of her body and particularly her pleasure in her arms.

Such ambivalences are manifested throughout women's bodybuilding, and importantly, the reproduction of this world in bodybuilding magazines. An article on Laura Binetti in *FLEX* informs us that there is nothing in her flat except one lone photo to indicate that Binetti or her flatmates are bodybuilders. There are no dumbbells in the living room and all her trophies are on display in the house of her parents. 'As a matter of fact, most people have trouble believing that Laura is a bodybuilder, let alone a champion, when they see her at work as a downtown Toronto insurance agent'. Part of the reason for her low-key self-presentation, the article informs us, is that Toronto is cold and 'when temperatures plunge to minus four, Laura stays hidden under quite a few layers of clothing'. The significance of this, however, is undermined by the fact that Laura prefers even when the sun is out to wear loose clothes both in and out of the gym. 'I do not want people to think I'm showing off. I'm just not like that'. The ambivalence is developed in her own commentary on her body.

I've got an overall package, muscular, but not overly muscular. I like women's bodybuilding, but there's also a point when it starts to look over-masculine. (*FLEX*, July 1990:126)

Binetti goes on to suggest that one of the ways this 'over-masculine' look is achieved by women is through the use of drugs. One of the most significant controversies in bodybuilding, both women's and men's, is over the use of anabolic steroids to increase both strength and muscle mass. We do not have the space in this paper to fully elaborate the nature of this debate, but it is necessary to make a number of points as it is a very significant question in relation to bodybuilding. Of all the products and pseudoscience hurled at the bodybuilder via consumer capital, particularly bodybuilding magazines, it is the 'natural' steroids, and powders and potions of various 'natural' kinds (or high tech, but legal kinds) that are most prominent. Clearly what is at stake here is what we might call the impurity of the chemical body, the unnaturalness of the steroid body — what Kristeva, in her work on abjection, for example, discusses as the tenuous boundaries of the body (Kristeva, 1982). Adverts for natural steroids are extremely common in all bodybuilding magazines, but it is not simply these advertisements that are significant. One could see much of the commercial discourse around bodybuilding products, methodologies and regimens as ways of making the kinds of gains in muscle mass attributed to illegal drugs. In this sense one could see a large part of bodybuilding discourse as over-determined by a steroidal imaginary and an absent centre of magical and illegal drugs. This discourse, as the fairly recent controversy over Ben Johnson illustrates, is as applicable to men as to women, and relates to the first part of the double structure of transgression of women bodybuilders that we discussed above, that is, 'cultured' muscle as opposed to natural muscle. (It also illustrates the more general relevance of drugs, and particularly steroid-use, to sport.) What interests us particularly here, however, is the way in which the discussion of steroids and their use is significantly gendered in relation to women's bodybuilding. In common with men, women are not supposed to use unnatural means, that is, anabolic steroids, to develop their bodies. What is most crucial, however, is the gendered nature of the prohibition against women. It is the transgression of gender difference that is most significant; the danger for women taking steroids is that they will become men. The effects of steroid usage in women are listed as including,

> enlarged clitoris, increased or decreased libido, decreased breast size, diminished menstruation, increased aggressiveness, acne, male pattern baldness and increased appetite. Some of these changes such as lowered voice and increased facial hair, may be permanent. (Ferguson, 1990:57)

In another article on steroid use by women Edge lists similar 'virilization' effects (Edge, May 1989:61). Both commentators are startlingly silent on other side-effects of these drugs, such as liver damage, which actually may be life-threatening. It seems in both cases that the danger of women becoming more like men is more significant than the possibility of them becoming seriously ill or even dying.

Cory Everson puts another perspective on this in an article interestingly titled 'Have We Created A Monster?' Everson, six times Ms Olympia, is responding to people who regard women's bodybuilding as unhealthy, unnatural, undesirable, or any combination of the three. She states,

> I have read a lot of baloney about steroids, muscularity and femininity . . . most people who write this garbage are incredibly stupid. Like, muscle development is uglier than mounds of blubber or skin and bones? And athletic tone . . . is less feminine than rolls of fat and puny weakness and frailty. (Everson, Summer 1990:20)

After pointing out some clichés of gender stereotyping Everson notes a prevailing attitude that men, those who are 'allowed' to have muscle, should not be tested for steroids since they are 'masculine' drugs. Women, in contrast, cannot take them because that would not be regarded as feminine. Beverley, in an article on nutrition for women bodybuilders, has this to say about steroid usage,

> It's bad enough for a man. For a woman to take drugs to increase male hormones, for that's what they're doing, seems to me to border on lunacy. What they must be doing in the long term to their hormone systems is unthinkable. (Beverley, May 1989:66)

This seems to support our contention that it is the gender-bodybuilding capacity of steroid use by women bodybuilders that society defines as most threatening, as precisely unthinkable.

Weights and Measures: Working the Edge

We would now like to turn our attention to the ideal of the women bodybuilders' body and the ways in which the interplay between the muscularity/masculinity fusion and notions of femininity are managed, particularly through the judging of women's bodybuilding contests. The proposition that the body is not an historical given demands an investigation of the discourses which produce the 'built' body of our text. This body, however, as has been pointed out above, is significantly gendered. The discourses involved in bodybuilding address the problem posed by the deviant and dangerous muscled female body by a differential construction of acceptable form between men and women.

Much has been written in recent years about the ways in which the idealized women's body has shifted from the 'womanly' ideal most lately seen in the fifties to the androgynous (or more accurately boyish) look of the past thirty years or so. Bordo claims that both the extreme thinness of the sixties and the more 'athletic' look of the eighties can be encompassed within a discourse of androgynous slenderness which is marked by a rejection of

> The most literal symbolic form of maternal femininity . . . represented by the nineteenth-century 'hourglass' figure, emphasising breasts and hips — the markers of reproductive femaleness — against a wasp waist. (Bordo, 1990:104)

When looking at something as radically challenging to conventional notions of the gendered body as female bodybuilding the superficiality of this shift is pointed up. Doris Barrilleaux, who has been involved in the bodybuilding world for over thirty years, explains what is at stake as women bodybuilders begin to exhibit extreme muscularity,

> I think it may ruin the sport . . . A lot of women tell me they don't want to look that (more muscular). I like the athletic look . . . broad shoulders but small waists . . . I like the hourglass look. The V-shape is traditional to the male. (Bugg, June 1989:51)

When the crunch comes, the masculine counterpoint is an archetypal feminine unrelated to any notions of boyishness. Recognizable markers of femininity were needed, the very breasts, hips and waist of the maternal woman, accompanied by hair and make-up styles which add up to a notion of idealized womanhood, which can in no sense be described as androgynous. Bev Francis, one of the key figures of *Pumping Iron II* was told to 'get feminine or get out of women's bodybuilding' (Pearl, May 1989:75). What Ross (Sept. 1990:45) refers to as the 'extreme emphasis on marketability' (of women's bodybuilding) has led Cory Everson to engage in a different kind of body work.

> Cory's biceps aren't getting any bigger but her breasts are. That's okay, the implants are enhancing her femininity and marketability. (Teagan, cited Pearl, May 1989:73)

If the apotheosis of bodybuilding is winning at physique contests, then we have a very simple method of enforcement of the notion of the correct body for a woman. If a woman does not conform to this standard she cannot win. Women's bodybuilding has been the site of struggle over the construction (in both senses) of its proponents' flesh. The judging of female physique contests brings together all the ambivalences about women and muscularity and these have been expressed in the controversies which have raged within and about women's bodybuilding since the late 1970s. Responses have ranged from condescending patronage to outright hostility, but as Pearl suggests, 'as the sport has grown, issues have been raised about just how far women should be allowed to build and about judging criteria' (Pearl, May 1989:72). The use of the term 'allowed' here is noteworthy, suggesting that the muscular woman is threatening and needs in some way to be controlled and contained.

There is evident confusion (on the part of contestants, audiences and judges) over the judging criteria in women's contests. It is clear that bodybuilding, for women at least, is not just about being 'allowed to gain as much muscle as is humanly possible whilst at the same time retaining good symmetry and a healthy condition' (Pearl, May 1988:72). An article on Dorothy Herndon, a relative new-comer on the competitive scene, exemplifies this,

> Her quest for size . . . has been the biggest drawback in her competitive career. In 1986 Dorothy's massive upper body turned heads, but managed only twelfth place position at the USA. In 1987 an even bigger Dorothy sat crying in the audience as she watched the top fifteen vie for the title — she hadn't even been placed in the running. (Dayton, Summer 1990:46)

Another important feature of the bodybuilder is the body vascularity, described by Ross as the 'icing on the cake of a muscular physique . . . veins pop to the surface of the skin, zig-zagging like metal cords in/out of deep muscular furrows' (Ross, Sept. 1990:45). However, the desirability of vascularity for women is seen somewhat differently. Despite the fact that nearly all the top women stars including Cory Everson, Bev Francis and Tonya Knight have these 'river maps' on their arms,

> for women, the criteria are somewhat different. With the extreme emphasis on marketability, a vascular woman may turn the average pencil-neck off and thus hurt her own chances in a big pro show. (Ross, Sept. 1990:45)[11]

Cory Everson, talking about the 1989 Ms Olympia, further illustrates the problems faced by competitors,

> There was a lack of depth in the contest and outstanding competitors were the really muscular ones and they outnumbered those who are symmetrical . . . I don't want to say 'feminine lines' but less muscular physiques . . . There's the difficult decision the judges are going through. Do they score Marjo and Janet higher because of their symmetry and beauty even though they are not in great shape? . . . What's going to happen next year since this year's bigger more muscular women are scored higher? Will everyone come in another twenty pounds heavier? If

they do, will the judges score them first or last? So does Sandy think she
has to be bigger next year to beat me or smaller and symmetrical to beat
me? (Manion, July 1990:103)

The inconsistencies and contradictions in the placings given to women
contestants are exemplified by the commonly reported situation whereby the
same woman can receive a first place position from half the judges in a particular
contest, and yet be placed at the end of the field by the remainder.[12] The search
for criteria for the ideal female bodybuilder's body examined in *Pumping Iron II*
seems then to have been unresolved, and yet Everson has won the most important women's physique contest in the world six times in succession. A case of
safety in numbers? An irony only to be expected? Everson, in common with
many other women at the top of the sport, has adopted the blonde, 'Barbie doll'
look of the hyper-feminine, her body is heavily muscled, but has not gone
beyond the point at which (in the bodybuilding world) it would be regarded as
'too extreme' for a woman. She, more successfully than others, has walked the
thin line between muscularity and acceptable femininity by working her body in
a particular way to produce the ideal size and proportions, by adopting a posing
style emphasizing dance, grace and creativity, and by trappings of hair and make-
up and the like reminiscent of the style adopted by the fictional women of Dallas.[13]
A British competitor, Donna Hartley, gives her version of what is expected:

> *Sport and Fitness* magazine started to say that the women who are tending
> to look more masculine will be marked down. What they are saying is
> that some women are tending to take it too far. They are trying to stop
> it. They want you to be muscular but still retain your femininity . . . If
> you have a wide waist you can look a bit on the masculine side. A
> narrow waist always looks feminine . . . Also little things about going
> on stage are vital. Some people don't bother to tan up properly, they
> don't do their hair or nails. It's important that all these things are done as
> they all add up to the end package. I also think if women bodybuilders
> have cropped short hair and they are muscular they look mannish.
> (Donna Hartley, cited Pearl, May 1989:75)

It would be difficult to find a more powerful commentary on the way in which
the woman bodybuilder constructs her body to fulfil the twin constraints of
aesthetic and safe femininity than the career of Bev Francis, and the changes she
has made to her body in order to become a successful bodybuilder. Over the
years her waist and hips have become more slender, and the proportions of her
body have changed to become more symmetrical, the development of her leg
muscles has been toned down, she has brought out the 'detail' of her musculature
rather than concentrating on pure size or mass, she uses make-up and nail polish
and has grown, lightened and curled her hair.

It seems that the one criterion for success about which there is no ambiguity
in women's bodybuilding is the necessity to adopt the soft touch. It is these
traditional markers of the feminine which have been adopted by women as a
counterbalance to their musculature. Mandy Tanny, also commenting on the
1989 Ms Olympia, in which, as Everson explained above, the more heavily
muscled women were successful, enthuses,

> Instead of the usual racehorse lineup . . . the whole presentation was like
> a muscular beauty pageant, and the audience loved it. (Tanny, April
> 1990:128)

It is as though, when pushing at the limits of gender identity, lipstick and blonde
locks are as necessary for the woman bodybuilder as they are for the female
impersonator. There are a wide variety of styles of dress and personal presentation available to Western women of the late twentieth century to the extent that
the notion of female-to-male cross-dressing has become almost meaningless.
However, in the same way as it is necessary for the extreme gender markers
of the hyper-feminine to be adopted by the male cross-dressers in order to make
it clear that they wish to be recognized as 'women', so too is it necessary for
women bodybuilders.[14] It is the adoption of the caricature features of femininity which allows a recognition of the familiar, the non-threatening. So long as
women remain powerless, it is acceptable for them to ape the boys wearing their
jeans and haircuts, but any incursions into the 'strict territory of a special kind of
man' (Lyon and Kent Hall, 1981:2) requires, in the words of Cory Everson, that
these women 'act and speak like ladies' (*Musclemag*, July 1990:103). It seems that
the female muscled body is so dangerous that the proclamation of gender must be
made very loudly indeed.

 These strategies for asserting gender should be viewed as falling within a
discourse which holds 'woman' to be 'non-man', which produces the masculine
as 'given' and the feminine as 'other'. Male gender is taken for granted, or
occluded altogether as being unproblematic, not a subject for viewing or examination, whilst women are visible firstly as women and only then as (gendered)
bodybuilders.

> As far as judging goes; many a judge has told me that they hate judging
> women and find it most difficult. One in fact openly admitted that he
> did not like women bodybuilders and could never get used to women
> having so much muscle, much preferring his women to be 'soft and
> cuddly'. (Pearl, May 1989:72)

Conclusion: The Battle of the Bulges

> I really changed my body, more than I realised at the time . . . it's a lot
> different . . . I guess I was a little too much before, but I was in love with
> getting big, with size . . . I just wish it hadn't taken me so long to figure
> out what I was doing wrong. (Dayton, Summer 1990:46)

> The Ms Olympia . . . probably every woman's dream. (Bodybuilding
> Monthly, July 1989:69)

We have taken bodybuilding to be a limit case of the trainable body, a physical
body which is situated within a pattern of social power which both enables and
directs its production in a particular form in a definite historical moment. This

social power, we have argued, is expressed through powerful panoptic techniques of self-monitoring, where 'the word' is, literally, 'made flesh', and the state of the physical body comes to operate as a symbol for the health, and thus the worth of, the 'soul'.

The body of the woman bodybuilder, then, becomes the site (sight) of the intersection of the discourses of bodybuilding and of gender. Because muscularity has been coded as a fundamentally masculine attribute, its adoption by women has offered a threat and a challenge to notions of both the feminine AND the masculine. It seems that the possibility of the equation of muscularity with femininity is, in both senses, unspeakable.

Ros Coward, in a discussion of women and dieting, puts this another way:

A large woman who is not apologising for her size is certainly not a figure to invite the dominant meanings which our culture attaches to femininity. She is impressive in ways that our culture's notion of the feminine cannot tolerate. (Coward 1984, 1984:41)

Fat is equated with the libidinous, female sexually-mature body, and thus with lack of control. Coward suggests that women suffer for this by adopting a masochistic, punitive attitude to their bodies. Paradoxically, women bodybuilders, through exerting extreme self-control, fragmentation and objectification of their bodies, achieve the 'impressive' body, which takes up more space than is proper for a woman. The irony is that the fruits of self-control become, in this case, highly visible, not to be viewed without discomfort. Yet women bodybuilders speak of their bodies with pleasure, rather than the self-hatred of the discourse of dieting, enabled by the valorization of moral worth displayed as a physical attribute, so noticeable in the 'body age' of the 1980s and 1990s. However, as Bordo suggests, this correct management of desire, what she terms '"virile" capacity for self-management' (Bordo, 1990:101) is equated with accepted notions of masculinity. Women have adopted physical attributes strongly coded as masculine, by the use of regimens of self-management which are themselves so coded. The doubly-transgressive position of the woman bodybuilder comments ironically on this masculinity.

In the early 1980s, Robert Mablethorpe photographed Lisa Lyons' muscular arm wearing a lace glove, for its subversive and mocking effects on received notions of masculinity and femininity. This juxtaposition of masculine and feminine attributes on the bodies of muscular women has become a commonplace image in the bodybuilding world, even, we have suggested, necessary and desirable for the process of making the body 'safe'. This contradictory coding does, however, remain subversive. In drawing attention to the very power it aims to soften, it pumps the ironies of gender relations.

The beauty of bodybuilding is you can change your appearance. By your own efforts you can add or subtract pounds of bodyweight. You can build your arms, shoulders, legs, chest, back, and in so doing, you can get a pleasure from training you might never have dreamed possible. Even the pain has its reward: it is invariably followed by the most desirable effect of all — the pump. (*Female Bodybuilding*, July 1989:4)

Notes

1   Bodybuilding raises also most graphically the need for other ways of talking about the body. In this essay we are primarily concerned with the body as a surface of inscription. It is the discourse particularly of bodybuilders themselves, however (and our own experience of the gym) which reminds us that the body is more than simply a text on which the social is written. Bodybuilders talk consistently about 'the pump' and an erotics of the gym. We hope to deal with this in subsequent articles.

2   Bev Francis makes the difference between powerlifting and bodybuilding clear. In powerlifting the aim is to lift the heaviest possible weight, and you try to use as much of your body as you can to achieve this aim, concentrating on the weight and not on the muscles or groups of muscles being used. This is a completely different method of training from that used by bodybuilders. As Bev Francis states, 'I try to isolate the movement so that the rest of my body is completely still. I try to feel the muscle through the entire movement' (Francis, 1989:11–13).

3   We do not have space to elaborate the complex positioning of bodybuilding within and across other fitness discourses, but our analysis thus far shows this positioning to be gendered, dynamic and tied in significant ways to both the current 'fitness craze' (an obsession with the 'hard body') and wider social developments of the 1980s and 1990s. The many new magazines on fitness and 'superfitness', for example *Excel*, reveal many of these developments.

4   The materials presented in this essay exclude one whole section of our writing on the specifics of bodybuilding discourse, a section entitled 'From calves to cows'. Exigencies of space prohibit extended commentary on hypertrophy and hyperplasia (the latter being an increase in the actual number of muscle cells) or the techniques of blitzing, flushing, muscle confusion, giant sets, angle training and so forth.

5   This point, we feel, needs further research and discussion, but may well be connected with the gendered nature of panoptic technologies which form the conclusion to our paper.

6   This distancing between a 'hard body' image and bodybuilder's body can be seen in the more public and media-oriented representatives of gym bodies. Advertising, for example, in Britain, America and Australia, has a current fascination with bodybuilding images and paraphernalia. The international magazine on superfitness referred to above, *Excel*, is a good example. Again this process is gendered: the bodybuilding men represented have quite large muscles but are seldom 'pumped' and vascular, while the women represented are athletic but seldom bodybuilders (even more rarely 'pumped' or vascular). Bodybuilders are as unwelcome in magazines and advertisements as they are in health clubs. Nonetheless, at all of these sites the potential of bodybuilding is being mobilized, even if in a 'controlled' form.

7   Carol Adams has written a book-length commentary salient to this point (Adams, 1990, *The Sexual Politics of Meat?*).

8   Ewen has a number of interesting comments to make about the connections between human beings and machines, commodification and the idea of modernity. Like Jardine, Ewen sees working with weights as part of a new cult of the body, 'a yuppie body maintenance, where one plugs the body directly into the machine so as to "fix" it, to plug directly into capital . . .'

9   The concept of somatotype is interesting in this regard as it retains something of the earlier genetic typing. Bodybuilders (and other sportspeople) talk of three different types of body: ectomorphs, endomorphs and mesomorphs. These three types have more colloquial reference: the stringy body, the burly body and the sinewy body (Hix, 1983:13). Whilst in bodybuilding discourse it is clear that

mesomorphs have an advantage in attempting to gain the ideal bodybuilder's body, it is precisely the training and dietetic regimen, and a willingness to submit to them, that produce the bodybuilder. 'If you don't have a lot of motivation, whatever innate potential you actually possess will go to waste' (Francis, 1989: 56). Regardless of one's body type, then, in bodybuilding

> You get results in direct proportion to the amount of work and dietary dedication you put into the sport. So, if you don't have the best bodybuilding potential, don't use it as an excuse for not making good gains. Work hard, and you'll eventually build a great physique. (Francis, 1989:58)

10 The September 1989 edition of *20/20* magazine had an article on female bodybuilders entitled 'Broad Smoulders'. Even the title of this article seems to support our thesis on the making safe of women bodybuilders. It produces a conjunction of a hyperfeminine attribute (smouldering looks) to make unambiguous attributes which are either masculine, potentially masculine or ambiguous (broad shoulders).

11 Again space prohibits extended commentary but the concept of vascularity is enormously significant. It can be interpreted as a continuous search for increasingly specific definitions of bodily excellence. Although it is, as Ross's comments make clear, a significantly gendered phenomenon, the importance of vascularity in the world of male bodybuilding and to bodybuilding generally should not be underestimated. It is a new edge of the body, a boundary that significantly describes the difference between bodybuilders and others.

12 See, for instance, *Women's Physique World*, Fall 1990:46.

13 It is interesting to speculate that this may be why relatively few black women are at the top of the sport, this particular 'look' being a white prerogative.

14 It is interesting to note that powerful women in another sphere, that of business, are similarly enjoined not to mix short hair with shoulder pads.

References

BEVERLEY, B. (1989) 'Nutrition for Women Bodybuilders', *Bodybuilding Monthly*, Vol. 12, No. 8, Ossett, Yorkshire: Bodyshop, pp. 66–69.

BORDO, S. (1990) 'Reading the Slender Body', in JACOBS, M. (Ed.) *Body/Politics: Women and the Discourses of Science*, London, Routledge, Kegan Paul, pp. 83–112.

BRADFORD, R. (1990) 'Carol Mock: Body Business', *Female Bodybuilding and Weight Training*, No. 21, New York, Starlog Communications International Inc., pp. 28–29.

BUGG, L. (1989) 'Doris Barrilleaux: The World's Sexiest Grandmother', *Bodybuilding Monthly*, Vol. 12, No. 9, Ossett, Yorkshire: Bodyshop, pp. 50–51.

de CERTEAU, M. (1988) 'Tools for Writing the Body', in *Flesh: Intervention*, Nos. 21–22, Sydney, Interventions Publications, pp. 7–12.

CHESHIRE, C. and LEWIS, J. (1985) *Body Chic*, London, Pelham Books.

COWARD, R. (1984) *Female Desire: Women's Sexuality Today*, London, Paladrin Books.

DAYTON, L. (1990) 'Laura Binetti's Got the Giant's Secret', *Flex*, Vol. 8, No. 5, Keighley, Yorkshire, Weider Health and Fitness, pp. 125–126.

DAYTON, L. (1990) 'Dorothy Herndon: Bodybuilding with Passion', *Female Bodybuilding and Weight Training*, No. 21, New York, Starlog Communications International Inc., pp. 44–46.

EDGE, A. (1989)'Understanding the Female Body', *Bodybuilding Monthly*, Vol. 12, No. 8, Ossett, Yorkshire, Bodyshop, pp. 60–64.

EDITORIAL (1989) 'Woman and Weights', *Bodybuilding Monthly*, Vol. 12, No. 8, Ossett, Yorkshire, Bodyshop, pp. 57–58.

EVERSON, C. (1990) 'Have We Created a Monster?' *Female Bodybuilding and Weight Training*, No. 21, New York, Starlog Communications International Inc., pp. 20–21.

EWEN, S. (1988) *All-Consuming Images: The Politics of Style in Contemporary Culture*, New York, Basic Books.

FEHER, M. (1987) 'Of Bodies and Technologies', in FOSTER, H. (Ed.) *Discussions in Contemporary Culture*, No. 1, Dia Art Foundation, Seattle, Bay Press, pp. 159–165.

FERGUSON, J. (1990) 'Natural Women: Anabolic Steroids and the Female Body-builder', *Natural Physique*, Vol. 3, No. 2, New York, Cheo Publishing Inc., pp. 56–57.

FRANCIS, B. with REYNOLDS, W. (1989) *Bev Francis' Power Bodybuilding*, New York, Sterling Publishing.

HIX, C. (1983) *Working Out: The Total Shape-Up Guide for Men*, New York, Simon and Shuster.

JARDINE, A. (1987) 'Of Bodies and Technologies', in FOSTER, H. (Ed.) *Discussions in Contemporary Culture*, No. 1, Dia Art Foundation, Seattle, Bay Press, pp. 151–158.

JONES, D. (1990) 'Animating Awesome Arnie', *The Guardian*, June 16–17, London, Guardian Newspapers Ltd., pp. 18–20.

KENNEDY, R. (1990) 'The Pump', *Female Bodybuilding and Weight Training*, No. 21, New York, Starlog Communications International Inc., p. 47.

KRISTEVA, J. (1982) *Powers of Horror: An Essay in Abjection*, trans. Leon S. Roudiez, New York, Columbia University Press.

KUHN, A. (1988) 'The Body and Cinema: Some Problems for Feminism', in SHERIDAN, S. (Ed.) *Grafts: Essays in Feminist Cultural Theory*, London, Verso, pp. 11–23.

LYON, L. and KENT HALL, D. (1981) *Lisa Lyon's Body Magic, London, Bantam Books.*

MANION, J.M. (1990) 'Cory Speaks Out', *Musclemag*, No. 98, Birmingham, Musclemag UK Ltd., pp. 99–104.

NIXON, D. (1990) 'Robin Parker: Bodybuilding as an Artform', *Female Bodybuilding and Weight Training*, No. 21, New York, Starlog Communications International Inc., pp. 26–27.

PEARL, R. (1989) 'Woman and Men Judges', *Bodybuilding Monthly*, Vol. 12, No. 8, Ossett, Yorkshire, Bodyshop, pp. 72–75.

Pumping Iron II — The Women. (US 1985) directed by George Butler, British Distributor, Blue Dolphin, Video Distributor, Virgin.

ROSS, D. (1990) 'Vascularity', *Super Fitness Excell*, Vol. 1, No. 1, Playa del Ray, California, Kuliaikanuu Inc., pp. 45–47.

TANNY, M. (1990) 'Cory's Closest Win', *Muscle and Fitness*, Vol. 51, No. 4, Woodland Hills, California, 1 Brute Enterprises Inc., pp. 126–138.

WEIDER, J. (1990) 'Those Wonderful Female Bodybuilders', *Muscle and Fitness*, Vol. 51, No. 7, Woodland Hills, California 1, Brute Enterprises Inc., p. 6.

Chapter 5

You Too Can Have a Body Like Mine: Reflections on the Male Body and Masculinities

David Morgan

'Macho man with feathered knickers' (Caption to an illustration in a fashion article 'Bad Boy Struts His Stuff in Florence', The European, 18–20 January 1991).

'Charles Atlas Also Dies' (Title of a short story by Sergio Ramirez)

Introduction

If, in general, the sociology of the body is a relatively late arrival on the scene, the sociology of the male body would seem to be even more of a newcomer. Most of the examples treated at any length in Turner's *The Body and Society* (1984) deal with women, their bodies, complaints and conditions, and studies of the representation of the female body still clearly outnumber those dealing with the male body. Few of the articles in the three volumes edited by Feher *et al.* deal specifically with issues of men and male bodies, and the same applies to the comprehensive bibliography in the third volume (Feher *et al.*, 1989). This concentration on women's bodies is clearly apparent in that area of sociology most directly concerned with bodily matters, the sociology of health and illness. This is not simply a greater representation of issues dealing with women — childbirth, menstruation, eating disorders and so on — but the greater likelihood of a more gendered discussion where women are the subject of the research in question.

This tendency to see women as being in some way more embodied than men is reflected in popular culture and popular imagination. The body work carried out on Hollywood stars such as Marilyn Monroe could only ever really apply to women (McCann, 1988:67–71). Representations of women's bodies in advertising and soft pornography — the Page Three Girl being only one of the more obvious examples — are much more visibly obvious than any strict equivalents for men, and descriptions of women in popular fiction tend to be more embodied than descriptions of men.

This greater embodiment of women in contrast to men is also apparent in some feminist writings, as witnessed by the various versions and editions of *Our*

Bodies, Ourselves (Boston, Women's Health Book Collective, New York: Simon and Schuster). Equivalent volumes for men do exist but they are hardly as well-known or as widely distributed. Similarly, 'well-men clinics have been started, although as yet they have a marginal presence in popular medical understandings' (Achilles Heel, Summer 1991). An emphasis upon women and their bodies was clearly an important and necessary part of the feminist critique as women became increasingly aware of the various ways in which patriarchy entailed various forms of control over their bodies (Freund, 1983:24). Martin, for example, noted how, for the women in her sample, a central image was one of separation from self and body (Martin, 1987:77). None of this should be ignored or marginalized; nevertheless, it might be argued that one of the paradoxical consequences of this feminist critique has been the relative underemphasis on men and their bodies, thereby leaving some aspects of the exercise of men's power unexamined.

If it be the case that, at least superficially, women tend to be more embodied and men less embodied in social scientific, popular and feminist writings and representations, various reasons might readily be provided for such a bias. Very generally, it may be seen as part of a wider problem which has only recently begun to be rectified, namely one where women are more likely to be problematized than men. Wherever women are the subject of examination, directly or indirectly — whether it be health studies, cultural studies, the sociology of work and industry or criminology — the analysis tends to be more gendered than similar treatments where men are the research subjects. A greater emphasis upon women's bodies may, therefore, be part of this more general tendency. Further, a greater tendency to write and speak of women and their bodies may be seen as reflecting the well-known ideological equation between women/men and nature/culture (Ortner, 1974; Sydie, 1987).

It might also be added that where issues of men and their bodies do come under sociological examination, the consequences are often limited and disappointing. Thus, accounts with strong sociobiological overtones of body language or bodily abuse in discussion of young men and aggro, for example (Marsh, 1978), tend to present a relatively unproblematic and depoliticized equation of masculinity and violence. These kinds of emphases are, or were, sometimes to be found in writings associated with men's studies or more critical accounts of men and masculinity. Here, a somewhat one-dimensional picture of men and their bodies emerges, one over-concerned with hardness, aggression and heterosexual performance, a kind of 'over-phallusized picture of man' (examples in various degrees: Easthope, 1986; Hoch, 1979; Reynaud, 1983).

This chapter can only begin to suggest some of the complexities involved in considering men, masculinities and their bodies, in the hope that they may provide a research agenda for more detailed work. Contrary to what might seem to have been argued up to now, I begin with the argument that, in modern society at least, men and ideas of masculinity are both embodied and non-bodied. Clearly, bodily differences are taken as major signifiers of differences between men and women, and these physical differences are often read, in complex ways, as being the very source of essential differences between the masculine and the feminine. The popular linkages between penis and strength, hardness and action are well-known and have been the subject of critical deconstruction and satirical comment. Similarly, in many versions of popular masculine speech, to have balls is to have courage, nerve and to be, in a Goffmanesque sense, a man of action (Goffman, 1967).

Yet, just as it would be wrong to accept uncritically the idea that women are the more embodied gender, so it would be misleading to see men straightforwardly more embodied than women. Many images of men in sport, at war and in doing sex are highly embodied or, to be more exact, we are encouraged to read these representations in this way. Pictures of stockbrokers, bishops or dons might not seem as embodied as images of sportsmen or warriors, but if we fail to see their bodies in these cases this may be because of a prior framework of understanding that links men, bodies and action.

Moreover, many ways of understanding or constructing men and masculinity would seem to go to some lengths to exclude considerations of bodies. This is, of course, another variation on the nature/culture divide, especially where this shades into the mind/body distinction. Men, in this model, are reasonable, more clearly identified with rational activities, and are less emotional. This is not to say that men do not have emotions or feelings but rather that, within certain cultures at least, they are less likely to express these feelings in overt, visible and unambiguously embodied ways. Representations of the male body often seek to deny that body. The classic men's suit hides or minimizes the shape of the body (Byrde, 1979) and, even in the supposed age of the new man, men are less likely to be described as wearing figure-hugging clothes. Clearly, of course, such representations of the male body are subject to very wide cultural and historical variation.

Hence, divisions between men and women cannot simply be expressed in terms of degrees of embodiment. In some constructions it is the man who is more embodied, where women may be seen as the more spiritual or refined. In other cases, as we have seen, it is women who are more clearly embodied. Further, degrees and kinds of embodiment signify differences between men as well as differences between women and men. Some men have more balls than other men; some men are coarser, more overtly physical, than others.

Beyond Dichotomies

The papers in this collection, including the present one, seek to explore and deconstruct a variety of dichotomies. The major ones, running throughout this volume, are to do with mind and body and culture and nature. In this chapter, I have already begun to question the straightforward mapping of these dichotomies on to that between men and women.

Another popular opposition with strong gender connotations is that between the public and the private. This is not the place to explore the multiple complexities and ambiguities around these widely used, abused, and sometimes deconstructed, oppositions. However, it is instructive to consider some of the ambiguities in connection with the more bodily aspects of the constructed differences between men and women. At first, the matter seems to be straightforward. Men's power is exercised in the public arena and this power frequently, one might say always, takes on a bodily form. This is closely linked to the occupation and the use of space:

> To be an adult male is distinctly to occupy space, to have a physical presence in the world. (Connell, 1983:19)

Hooligans, subjects of popular fears and moral panics through the centuries (Pearson, 1983), are groups of, for the most part, young men occupying public space in a particularly loud and aggressive manner. The verb 'to swagger' dealing with a particular kind of male performance in public space could rarely be applied to women. Men, as women sometimes complain, take up more space on public transport, and men's bodies predominate in public parades representing state power or military might. Whether by right or by force, men come to occupy public space is a distinctly embodied fashion.

Yet this is not the whole story. Often men in public space are, officially or unofficially, uniformed as soldiers, policemen, clergy or stockbrokers. The nature of uniform is, among other things, to divert attention away from the particularities and idiosyncracies of specific bodies and to focus on generalized public roles and statuses. The disciplining of a body of men is at the expense of individual bodies. This is not to say that, for a wide range of societies, men do not tend to occupy public spaces with greater frequency and often greater freedom than women. However, the ways in which men occupy public space and the degrees to which such presences are licensed or circumscribed do vary considerably. Further, the claims to public spaces may be the subject of conflict and contestation between men and women, as we see in the debates around sexual harassment.

Rather than explore a whole range of other dichotomies and their interconnections with issues of gender and embodiment (a task which is explored at greater length in the introduction of the present volume), I shall here develop one particular theme in order to highlight issues of complexity and ambiguity. This is what I describe as the 'embodiment of reason'. As has already been noted, a major axis around which these issues are organized is between mind and body. This is not the place to explore complex philosophical issues but simply to raise some sociological themes. Whatever the complex term 'mind' signifies, it clearly overlaps with several other widely used terms such as 'thinking' or 'reason'. These terms have clear gender connotations in that they are more readily associated with men than with women in central ideological constructions. What is less readily appreciated is that they also have bodily connotations, despite the apparent location of the realms of thought, reason and mind in some trans-bodily space.

This is not simply a question of the obvious point that thinking is associated with a bodily organ, the brain. Let us consider Rodin's often reproduced (and parodied) statue, 'The Thinker'. Firstly, it is almost certainly no accident that the figure is a male figure; it is by no means certain if the statue would work if it depicted a woman in an identical pose. Further, it is clearly a matter of some importance that it is not any old male body that is being depicted. An obese figure or a skeletal figure would be as inappropriate as would be a female figure. Secondly, the figure clearly represents a special kind of unity of mind and body. The figure is not simply thinking; he can be said to be actively doing thinking.

Thinking, therefore, can be understood as being a particularly embodied way of being in the world. Insofar as intellectual labour is woven into wider patterns of the sexual division of labour, then to do thinking is to occupy a particularly distinctive and often privileged place in space, public or private. The thinker allows for no interruptions from the mundane world of domestic responsibilities or small children. Yet obligations are placed upon the thinker to be seen doing thinking, to occupy space in a particular watchful or concentrating manner. Certain props, extensions of the body may help such as the book-lined study, thick-rimmed spectacles or pipes, but the body has to be deployed in a way to legitimate the title of thinker.

Doing thinking also points out differences between men. Popular stereotypes locate the business of thinking in particular physical types such as egg-heads and pointy-heads, and these popular images reflect wider patterns of the social division of labour between mental labour and manual labour. Although such stereotypes often associate the former with the lack of any kind of physicality, it can again be seen that the distinction in reality deals with different bodily ways of being in the world. Thinking, being reasonable, doing rationality, are all closely interconnected and are all socially distributed not simply between women and men but between different classes of status groups of men. These bodily contrasts are given dramatic expression in conventional depictions of industrial disputes. On the one side we have the mass meeting where individual bodies merge into a body of men; on the other side we have more identifiable individuals moving in and out of offices. On the one side the embodiment of feelings, on the other side the embodiment of rationality and efficiency. The analysis of media representations of industrial disputes have perhaps had less to say than they might have about the bodily codes around which such conflicts are constructed.

Men, Power and Bodies

The processes whereby women's bodies have, generally, been more problematized than those of men or, to put it another way, whereby women have been constructed as being more embodied than men, is clearly not a simple error or oversight. Intellectual blindspots generally have social and political roots, and issues to do with men and their bodies provide no exceptions to this rule. Here, as elsewhere, we are in the simplest terms dealing with systems of patriarchy or male power. However this troublesome word might be understood, one deep-rooted and long-term feature of systems of patriarchal domination is the fact that men are not routinely required to reflect upon their positions as men in society or to consider themselves as gendered or embodied subjects. Throughout history, it is the relatively powerless who find themselves reflecting upon their identity in society and upon those social structural features that contribute to their minority, subordinate or marginal status within a given society. Only under certain situations of crisis do the relatively powerful find themselves engaging in similar processes of self-reflection.

It has frequently been argued that our present times constitute one such period of crisis for men and masculinity (see Morgan, 1992). What we need to do here is to explore the relationships between issues of power and issues of embodied gender. We should not assume that the connections between men's bodies and systems of patriarchal power (and other power) are identical in all societies. Further comparative discussion is clearly necessary. However, confining our discussion to modern societies, one clear point of departure is, as has already been indicated, the Weberian theme of rationality (Seidler, 1989). Where social systems come to be dominated by themes of rationality and where such themes become, covertly at least, to be identified with men, then issues of the body together with the associated issues of the emotions come to be marginalized. In many cases and in a variety of ways this has entailed being identified with women. This is not to say that bodies are inherently non-rational, but simply that the processes whereby rational systems develop tend, symbolically and often practically, to locate the source of that rationality outside the body in realms of pure thought, abstract reason or systems of logic, or, within but not of the body, in the realm of the mind. In the circle of men, power and rationality, men become less and women become more embodied. This may be seen as one of the covert themes of the analysis of the Protestant ethic (Morgan, 1992). Clearly matters are a lot more complicated than this and some of these complications will be explored later. One obvious qualification is that such a system revolving around power, masculinity and rationality is not static and that one of the sources of this chapter, indeed of the whole volume, is the challenge that has been presented to these equations from the feminist movement. Women do not simply come to an understanding of their lives as being significantly embodied in many ways, but also come to understand the systems of control and domination over their bodies (Freund, 1983:24). Women also come to look quizzically and critically at men's bodies and their representations, to represent these bodies in demystificatory ways:

> To subject the penis to representation is to strip the phallus of its empowering veil . . . (Schor, 1987:113)

With the growing, and sometimes problematic, interest in men and masculinities and the development of what is sometimes called 'Men's Studies', a movement clearly shaped by the impact of feminist critiques, it is not surprising that men should begin to look questioningly at their own bodies.

Thus there are intimate connections between issues of men's bodies and issues of men's power, and it has been the challenging of the latter that has led to the problematization of the former. Clearly, there are no difficulties in making the connections between patriarchal power and men's bodies. Popular or pornographic representations of the erect and thrusting penis; imperial representations of a glorious past or socialist representations of a glorious future; popular scientific discourses around body language: all these and many more features of modern culture make these equations without effort. The domination of men over other men, over women and over children (and indeed over animals and nature) are expressed in bodily terms, directly as well as indirectly. In his useful typology of body-use in action, Frank distinguishes between the Disciplined, the Dominating, the Mirroring and the Communicative Body (Frank, 1991). While issues of gender and masculinity are not absent from these other three types, the links are most clearly expressed in his discussion of the Dominating Body:

> . . . it is impossible to consider the dominating body without also questioning the construction of the masculine body. (Frank, 1991:69)

Without going into the details of Frank's analysis (which at times leans towards essentialism) some general points may be made about the dominating body and masculinity. In the first place, while the most dramatic examples of the dominating body come from war and physical violence (Frank deals with Theweleit's analysis of fascist power at some length) such examples do not exhaust the range of possibilities. Dominance may be established in the Board Room as well as on the battle-field and, as studies of proxemics maintain, such dominance can be expressed in terms of bodily posture and sitting as well as through the more overtly physical deployments of the body. The discussion about the connections between power, rationality and masculinity underlines this point. Linked to this consideration is the continuing need to stress that such discussions of dominance should not be interpreted in straightforwardly biological or deterministic terms. It is not the possession of a penis which provides the basis for male dominance over women. Rather it is systems of patriarchy which enable the penis to be represented or understood in ways that express domination. Thirdly, it is clear that the dominations that are being discussed do not simply refer to dominations of men over women. We are also dealing with dominations of men over other men, and the possible and complex links between these and other patterns of domination.

It is especially important, when exploring the relationships between gender, bodies and domination, to avoid too simplified an account of the interconnections. The links between them are the outcome of complex and diverse historical and social processes rather than determinate laws. Here, perhaps, an autobiographical example may serve as illustration. In much of the recent men's literature, I find accounts of penis anxiety on the part of young men. They are supposed to be routinely concerned about the length of their penis and to engage in covert or overt comparisons with other young men. Thus:

> The adolescent locker-room talk is in terms of inches, and we secretly (sometimes openly) compare sizes. (Lewis, 1978:107)

Certainly Hall's historical study of men's sexual anxieties unearthed some concerns about the size of the male organ (Hall, 1991:135) and the sheer volume of such accounts cannot be simply dismissed. But is it the whole story? For myself, despite the normal rituals of communal showers, a long period in the Boy Scouts and the experience of National Service, I cannot remember engaging in these kinds of comparative rituals nor can I remember ever having experienced any serious anxiety about the size of my member. The anxiety I can remember is to do with erections and the real or imagined embarrassment that might accompany such events. I can remember, for example, a patrol of Scouts lining up for inspection at a summer camp and the imperfectly suppressed giggles at the tell-tale bulge in the patrol-leader's shorts.

Such personal reflections can be useful not so much to prove a point but to serve as an aid to thinking through complexities. Erections are a source of embarrassment and humour not simply because they draw attention to the penis, something that is normally kept well out of the public gaze in most Western cultural situations, but because they are seen, rightly or wrongly, as an outer signifier of inner thoughts and desires. While all kinds of stimuli (not all of these sexual by any means) might produce erections, the meanings given to such an event are primarily sexual. What is particularly disturbing about such events is their apparently arbitrary and unpredictable character. In short, the erection has an irrationality about it which contrasts markedly with Western, and especially middle-class, one might assume, themes of control and predictability. The erection is a jester in the wings of the civilizing process.

What has this to do with power? Superficially, it would seem to suggest that modern man, far from wishing to flout his erect penis, wants, in most situations apart from the overtly sexual, to keep it very much out of sight if not always out of mind. Yet, even if this is true, it does not necessarily signify a straightforward reduction of embodied power. Apart from considerations to do with the preserving of the mysteries of power for private sexual encounters, there is the idea that power as much resides in the control of bodily activities as it does in the overt deployment of the body. As Elias classically argued, self-control and societal control went hand in hand (Elias, 1978), although this is not to be understood in terms of some simple and determinate flow between the two. Rather it is to be understood in terms of the linkages between rationality, power and gender discussed earlier and the ways in which these are historically situated. Similar arguments may be made in relation to physical violence, where power may lie in the manifest control over the expression of anger in physical terms rather than in the straightforward deployment of physical aggression. As a character in the Howard Hawks Western, *Rio Bravo*, remarks: 'He's so good, he doesn't have to prove it'.

Sites of Bodily Power

In almost any society, it is relatively easy to think of those sites or arenas where men's power, expressed in bodily terms, is exercised. In most modern societies, for example, we might routinely think of the sports arena or the battle-field even if, in the case of the latter, modern technology might seem to erase the sheer physicality of human combat. Other obvious sites would be to do with sexual encounters. While many of these encounters are conventionally understood in terms of the 'private', others, for example those to do with sexual representation and sexual display, have a more strongly accented public dimension. It soon becomes readily apparent in following through these and other examples, that these by no means exhaust the possibilities and that, in principle, any physical or social space may be understood as a potential site for the intersection of gender, power and men's bodies. Feminists, for example, have clearly identified the street as one arena where male power conventionally is exercised and it is clear that this power may still be exercised in bodily terms even where no direct physical encounter takes place. Conventional discussions of body language, especially where these are allied to questions of managerial or executive power, are clearly also gendered even where they are not specifically signified as such. Similar observations may be made about all such sites, public or private, physical or symbolic.

A recognition of the multiplicity and diversity of sites where men, bodies and power converge should serve, yet again, as a warning against any kind of essentialism. While some sites are more obviously embodied than others (at least for a given culture) embodiment is a feature of all sites, certainly in those sites where gender and power interact. To illustrate this, I take a site where, to the superficial observer, issues of bodies and physicality would seem to be at their minimum, namely that of angling. I must be a little more specific here. While deep-sea fishing as a sport and fishing as an occupation have very strong associations with conventional constructions of masculinity, these considerations would seem to be at their minimum when contemplating the solitary figures on the banks of many English rivers or canals. Here there would seem to be no Hemingwayesque battle between Man and Nature and no collective camaraderie in the face of danger and uncertainty. Putting aside any of the more obvious and reductionist phallic connotations of the fishing rod or the emphasis upon the size of the catch, where are the bodies? Where is the masculinity?

In the absence of any specific research on this topic, what follows is simply suggestive. In the first place, angling very obviously takes place in the public space, even though the activity itself might seem to be highly privatized. An unproblematic occupation of a piece of public space which appears to be so characteristic of leisure angling, is part of a wider phenomenon, the clear gender divide when it comes to the deployment of bodies in public or open spaces. Part of the reason why there appear to be so few women anglers is simply to do with expectations about the occupation of public space, free from sexual, or other, harassment.[1]

In the second place, angling is very obviously the deployment of a set of skills which, in common with all such skills, are to do with the control and deployment of the body. The fact that these skills are linked, directly and symbolically, with strong masculine traditions is also a matter of some significance. However, in keeping with some earlier observations in this chapter, I should emphasize the theme of control, the emphasis upon the development of particular sensitivities and the deployment of watchful patience, rather than the obvious deployment of brute strength.

Finally, angling has clear associations with what Goffman calls 'action', that is with situations where outcomes are problematic and consequential (Goffman, 1967). Action in this sense, as I have recorded elsewhere (Morgan, 1990), has strong gendered, indeed masculine, connotations. Matters are more complex in the present example. The author of *The Compleat Angler* or the *Contemplative Men's Recreation* (Walton, 1983) argued that angling represented the meeting point of action and contemplation, locating the activity in well-established but highly, if covertly, gendered philosophical debates. Hence, even in something like angling, the interplays between bodies and gender, and hence also power, are a complex and over-determined phenomenon.

We may perhaps conclude, therefore, that there are no social sites or arenas which are unembodied just as there are no sites that are ungendered and that, in such sites, gender, power and bodies interact. This is not, of course, the same as saying that all sites are equally or similarly gendered or embodied. In order to begin to explore the nature of variations in embodied locations, we may first consider the extent to which, in a given culture, bodily deployment or display is licensed, permitted or required. Following the arguments of Elias about the associations between the civilizing process and bodily control (Elias, 1978) both in terms of the internal and external controls, we may argue that certain forms of bodily expression or deployment are, in modern society, licensed or legitimated, but only for particular times and particular spaces. This is especially true where physical violence is concerned. The overlapping arenas of war and sport (especially physical contact sports such as boxing) are clear examples where particular kinds of bodily conduct are licensed or even required. Such conduct would be liable to negative sanctions were it to take place outside these arenas.

Yet we should not confine such arenas to those involving the deployment of physical violence. The world of fashion, for example, may often be an arena where certain kinds of display are permitted which might be the subject of negative or satirical comment were they to take place away from the catwalks. Thus, the captions on one article on men's fashions read:

'Cowboy-style chaps over blue denim'
'Macho man with feathered knickers'
'A gaucho look, along with white gloves'
'Chinese ideographs on a streamlined silhouette'
(All from *The European*, January 18–20th, 1991).

Similar observations may be made, perhaps more strongly, about the world of male strippers (Barham, 1985).

Thus there are certain arenas where bodily deployment and display on the part of men may clearly be permitted. Overlapping with these are those arenas where bodily performance will be required. The distinctions here are often matters of degree. For example there are certain work contexts where it would seem obvious that bodily skill and deployment will be required: policing, deep-sea fishing, extractive industries, etc. Even here, however, it is often difficult to distinguish between those features of bodily deployment which are strictly required by the work and those which are part of a masculine occupational context. Less obvious, perhaps, are the more private arenas where more particular expectations are made in terms of bodily performance. Chief among these must be those sites associated with sexuality where, conventionally, physical expectations come to the fore. While sexual advice, from manuals, magazines or therapists will now routinely bracket the physical and the emotional, the emphasis will still tend to be around genital sex and intercourse. Conversely, sexual dysfunction (itself often seen as a signifier of relational or emotional problems) is conventionally understood in terms of such indicators as failure to achieve erection, failure to achieve orgasm or premature ejaculation (see Clark, this volume).

Just as there are arenas or sites where bodily deployment may be both required and approved, in varying degrees, so too are there those sites where bodily considerations are expected to be kept at a minimum. Strictly speaking such sites are not so much embodied as sites where bodily control is very much required. We are much into Elias country here, a reminder that such situations are the outcome of long and complex histories. As an illustration, I shall mention a series of advertisements which appeared in *The Listener* and similar publications during the early 1960s and possibly before. The product was a kind of up-market chewing-gum and the advertisements consisted of a series of drawings depicting certain public events such as Ascot, Henley or upper-class garden parties. 'Certainly Not!' the advertisement proclaimed, making it clear that chewing-gum would be decidedly off-limits in such contexts. However, the advertisements went on to suggest that in certain other, undepicted contexts and used with discretion, chewing gum could be a legitimate pleasure as well as 'an aid to oral hygiene'.

While there are numerous ways in which this chewing-gum advertisement might be interpreted (for example, gum chewing might indicate or encourage a withdrawal of attention from the serious business to hand) one important theme would be to do with the drawing of attention to the body in contexts where the body is supposed to be kept strictly under control.

It may be suggested that we are dealing here with contexts, often ceremonial contexts, where the generalized social body clearly takes precedence over the individual physical body. This is presumably why the soldier who faints on parade will be the object of censure or discipline. While such situations clearly impose their constraints on both women and men (one might think of the long periods of grooming and corsetting that must have preceded ceremonial events in the upper-class season in late-Victorian England) it is likely that, generally speaking, the expectations of bodily control fall more heavily upon men than women. This is partly because men are more likely to occupy centre stage on ceremonial and public occasions than women, and partly because in the last two centuries at least, the formal dress of British men has tended away from the physical body and very much towards the social body.

It is possible, therefore, to think of a kind of continuum running from those situations where bodily deployment is both required and legitimated to those where it is neither required nor approved. Between these two extremes there are some more ambiguous situations. There are sites where bodily action is clearly required although not necessarily approved (arm wrestling, for example) or approved but not necessarily required (recreational walks). The ambiguities in this area reflect the complexities of a modern society, the multiplicities of overlapping reference groups or fields of meaning and the struggles and negotiations around the legitimacy or otherwise of different forms of embodied activities.

The point of this analysis is, as has already been stressed, not to provide a list of particular sites where embodiment, masculinities and power meet, but rather to suggest some of the principles upon which such sites might be constructed. To use another metaphor, the aim is not so much to point to a particular spot on a map but to suggest some rules by which this, and similar, maps might be constructed and read. One set of rules or principles, therefore, has been to do with the degree to which bodily deployment is required or is legitimated. Another set of principles might be to do with the ever-problematic distinction between the public and the private. There is, as has been stressed elsewhere, need for caution here partly because of the ambiguities built into the opposition itself and partly because such oppositions are in part ideological constructions which are used and called upon in difficult circumstances. Here, I am arguing that just as social situations may be described as being more or less embodied, so they may also be described as being more or less open to the scrutiny of others. Such scrutiny may be direct or indirect or potential or actual. Thus speaking on a soap box in Hyde Park is a public act, whether or not it attracts an audience. Putting these two sets of principles together or cross-cutting the two continually shows the various ways in which social contexts may be more or less embodied and more or less public. Thus a football match is both embodied and public while the training for such a match may well be equally embodied but much less public. Similarly (and putting to one side for a moment the approaches of Foucault and popular understandings of permissiveness) sexual intercourse is both embodied and private.

Hence, while in modern society there are clearly certain sites where embodiment, gender and power meet, the aim of this section has not been to provide a list of such sites, but to argue that all sites are in principle open to such an analysis, and to provide a provisional guide to some of the investigative strategies that might be adopted in exploring such sites. To return to our solitary angler: he is both public and private and his activities, while embodied, are as much to do with bodily control and the art that conceals art as with more overt bodily display or deployment. And in his own rather unspectacular way he exercises power, not only power over nature but also the power to define his time and his space.

Types of Men's Bodies

Just as we should beware of seeking to provide a list of sites where embodiment and gendered power meet (with the implication that such a list provides a set of fixed or essential locations) so too we should be wary of establishing a typology of men's bodies. Assuming that we are not interested in simple physical descriptions of men's bodies (although the meanings given to such classifications may well be of interest) we are left with accounts which either provide for a plurality of masculinities and their bodily signifiers or concomitants or, more contentiously, with accounts which argue for embodiment being strongly or weakly associated with types of masculinities. In other, simpler, words, some bodies may be seen as more masculine than others.

Something of this kind of assumption appears to inform Frank's typology of body-use in action (Frank, 1991). As already noted, he draws up a typology around the words 'Disciplined', 'Dominating', 'Mirroring' and 'Communicating'. Insofar as issues of gender, especially masculinity, enter into the discussion, it is around the second of these terms, 'Dominating'. It is likely that such a linkage is drawing upon commonsensical notions of masculinity or upon the more overt and obvious manifestations of embodied masculine power. Yet it is likely that issues of masculinity arise in all four although in different ways and to different degrees. Put another way, all four types of body-use in action may be seen as being gendered.

After 'Dominating', the next type of body-use in action which is most obviously associated with masculinity is probably 'Disciplined'. Here the medium which Frank cites is 'regimentation', something with clear associations with the military and with religious orders. The former has strong masculine connotations of course, while the latter applies to both men and women. While the disciplined body can be strongly associated with some aspects of femininity (Frank instances the example of fasting) it is clear that this is a theme strongly associated with the developments of masculinities, especially within the early and middle stages of capitalism.

As has already been noted, the Dominating body, where the medium is that of force, is most closely associated with masculinity in many societies. However, it would be misleading to suggest that the Dominating body was anchored firmly and exclusively to men and to masculinity. Woman can and do use force and exercise domination, over children, over other women, and sometimes over men. Such instances are certainly less frequent for women than for men, although in many cases it would seem that the difference is not so much one of whether women are capable or not of exercising force, but the wider frameworks of meaning within which the exercise of force by women is conventionally understood.

The other two types of body-use in action would seem to have much stronger feminine connotations in modern society. The Mirroring Body, where the medium is consumption, would seem to have stronger feminine associations since the wider gender division of labour tends to allocate the consumption function, generally speaking, to women rather than to men. Further, women are more likely to be directly involved in the commodification of their bodies, in the presentation of their bodies as objects of consumption. Again, there is nothing inevitable about this and recent research has provided plenty of examples of the ways in which the links between consumption and the male body develop in modern society (e.g. Featherstone, 1991). In the case of the Communicative body, where the medium is that of recognition, Frank argues that in present times we have only hints as to what this may mean. Certainly, his account of this type of body (using the illustrations of dance) does have strong feminine connotations with the stress on the mutual interplay between dyadic other-relatedness and self-recognition. Yet, while perhaps the strongest intimations in modern society come from relations between or involving women, there are also hints of the Communicative body in relationships between men, sometimes under the most extreme of circumstances in the face of danger or at time of battle.

The purpose of this elaboration of Frank's types is partly to continue the exploration in terms of gender, which Frank himself began, but mainly to make the more general point that while certain types of body or bodily use in action have, in present cultures at least, strong masculine connotations, this is by no means inevitable. Indeed, if certain modes of bodily use readily conjure up images of men (such as Dominating) this may be because such understandings are ready to hand, deeply embedded in the culture. In contrast, an approach which stresses a plurality of masculinities will also allow for a range of bodily uses to be associated with men, some less obvious than others. This seems to suggest a cafeteria model of masculinities, whereby it is claimed that there are a variety of forms of available masculinities within modern society and that men may choose from these masculinities more or less at will. This is, of course, a model which is in keeping with some aspects of the post-modern debate as applied to issues of gender. Somewhat more structured, and more sociologically appealing, is the model suggested by Connell (and adopted by many writers on men and masculinities) whereby certain masculinities are seen as more dominant or hegemonic than others within any particular society (Connell, 1987). Thus, generally speaking, the warrior is more hegemonic than the wimp. While there is clearly value in arguing for a hierarchy, rather than a simple plurality, of masculinities, the relationships between hegemony, embodiment and gender are by no means straightforward.

As an illustration of some of these complexities, I shall consider a distinction which derives from Bakhtin and which has been used by Stallybrass and White and, to a lesser extent, by Featherstone (Bakhtin, 1984; Featherstone, 1991:79; Stallybrass and White, 1986). This is a distinction between the grotesque body and the classical body. Generally speaking and with some simplification, classical bodies are controlled, in conformity with dominant (in this case European, Western?) aesthetic standards, and are constructed as being much closer to culture or to the civilized. In contrast, the grotesque body is uncontrolled, unappealing according to dominant aesthetic standards, and constructed as being much closer to nature. Almost, one might say, the distinction is close to that between the sacred and the profane. There are clear, historically located, class connotations to this distinction, the classical body being much closer to models prevailing amongst the aristocracy or the Court society, while the grotesque body is more likely to be represented as a member of the peasant or the lower classes. Such bodies were also identified with particular spatial sites. In eighteenth century England, classical bodies were more associated with the coffee houses, the grotesque bodies with taverns (Stallybrass and White, 1986).

Generally speaking, the contrast between classical and grotesque (which clearly has both masculine and feminine variations) was developed and probably applies best in relation to pre-industrial European society. In a relatively stable hierarchical society, the relationships between embodiment and distinction could be relatively straightforward. The contrast between the more physical, more 'natural' and relatively uncontrolled peasant on the one hand, and the cultivated and controlled member of the court society was almost an absolute one and it was the starkness of this contrast which enabled it to be subverted in carnivals and saturnalia as well as in literature. The contrast, for example, between the members of the court and the 'rude mechanicals' in *A Midsummer Night's Dream* is subverted both by the mechanicals' aping of classical drama and by the lack of control on the part of some members of the court as a result of magical intervention.

At this point we may also consider another figure of European imagination which has some relevance to this discussion, that of the 'wild man'. He appeared in various guises such as the construction of the Indians in North America or the case of 'Peter', discovered living in a state of nature in the woods near Hamelin in 1724 (Dudley and Novak, 1972). 'Peter' was, of course, one of several such sightings who aroused the intellectual curiosities and imaginations of members of the literate classes from the eighteenth century onwards. The 'wild men' were, obviously, not the same as the grotesque bodies of the peasantries and lower classes, who were much closer to home. Nevertheless, like the grotesque body in some respects, the wild men were the objects of both desire and anxiety (Dudley and Novak, 1972). Further, the body of the wild man served as a site where constructions of nature, and by implication civilization, were worked and re-worked.

In a more industrial society, the boundaries become less clear and it may be suggested that the contrasts between the classical and the grotesque are of reduced significance. Nevertheless, their variations as models of masculinity still persist and still have their significance. In the face of the disciplines of capitalism and bureaucracy, the classical body becomes the rational body but the grotesque body still, at least symbolically, tends to be associated with the working or the lower classes. Yet today, as in former times, the grotesque body is by no means wholly stigmatized. Beer-bellied, prone to fits of violence or uncontrollable mirth and lacking any of the conventional signs of self-discipline, the grotesque body can serve as a warning to society as a whole. This is certainly the case in some public health advertisements, highlighting the links between beer drinking, smoking, lack of exercise and chip eating with a proneness to heart complaints. Yet, at the same time, the grotesque body's symbolic closeness to natural instincts, its apparent rejection of the conventional limitations of a proper time or place may be a source of admiration, an ironic comment on the 'unnaturalness' of respectable or civilized society. The symbol of this covert celebration of naturalness may be the fart or the belch which, instead of being disguised or apologized for, is acknowledged as a source of pleasure or relief.

It is clear that, firstly, the distinction between classical and grotesque cannot begin to cover all the variations in masculine bodies in modern times, and that, secondly, they cannot be simply mapped on to class distinctions. Indeed, it is likely that both working- and middle-classes have their variations on the classical/grotesque theme. Thus working-class cultures may include variations on the classical body theme in the case of the 'hard man' who knows how to take care of himself in a clear and disciplined manner, or the 'sharp dresser', taken up as a feature of many, largely working-class, youth cultures. Similarly, various manifestations of respectability should be seen not simply as desires to imitate middle-class class, but as attempts to develop an authentic variation on working-class experience.

Middle-class or bourgeois culture also, it may be suggested, has its own variations on the grotesque body theme. There is, of course, the familiar, if often stereotypical, figure of the bohemian or the artist who is accorded some licence by the largely middle-class society in which he moves and from which, to a large extent, he derives his livelihood. In various ways figures such as Augustus John, Dylan Thomas, Brendan Behan and more recently, Jeffrey Bernard, manifest some features of the grotesque male body in the sense of individuals being allowed to manifest a certain lack of control in certain areas, especially in relation to alcohol. Another variation may be the well-rounded belly of the successful man, the apparent excess here being an obvious manifestation of conspicuous consumption, even where control and discipline might well be exercised in other areas of his life.

It should be stressed that the grotesque and the classical or rational bodies (at whatever social level) have particular if different relations to masculine power. The grotesque body represents the symbolic power of the natural, a capacity for violence and sheer physical domination, highlighting the potential fragility of respectable society. In reversal of the conventional equation, it is a man's apparent unmediated links with nature, in all its earthiness and unpredictability, that provides the power of the grotesque body. Respectable, cultured society in this context becomes feminine or effeminate. The classical or rational body represents the power that resides in control, control over self and control over others. The aesthetic order of the classical body both mirrors and is a metaphor for the social order.

It may be suggested further that there are relationships, often covert, between the two manifestations of bodily power. The power of the controlled classical body, through the very emphasis upon control and discipline, suggests a capacity for violence which the classical body shares, although less obviously, with the grotesque body. The rituals of Officers' Messes or all-male colleges symbolize the subterranean links between the two types. And similarly, although this is perhaps less well explored, the power of the grotesque body derives in part from the licence it is accorded by the classical body. Upper- and middle-class patronage of bohemian society may be one example of this. At the very least, the grotesque body may serve as an abiding warning to respectable society as to what may happen if matters are allowed to get out of control.

It is not being claimed that this contrast between the classical (or rational) and grotesque body exhausts the range of types of male bodies which may be called upon in any given society. Rather, the contrast can be seen as representing one major theme around which modes of embodied masculinities can be analyzed. It is designed to serve as a reminder that there are many ways, just as there are many sites, where gender and bodily power interact.

Conclusion: Men, Bodies and Social Change

It has been one of the main themes of this chapter that, while there has been relatively more scholarly and other attention paid to women's than to men's bodies, it cannot be maintained that women are more embodied than men. Nor, indeed, can the reverse be argued. The relationships between men and women and embodiment are different in character rather than degree, and the difference lies in the complex triangular relationships between gender, embodiment and power rather than in any straightforward physiological determination.

Another consequence of a more sociological approach to the study of men's bodies is to focus on the variations between men, on masculinities in the plural, as well as upon the variations between women and men. Again, such differences cannot be reduced to any straightforward differences in terms of, physical strength, weight or height. Rather, these differences are to be sought, firstly in the different sites within which masculinities are constructed and reproduced. These sites are not, as might be understood in a more functional model, to be seen as fixed places or institutions but rather as shifting points of convergence around a variety of themes, such as those to do with the public and the private or in terms of the degree of legitimacy accorded to bodily action or display. Within many societies, some sites emerge with considerable frequency, such as those to do with war and sport. Yet even here, the strong linkages between gender, power and bodies are undergoing change and facing challenge.

In the second place, the differences between men can be seen in terms of the variety and the hierarchies of masculinities within a particular society. Over-use of the term 'hegemonic masculinities' might suggest that these are relatively straightforward, perhaps even fixed, hierarchies. However, even a brief consideration of the ideal-typical contrast between the classical and the grotesque bodied suggests that the relationship may be more complex. However, it may be said that the sheer physicality of the grotesque body loses out, in the long run, to the control of the rational or classical body.

One major historical theme has not been so much the shift from nature to culture or from the embodied to the less embodied. Rather, the emphasis may be better formulated in terms of a greater degree of control over bodies, both internally and externally. This, of course, is a major strand in the analysis of the civilizing process. The complexities of these controls cannot be explored in detail at this point: they include not only the well-known processes of societal rationalization and bureaucratization but also a greater degree of surveillance, particularly in the processes generally defined as medicalization. Clearly, these processes affect women as well as men and often more directly, although it may be suggested that these processes have a peculiar significance in the lives and experiences of men, given the strong historical links that may be made between masculinities, rationality and the growth of scientific discourses. It is this greater degree of emphasis upon issues of control and discipline that might have led, misleadingly, to the belief that men were less embodied than women.

These long-term historical processes, much over-simplified in the context of a brief essay, do not proceed with an inexorable logic detached from human critique or praxis. Thus, in recent years, very often directly or indirectly as a consequence of the women's movements, some men have begun to look critically at certain bodily aspects of men's behaviour and men's lives in general. At least four aspects of this critique may be noted:

1   The oppressing body.
    More critical accounts of men and masculinities, that is those accounts which take the feminist critique as their main point of departure, have looked at the male body as a site for the oppression of women. There have been several manifestations of this, including critiques of conventional models of male sexuality (both heterosexual and homosexual), searching examinations of men and sexual violence, and more general critiques of the role of men's violence, against both women and men, as one of the institutions or mechanisms of patriarchy (see, for example, Hearn, 1987). Considerable attention has been paid to issues of pornography which, while overtly dealing with the objectification and commodification of women's bodies, simultaneously construct simple and essentialist models of men's desires and embodied sexualities. The common definition of a pornographic book as being one which is read with one hand reflects the way in which men's bodies are constructed through pornography. Another illustration is to do with all aspects of sexual harassment and the way in which, in certain contexts such as public places at night, men's bodies are perceived as potential threats to women. It may be argued that these discussions of the various embodied ways in which men's oppression of women operates has tended to focus upon the details of individual cases while failing to bring them together in a thoroughgoing theoretical analysis of the links between embodiment and power in men's routine and everyday practices.

2   The body as a site for the emotions.
    It is by now a commonplace that men have difficulty in expressing their feelings and their emotions. Sometimes this understanding is linked to a general feminist-inspired and historically-based critique while elsewhere it might be simply part of a diffuse therapeutic understanding of the self and personal identity in modern society. The lack on the part of men is sometimes understood to be an inability or a deeply structured unwillingness to verbalize feelings, but it may also include a critique of a failure to give non-verbal, more embodied expression to one's emotions. The common phrase 'to get in touch with one's feelings' has significantly embodied connotations. The paradigmatic example of the bodily expression of emotion is, of course, the ability to shed tears or to weep in public. It is as if, in the face of a lot of comparative historical and anthropological evidence, the shedding of tears were the guarantee of authenticity, the embodiment of a true self.

3   The body and fraternity.
    Part of the contemporary search for male identity is an exploration of the
    positive aspects of being a man. This search may be more or less directly
    anti-feminist or it may be, more ambiguously, a response to a perceived
    lack in comparison with the more overt expressions of sisterhood that
    feminism has been seen as emphasizing. Positive virtues of masculinity
    are perceived to be in fraternity and male-bonding, the direct expression
    of which may be in uninhibited bodily contact or a collective sharing of
    bodily experiences:

> We were chanting and sweating and screaming and hollering. It
> was fun and uplifting because it involved prayers and a lot of
> affirmation. People talked about pain. (Account of men's week-
> end retreat, Newsweek, June 24th, 1991)

4   The healthy body.
    Concerns about the body are scarcely new nor are they confined to men.
    However, there are some signs that recent concerns do have some overt
    links with a critical understanding of men's routine practices. In the first
    place, a simple recognition of the male body as a site for concern may be
    a relative novelty:

> The sum of my knowledge about the male body, its structure
> and functioning was the fact that I had one. It worked very
> satisfactorily for me, performed most of the tasks that were
> required of it and without too much difficulty. It never seriously
> bothered me, and consequently, I never seriously bothered about
> it. (Lewis, 1978:ix)

> Further, this recognition may contribute towards a critique of some
> routine manifestations of the 'grotesque body' in terms of consumption
> and everyday lifestyle: drinking, eating conventional masculine foods and
> failing to subject oneself to the disciplines of regular exercise.

It should not be imagined that this list exhausts the various ways in which
reassessments of men's bodies have been taking place in recent years. We might,
for example, wish to add to this list some modern version of the more traditional
dandified body, a theme much emphasized in some recent men's magazines.
Further, it should be stressed that these various modes of problematizing men's
bodies do not necessarily add up to a coherent or widespread critical understanding of men and their bodies. Certainly, we should not see them in terms of any
straightforward linear progressive model. While there have been critiques of both
the apparent inhibitions of the classical or the rational body and the apparent
excesses of the grotesque body, theories of post-modernity have called into question any idea of progressive development and might instead seem to suggest that
the classical and the grotesque bodies are being placed alongside or mixed with
bodies based upon consumption and commodification:

Postmodernity then is no longer an age in which bodies produce commodities, but where commodities produce bodies . . . (Faurschou, 1988:82)

Again, this process is not one that is confined to men, and indeed, it has been one in which women have often predominated. However, a growing emphasis on men's fashions and the proliferation of non-pornographic men's magazines certainly points to the elaboration of consumption-led masculinities. The healthy body, the stylish body and the athletic body become part of a range of bodies that are available in commodified form. Even some apparently traditional heroic models of men's bodies, in the films of Arnold Schwarzenegger for example, tend to be ironic parodies of the traditionally heroic.

Here too, it would be wrong to read too much into the signs. A little bit of unease with the grotesque body here or a bit of a critique of the classical body there, mixed up with a few men's magazines, hardly adds up to a total transformation or even a fully articulated critique. However, it is clear that some kinds of changes are taking place and that the links between embodiment and power and gender are being loosened, perhaps even as a consequence of being recognized as links.

Note

1   By way of illustration, consider a recent edition of a publication called *The Complete Angler's Guide* (no. 5 (3), July/August 1991). Here there were some forty-seven photographs featuring humans, the most common picture being that of a man holding his catch. These forty-seven pictures contained seventy-seven men, three women and five who were probably men. The three identifiable women were instructive. One was the writer's daughter in an article about a family angling holiday ('Erica and Heather walked off to the village just down the road to get some groceries. . .'). A second was on a page dealing with 'Pollution Free Game' and the third was part of a husband and wife angling team.

References

ACHILLES HEEL. (1991) 'Health Matters', *Achilles Heel*, No. 11, Summer 1991.

BAKHTIN, M. (1984/1965) *Rabelais and his World*, Bloomington, Indiana University Press.

BARHAM, S.B. (1985) 'The phallus and the man: an analysis of male striptease', in MANDERSON, L. (Ed.) *Australian Ways*, Sydney, Allen and Unwin, pp. 56–66.

BYRDE, P. (1979) *The Male Image: Men's Fashion in Britain, 1300–1700*, London, Batsford.

CONNELL, R.W. (1983) *Which Way is Up? Essays on Class, Sex and Culture*, Sydney, Allen and Unwin.

CONNELL, R.W. (1987) *Gender and Power*, Cambridge, Polity Press.

DUDLEY, E. and NOVAK, M. (Eds) (1972) *The Wild Man Within*, Pittsburgh, Pittsburgh University Press.

EASTHOPE, A. (1986) *What a Man's Gotta Do: The Masculine Myth in Popular Culture*, London, Paladin.

ELIAS, N. (1978/1939) *The Civilizing Process, Volume 1: The History of Manners*, New York, Urizen.

FAURSCHOU, G. (1988) 'Fashion and the cultural logic of postmodernity', in KROKER, A. and KROKER, M. (Eds) *Body Invaders: Sexuality and the Postmodern Condition*, Basingstoke, Macmillan, pp. 78–93.

FEATHERSTONE, M. (1991) *Consumer Culture and Postmodernism*, London, Sage.

FEHER, M., NADDAFF, R. and TAZI, N. (Eds) (1989) *Fragments for a History of the Human Body*, Vols. 1–3, New York, Zone.

FRANK, A.W. (1991) 'For a sociology of the body: An analytical review', in FEATHERSTONE, M., HEPWORTH, M. and TURNER, B.S. (Eds) *The Body: Social Processes and Cultural Theory*, London, Sage.

FREUND, P.E.S. (1983) *The Civilised Body: Social Domination, Control and Health*, Philadelphia, Temple University Press.

GOFFMAN, E. (1967) 'Where the action is', in GOFFMAN, E., *Interaction Ritual*, New York, Doubleday Anchor, pp. 149–270.

HALL, L.A. (1991) *Hidden Anxieties: Male Sexuality, 1900–1950*, Cambridge, Polity Press.

HEARN, J. (1987) *The Gender of Oppression: Men, Masculinity and the Critique of Marxism*, Brighton, Wheatsheaf.

HOCH, P. (1979) *White Hero, Black Beast*, London, Pluto.

LEWIS, A.A. (1978) *The Male: His Body, His Sex*, New York, Doubleday Anchor.

MARSH, P. (1978) *Aggro: The Illusion of Violence*, London, Dent.

MARTIN, E. (1989/1987) *The Woman in the Body*, Milton Keynes, Open University Press.

MCCANN, G. (1988) *Marilyn Monroe: The Body in the Library*, Cambridge, Polity Press.

MORGAN, D. (1990) 'No More Heroes'? Masculinity, Violence and the Civilizing Process', in JAMESON, L. and CORR, H. (Eds) *State, Private Life and Political Change*, Basingstoke, Macmillan, pp. 13–30.

MORGAN, D. (1991) *Discovering Men*, London, Routledge.

NEWSWEEK (1991) '*Drums, sweat and tears*', June 24 1991, pp. 42–48.

ORTNER, S. (1974) 'Is female to male as nature is to culture?' in ROSALDO, M.Z. and LAMPHERE, L. (Eds), *Women, Culture and Society*, Stansford, Stansford University Press.

PEARSON, G. (1983) *Hooligan: A History of Respectable Fears*, London, Macmillan.

REYNAUD, E. (1983) *Holy Virility: The Social Construction of Masculinity*, London, Pluto.

SCHOR, N. (1987) 'The portrait of a gentleman: representing men in (French) women's writings', in *Representations*, Vol. 20, Fall 1987, pp. 113–133.

SEIDLER, V. (1989) *Rediscovering Masculinity: Reason, Language and Sexuality*, London, Routledge and Kegan Paul.

STALLYBRASS, P. and WHITE, A. (1986) *The Politics and Poetics of Transgression*, London, Methuen.

SYDIE, R.A. (1987) *Natural Women/Cultured Men: A Feminist Perspective on Sociological Theory*, Milton Keynes, Open University Press.

TURNER, B.S. (1984) *The Body and Society*, Oxford, Basil Blackwell.

WALTON, I. (1983) *The Compleat Angler, 1653–1676* (ed. by J. Bevan), Oxford, Clarendon Press.

Chapter 6

Selling the Body, Keeping the Soul: Sexuality, Power, the Theories and Realities of Prostitution

Susan S.M. Edwards

Introduction

Prostitution is, in the public mind, defined as the sale of sexual intercourse. Women who sell sex become prostitutes in the commodity exchange of sex for favours in kind or for money. Prostitution in both everyday and legal discourse, however, does not always result in the sale of sexual intercourse. In legal discourse this point was illustrated in the case of *R versus de Munck* (1918) 1 KB 635, where Darling described a prostitute as 'a woman who offers her body for acts of lewdness for payment'. The law then well understood the plethora of male requests for sexual and related services. Yet, for the most part studies of prostitution have rarely addressed the specific forms of services demanded of women or the nature of the prostitute's encounters with male clients, or how women try in these apparently 'intimate' sexual incidents to retain their autonomy whilst segmenting and selling parts of their body as commodities. Prostitute women, in their effort to retain their autonomy and private space, demarcate and rigidly define quite precisely certain conduct and behaviour as beyond bounds in the truly intimate encounters, thereby placing boundaries around certain parts of the body, and certain symbolically significant acts, privatizing specific aspects of so-called sex and intimacy. Such boundary defining is essential for survival and whilst this has little bearing on the fundamentally exploitative characteristic of prostitution, it is an essential survival strategy for women who sell sex.

In debates dealing with prostitution as exploitation there are those who argue that if prostitution were to be accepted within society and prostitute women assimilated and treated as any other women this would negate any exploitation, because women would be in control of their lives. Some prostitute organizations, notably the International Committee for Prostitutes Rights (ICPR) (cf. Pheterson, 1989), campaign for 'rights' for prostitute women, including the right to work as prostitutes. This, of course, like the parody of Plato's 'happy slave', is flimsy embourgeoisement, and cannot alter the fundamental exploitation that exists nor the indisputable fact of commodity exchange, nor the enduring fact of patriarchy, however improved are the work conditions or social status of the prostitute. As Evelina Giobbe, a former prostitute and founder member of WHISPER, (Women

Hurt in Systems of Prostitution Engaged in Revolt), writes in countering these arguments, 'This mythology, which hides the abusive nature of prostitution, is illustrated by the ideology of the sexual liberals which erroneously claims that prostitution is a career choice' (Giobbe, 1990:67).

This article proposes to examine theories of male sexual need, desire, power, hatred and despite of women through an ethnographic analysis of the sexual services and encounters men seek. The object is to closely examine the system of prostitution not only from the viewpoint of the provider of the service, but also from the viewpoint of the consumer in the context of prostitute/client encounters. This is achieved by first looking to the several theories of male and female sexuality and prostitution as a backcloth, sometimes in contradistinction and sometimes in reaffirmation of the experiential level of women's lives revealed through their voices and through research observation.

First, I shall address and evaluate the materialist accounts of prostitution which locate the organization of prostitution in the fundamentally exploitative power relationship between men and women. Second, I move on to consider the structuralist accounts of sexuality from which an understanding of the sexuality of men and women and, by extension, those involved in prostitution is drawn, and examine their limitations. Third, I shall consider the several contributions of feminism to an understanding of sexuality and prostitution. Fourth, through ethnography I hope to cast some light on this area in exploring some case study observations depicting what is sold and how the vendor retains her autonomy in this sale and exchange.

A Materialist Approach to the Sale of Sex

Materialist analyses of prostitution have focused on the system of prostitution, its relation to the nuclear family and especially to capitalism, where fundamental economic inequality and subordination place women *per se* in this potentially exploitative position. Here, prostitution is explained as a necessary system which supports capitalism (Engels, 1972). The sociologist Kingsley Davis adopts a similar economic perspective: 'The division of labor by sex inevitably makes women dependent to some extent on their sexual attractiveness and puts men in control of economic means. Since the economic means are distributed unequally between classes but female attractiveness is not, some women of lower economic means can exploit their attractiveness for economic gain' (Davis, 1971:345).

Materialist accounts explain prostitution as arising from the need women have to sell the body because of economic deprivation, although, apart from seeing men as the class with the money, very little is offered by way of explaining the demand part of the equation. Yet, insofar as a materialist account has offered an explanation of some women's involvement in prostitution, it has made several important gains for the understanding of prostitute women, over earlier accounts. Since, in locating prostitution as a response to material (economic) need and not as a reflection of some perverted or atavistic sex instinct, women are treated as responsible for their choices and not determined. Some nineteenth century theorists acknowledged that many young women turned to prostitution as a means of escaping poverty, and as a means of supporting their families. This realization was shared by several social commentators, including Henry Mayhew and Charles Booth, as well as by feminist campaigners, many of whom strove to repeal the Contagious Diseases Acts of 1864 and 1866, as well as bring the horrors of White Slavery to the attention of the world. Josephine Butler and the Ladies National Association (LNA) amongst others, argued that prostitute women were the victims of male pollution, men's laws, and by the 'steel penis' (the forcible examination by speculum reserved for registered prostitutes). This reality was further extended by William Stead's exposure of female sexual slavery, when in July 1885 the *Maiden Tribute of Modern Babylon* was printed in the *Pall Mall Gazette*. The impact was considerable: a public demonstration of some 250,000 people gathered in Hyde Park demanding raising the age of consent. Prostitution however is not just about the hardship of women forced to enter prostitution as a means of survival. Even where women had the opportunity for work and a good level of living, prostitution would still persist. The fundamental inequality in power relations means that even if there were not a class of poor women then prostitution would still exist as a means of men controlling women.

Prostitution represents the interface of two arenas of power and powerlessness, gender and class. Rich men have always used, abused, insulted and exploited poor women, working-class women and black women. And bourgeois men have vociferously defended their privilege to exercise this power over all women. For example, many in the House of Lords in the 1880s opposed the raising of the age of consent from fourteen to sixteen, lest their indiscretions with young working-class adolescent girls whom they regarded as playthings would be criminalized (Edwards, 1981:128). The history of black female slavery (Joseph, 1981, Davis, 1984), and the revelations of sexual slavery worldwide attest to the undisputable fact (Barry, 1984, 1991) that race constitutes a fundamental class dimension which places certain categories of women (black, Asian, Third World) as women to be sexually exploited and abused. (As a note in parenthesis, 75,000 American soldiers disgorged from ships on their way home from the Gulf into Olongopo in the Phillipines for Rest and Recreation; Olongopo is a prostitute city where prostitution is entirely dependant on US naval and military servicemen.)

This theme of rich man/poor girl upon which the institution of prostitution is founded is a recurrent theme in literature, art and pornography. Nineteenth century pornographic literature (*Index Librorum Prohibitorum*) reveals the perennial extent of this recurrent theme. Moreover, this fundamental power relationship of rich man and poor girl has been eroticized. In the nineteenth century the investment of sexual pleasure in class differences, as Heath (1982) writes, ' "Slumming" with working class women', was both a recurrent theme in pornographic literature and a reality. Examples are found in numerous pornographic books of the time. This is detailed in Walter's '*My Secret Life*', where a wealthy gentleman describes in specific detail his purchase of a juvenile girl for the purpose of prostitution (Marcus, 1971). Heath cites the example of Arthur Munby, a London barrister who collected and commissioned photographs of 'labouring women' whom he described in his voluminous diaries and notebooks.

Munby had a long relationship with a 'maid of all work' named Hannah Cullwick whom he finally married in 1873, keeping the marriage entirely secret and requiring Hannah to alternate between the roles of a servant and a lady. The relationship depended on Munby's erotic perception of nobility and 'degradation' and their ritual exploitation. Sessions are arranged in which Hannah is photographed as this or that type of working woman or posed as half naked, blackened chimney sweep with Munby towering over her; in which she is humiliated before Munby's eyes and for him by the photographer who treats her as socially inferior, pushes her roughly into position, rubs dirt on her for greater realism. She obeyed him as a thing of course, and [I] saw him blacken and besmear her . . . It made my blood tingle; but it made me bow in spirit more than ever, before so divine an abnegation of self. (Heath, 1982:12)

The lawyer Jelinger Symons from the clerical gentry, subcommissioner in the Yorkshire coalfield, and an early educational specialist, in his report from New Mills lingered over the fact that '. . . the chain, passing high between the legs of two girls, had worn large holes on their trousers, and any sight more disgustingly indecent or revolting can be scarcely imagined . . . No brothel can beat it' (quoted in Mort, 1987:49).

This eroticized pastiche of the world of the respected never fails to intrigue and to provide good copy for the newspapers. A century later, in 1980, in Madame Cyn's 'brothel' so-called, where working-class girls provided a service in a house frequented, as the defence case cryptically exposed, by *haute culture*, high society, professionals and paragons of the establishment, the intrigue continues. Here, Mr Robertson, for the appellant (Cynthia Payne) examined the police officer in charge of the case, a Superintendent Carroll:

> Q. As far as the clients were concerned, the 53 men I think, who were found and men who were observed going into the house on 6th December, they were broadly speaking middle-aged and elderly men?
> A. There was a good cross section, but principally middle-aged and elderly.
> Q. Of that cross section, you had businessmen, managing directors and accountants?
> A. Yes.
> Q. You had barristers?
> A. Yes sir.
> Q. And solicitors?
> A. Yes.
> Q. . . . you had a member of parliament from Ireland?
> A. Yes.
> Q. You had a member of the House of Lords?
> A. That is correct.
> Q. You had several vicars?
> A. Yes.

(Criminal Appeal Reports 1980 Vol. 2:165)

Essentialist Accounts

Whilst womens' economic need and the differential power relation between the sexes has often explained the persistence of prostitution, many theorists have condoned at least men's involvement or 'need' for prostitution by reference to its intransigent essentialism. And here it is the immutable accounts of male and female sexuality which create a climate which sustains prostitution by its explanation of the individual prostitute and the client. Within all essentialist accounts, male sexuality is considered instinctual, not social, nor learned; thus rape, sexual assault and the use of prostitute women by men is exoneratable since men have no rational choice nor free will. Such a construction of male sexuality mitigates not only rape, but child sexual abuse and other forms of sexual conduct. And the transcriptions or translations and thereby assimilation of essentialist theory into everyday and legal theorizing are not hard to find. Judge Cassel recently exonerated a man for the rape of his 12-year-old stepdaughter when the man's wife was pregnant. Lord Lane, the Lord Chief Justice, said of the paediatric surgeon Oliver Brooke that his collection of child pornography 'was akin to young boys collecting cigarette cards in olden times'.

Yet whilst regarding men as instinctual, part of this same construction has been to regard women both as rational and as instinctual. On the one hand women are expected to be cognizant of men's inability to control their sex needs and are thereby appointed as 'gatekeepers'. Once women have failed to effect this 'gatekeeper' function, for instance when battered, raped or abused by men, women are, at that moment, portrayed as fundamentally masochistic. Even the extensions of essentialism into the arena of social learning continue to exonerate the excesses of male power and violence; arguments which derive from individual, pathological and social explanation tended in the past, as they do now, to justify male sexuality as predatory because it is innate or learned. By extension, man's abuse of women in sadism and violence is natural too, a thesis central to the 'scientific' discourse. And women who make no attempt to exercise any role as 'gatekeeper', such as prostitute women, are regarded as fundamentally masochistic. Krafft-Ebing (1901) and Ellis (1936) amongst others, argued that sadism was instinctual. This view found its complement in the argument that masochism in women was similarly instinctual, thus in effect lending a specific kind of legitimacy to male sadism through making the masochistic woman in her pursuit of hedonistic sexual pleasure responsible, and masochistic women as the causative variable. Again this juxtaposition finds expression in pornography, and it is this scenario in real life too which is frequently sought by men in their search for prostitute women. Thus for essentialists sexual conduct and practices had very little to do with the social or political world, but instead had an immutable character framed and determined by an innate biology. These presentations are fundamental to sustaining the ideology of prostitution, and it is within and outside of prostitution that these encounters emerge.

For many of these writers, however, the sadistic and masochistic aspects coexisted within one person as two opposing forces. Ellis wrote:

We thus see that there are here two separate groups of feelings: one, in the masculine line, which delights in displaying force and often inflicts pain or the simulacrum of pain; the other, in the feminine line, which delights in submitting to that force, and even finds pleasure in a slight amount of pain, or the idea of pain, when associated with the experiences of love. (1936, Vol. 3:104)

Freud had already developed this deterministic sadistic/masochistic narrative in 1905 in *Three Contributions to the Theory of Sex*:

> The roots of active algolagnia, sadism, can be readily demonstrable in the normal individual. The sexuality of most men shows an admixture of aggression, of a propensity to subdue, the biological significance of which lies in the necessity for overcoming the resistance of the sexual object by actions other than mere courting. (Freud, 1962:22)

He explained further that there is an intimate connection between cruelty and the sex instinct. For Freud a 'sadist is always at the same time a masochist'.

In the more exaggerated archetypal forms sadism and masochism often emerge as sex-specific. According to Ellis, Krafft-Ebing, Freud and later sexologists, men instinctually wish to dominate in various guises, and women instinctually desire to be dominated and subjugated. Krafft-Ebing, writing on his clinical findings on masochism which were manifestations of 'a diseased condition of the mind or body' (1901:vii), provides many accounts of both female and male masochism. And the sexual perversions clinically documented by Krafft-Ebing are found enacted on picture and on film, and requested of prostitute women by men. 'She makes me perform the lowest menial work, wait upon her when she arises, in the bath *et inter mictionem*. At times she uses my face for the latter purpose and makes me drink of the voidance' (Krafft-Ebing, 1901:129). Although an example from clinical experience, this forms the basis of contemporary dominatrix pornography. In 1924, in *The Economic Problem of Masochism*, Freud identified three kinds of masochism, erotogenic, moral and feminine. Here masochism was the result of a psychical response to the fundamental biological distinction between the sexes. On the subject of female masochism he has this to say:

> In both cases — for the real situations are in fact only a kind of make believe performance of the phantasies — the manifest content is of being pinioned, bound, beaten painfully, whipped, in some way mishandled, forced to obey unconditionally, defiled degraded . . . in them the subject is placed *in a situation characteristic of womanhood*, i.e. they mean that he is being castrated, is playing the passive part in coitus, or is giving birth. (Collected Papers, vol. 11, Freud, 1954:258; my emphasis)

Pornography depicts women in masochistic situations described here as bondage, violence, domination and degradation. And in transvestite 'TV' porn, men are placed in a situation characteristic of womanhood (cf. Kaite, 1988:160).

On sadism Krafft-Ebing (1901:82–83) provides a compendium of accounts from violence to murder.

> 'I opened her breast and with a knife cut through the fleshy parts of the body. Then I arranged the body as a butcher does beef, and hacked it with an axe into pieces of a size to fit the hole which I had dug up in the mountain for burying it. I may say that while opening the body I was so greedy that I trembled, and could have cut out a piece and eaten it.'

'I am fond of women, but it is sport for me to strangle them after having enjoyed them'.

Essentialist arguments for the fundamental role of men and women in relation to one another and sexual pleasure explain the sexual subordination of women as fixed, immutable and, above all, the natural state of things.

Structuralist Critique

Yet it is patriarchal power and male privilege which define the narrative of prostitution, and also the narrative of rape, sexual abuse and pornography, by inverting, truncating and distorting reality so that we learn about prostitution as a sexual encounter between men and women, which is precipitated by women, where women have freedom, choice, to engage in it or not, and where men simply respond to the supply and to their own instinctual needs. The structuralist contribution and critique of essentialism provides for an appraisal of the juxtaposition or *prise de position* of the sexes in an entirely different way. The central endeavour of the structuralist enterprise is to identify the underlying structures which organize and arrange sexual difference. Here I wish to focus on the contributions made respecting the role of discourse and language in defining and prescribing the relations between the sexes. Foucault is often cited insofar as his work directs us to the examination of structures of language and discourse in the articulation of sexuality.

> . . . instead of studying the sexual behaviour of men at a given period (by seeking its law in social structure, in a collective unconscious, or in a certain moral attitude), instead of describing what men thought of sexuality (what religious interpretation they gave it, to what extent they approved or disapproved of it, what conflicts of opinion or morality it gave rise to), one would ask oneself whether, in this behaviour, as in these representations, a whole discursive practice is not at work; whether sexuality quite apart from any orientation towards a scientific discourse, is not a group of objects that can be talked about or is forbidden to talk about, a field of possible enunciation (whether in lyrical or legal language), a group of concepts (which can no doubt be presented in the elementary forms of notions and themes, a set of choices (which may appear in the coherence of behaviour or in systems of prescription). (Foucault, 1972:193)

But despite the use to which his work has been put by feminist scholars, and apart from his addressing sexuality, his work is not feminism. 'Foucault's work has become controversial as a feminist resource perhaps as a result of his explicit disinterest in feminist politics' (Grbich, 1991:66). Nevertheless, Foucault provides useful insights into patriarchy. In this way the 'domain of prostitution' is also proscribed, defined, articulated in a given way, though not by prostitute or non-prostitute women, but by clients and by the public image and male medical and cultural discourses. Luce Irigaray, in *This Sex Which Is Not One*, examines how in sexuality woman is an 'obliging prop for the enactment of man's fantasies' (1986:25). She writes of her further:

That she may find pleasure there in that role, by proxy, is possible, even certain. But such pleasure is above all a masochistic prostitution of her body to a desire that is not her own, and it leaves her in a familiar state of dependency upon man. Not knowing what she wants, ready for anything, even asking for more, so long as he will 'take' her as his 'object' when he seeks his own pleasure.

It is in discourse that women are subordinated, whereby there is a 'staging of representation according to exclusively masculine parameters, that is according to phallocratic order' (Irigaray, 1986:68). And here,

the use, consumption, and circulation of their sexualised bodies under-write the organization and the reproduction of the social order, in which they have never taken part as subjects. Women are thus in a situation of specific exploitation with respect to exchange operations; sexual exchanges, but also economic, social and cultural exchanges in general. (Irigaray, 1986:85)

For Lacan (1977) it is language and culture which precede the development of each individual consciousness where the conscious and unconscious mind is construed as the effect and not the cause of language. Theweleit (1987), similarly in his examination of male fantasy, argues that the subject is produced in language, where it is male desire which is signified in the 'I' of Western and Germanic culture where women are placed as the 'object', the other. Male objectification of women, male desire, and male sadism are all interlinked in this account. Similarly, masochism is also socially constructured by patriarchy, through, by and in its naming processes.

Feminist Critique

From the perspective of the feminist critique, structuralism has a way of dealing with all underlying structures equally. The cultural climate which defines male and female sexuality and thus pornography, in the visual representation, and prostitution in the actual representation, involves a whole iconography of cultural representations in language, theoretical and academic explanations and discourses symbolized in and by law, reproduced in and by law, and defined by men. And it is to the questions relating to inequality between those who define sexuality as well as the content of that sexuality that they address themselves. It is the articulation through modes of expression, whether language, art or literature, whereby men come to define the world they see and desire. Dworkin (1981:18) writes, 'It is the naming by decree that is power over and against those who are forbidden to name their own experience. . .'.

Feminist accounts of prostitution and pornography and male sexuality (Barry, 1984; Cameron and Fraser, 1988:164), are particularly critical of essentialist accounts, arguing that both individual pathological and social role explanations of male sexuality, propagate a culturally sanctioned misogyny where male definitions of women prevail. Central to this is the belief supported in discourse, scientific and cultural, that men should have unrestricted sexual access to women. Freud provided an explanation of sexual relations and power which was fixed and immutable, where man '... always feels his sexual activity hampered by his respect for the woman and only develops full sexual potency when he finds himself in the presence of a lower type of sexual object' (Freud, 1974:649). Such propaganda allows for and legitimates patriarchy and male supremacy in many of its grosser manifestations thereby lending support to the 'cultural ideology of sadism'. Barry explains how the representation of female sexual slavery through the media is a definite and established part of masculinist culture: 'Cultural sadism is a distinct social form that consists of practices which encourage and support sexual violence, defining it as normal behaviour' (1984:226).

Sadism is the dominant theme in pornography and part of the lived experience of prostitution, argues Barry, and sadism has been assimilated into the theory of sexuality. Male desire has been explained as natural, immutable, biological, physiological. In drive theory men are seething volcanoes of sex, and there is little any of us, least of all they themselves, can do about it. Dworkin calls this 'supremicist biology', which she sees is part of the modern legend of terror, the idea that man is biologically ordained. Thus, given this intractable version of male sexual behaviour, it is up to women to change or modify men's behaviour in the name of our own protection. This idea is rife in literature and discourse. Coventry Patmore in the '*Angel in the House*' (written in the nineteenth century) stated that women were the fault of man's trouble, and 'had made brutes men and men divine'. In this formulation, since men cannot help themselves and women are made responsible for male conduct, good or bad, women are encouraged to take this responsibility seriously by modifying their own behaviour. In addition, in order to assist women take on this responsibility for male conduct, women's behaviour has been the subject of regulation and control. When women resist these various regulations and forms of control then their right to protection from men is forfeited. Acquiescence with the symbolic curfew which silently and insidiously exercises control on women is one of the first rules of social conduct that the little girl child learns (cf. Hudson, 1987). A further extension of that terror Dworkin describes is that man is placed with the divine right to define the world of sexual relations in a manner which allows him to act exactly as he wishes. Dworkin argues that the male colonization of representation allows men to rape, and to use violence and force:

> It is the naming by decree that is power over and against those who are forbidden to name their own experience; it is the decree backed up by violence that writes the name indelibly in blood in male dominated culture. The male does not merely name women evil; he exterminates nine million women as witches because he has named women evil. He does not merely name women weak; he mutilates the female body, binds it up so that it cannot move freely, uses it as a toy or ornament, keeps it caged and stunted because he has named women weak. (Dworkin, 1982:17–18)

Critics like Cameron and Fraser argue that sadism and masochism are categories of our language (1988:174). Like all linguistic signs they cannot be taken as unproblematic reflections of experience, and especially not of the chaotic emotions of infancy, before language is acquired. It is in the representation and in the fairy tales that Dworkin argues that women are defined as masochistic and learn within that to fulfil their destiny. She quotes from the *Story of O*:

> . . . . as long as I am beaten and ravished on your behalf. I am naught but the thought of you, the desire of you, the obsession of you. That, I believe, is what you wanted. Well, I love you, and that is what I want too. (Dworkin, 1974:58)

Ethnographies

Perceptions and understandings of prostitution and of male desire are shaped by the several discourses on sexuality. What men want and how women survive is best explained through the voices of prostitute women and ethnographic observation. The problem with other accounts is that prostitution and prostitute-client relationships are treated as a unitary phenomena. The belief that, for women who supply the service, 'anything goes', is widespread, as women who sell sex forfeit their right to say 'No', to refuse and further some would say such women forfeit their right to protection. On the contrary, while sections of the public world may hold to this view, the selling of sex by prostitute women is carefully circumscribed, certain behaviour and actions are taboo, certain bodily zones are out of bounds, and certain symbolic acts are reserved for loved ones. These prostitute-client negotiations teach us not about 'what is sex', but 'what is intimacy', the latter often dislocated from the act of sex itself. It is here that prostitute women develop strategies or coping mechanisms to enable them to sell parts of their body in mechanistic transactions whilst keeping themselves whole and treating parts of their bodies as private and sacred. Yet the private and sacred are not necessarily the private and sacred in traditional accounts of sexuality. Prostitute women care less about the genitals and breasts, and much more about the mouth, the lips, the kiss and tenderness, for them the truest meaning and expression of intimacy.

Few studies have asked the prostitute herself about male power, sexuality or what men want (cf. McLeod, 1982; Jaget, 1980; Roberts, 1986). In order to gain a deeper understanding of the interface between sex/power the author built on interviews conducted with fifty women prostitutes in 1988 in London and Birmingham. Were 'punters' perverse power-crazed exploiters of women reflexing to their own innate instinctual craving? Were they pathetic and sexually inadequate? Or were they ordinary men? Are the demands made of prostitutes separate and different from sexual demands or manifestations of male sexual desire, or instead are these encounters but caricatures of wider versions and visions of male power and desire? And how should we view these manifestations in the exploitation, sadism and objectification of women? Is male sexual desire constructed in representation, discourse and language? Do these constructions precede the unconscious and indeed conscious desire, or are men creatures of instinct?

Prostitution is Alienation

Contrary to an archetypal belief about prostitute women, there is little job satisfaction. Women develop all kinds of strategies to keep themselves separated from their task. Unlike the worker who tries to fight against alienation and separation from the product of his or her labour, alienation and separation for prostitute women is essential to personal survival. Prostitution is the epitomization of alienation. Women must develop a split personality (Jaget, 1980:150). 'It kind of kills you but it's over fast, 'said a streetwalker talking about prostitution (Jaget, 1980:135). Nickie Roberts, a sex worker in strip tease, writes of the fear she experienced when stripping and the response of the men:

'All we got was the fear, the abuse. "GERREMOFF!" "SLAG!" "SHOW US WHAT YOU'VE GOT!" "SLAG!". The worst part was waiting up there in the dark for the tabs to open; the tape to start. That's when you prayed. Out there, you heard them; they sounded like wolves, you could breathe them. Wolves would've been kinder. Then when the tabs opened, my God; there was this wall of sweaty white faces, open-mouthed, glistening with booze, hate and fear. Yes — fear. I used to feel almost detached, sometimes, going through my routine, and — I couldn't help myself — looking into the punters' eyes (the part of me that wasn't scared shitless, that is). And they bewildered me, more than anything else. I felt like stopping the show and saying, "Listen: what's happening here?" ' (Roberts, 1986:83)

Masochistic Clients

a. flage
Speaking about their clients, London streetwalkers told stories of their liking for a bit of 'flage' — flagellation. 'Some are weirdos and some are kinky. You know they like to be spanked and they dress up in stockings and suspenders. I just think it's a bit kinky' (Interview 1).

Jaget (1980:105) noted that,

'The masochist clientele is something of a special breed, generally they're men who are cultured, who've got money and who've got some pretty incredible vices. They want us to hit them, stub cigarettes on their chest, stick pins through their penis, drag them round the room . . .'

As Krafft-Ebing extensively documented: 'As last I overcame the last vestige of my shyness, and one day to realize my dreams, had myself whipped, trod upon, etc., by a prostitute' (1901:121).

b. Urination and Coprophilia

As McLeod (1982:60) recorded, spoken through the words of Carol: 'Some of the things they ask you to do, you think this bloke needs to see a doctor, never mind a prostitute.! We're only ordinary women . . . This bloke wanted us to stand over him and shit over his face.'

Are these men ordinary, perverse, amongst us, or great writers? Havelock Ellis's biographer, Calder-Marshall, wrote (1959:21) 'Ellis confessed to the "germ of a perversion" in what he called urolagnia.'

c. Bondage

Bondage was not an untypical request made by clients, although most women explained that the client would be required to supply the gear. Many women actually preferred offering some kind of bondage relief, as they could be completely detached and were not required to have any physical contact with the client or with body fluids. Bondage is often favoured by individual clients approaching street prostitutes and by men seeking out bondage in establishments specifically catering for this.

In Hamburg, clubs for lesbians, male homosexuals, transvestites and hetero-sexual sadomasochists flourish. 'Justine's' near the Reeperbahn provides for sadomasochistic clients: one of the two entrances is through a side street and is symbolically fitting, a white stuccoed narrow passage, with a low ceiling like a birth canal opening out into a series of chambers resembling the crypt of a medieval church. The first vestibule contains the bar complete with videos of various sexual activities. At the time of my visiting, a women in leather and chains was having clothes-pegs put on her nipples. In the bar clients could look downwards through the slats of a wooden medieval screen to a bed below where other customers and hostesses could be viewed, although no-one was there at the moment of my looking. In this lower, dimly lit chamber, were various gadgets, from reproductions of medieval stocks, whips, canes, a medieval rack, chains, ropes and pulleys in an aura and orgy of medieval religiousness. Crucifixes adorned the walls, and altars and candlelabra combined with the clammy cold-ness of a crypt. Later, downstairs, as if into the very bowels, was a closed soundproofed chamber. Complete with oak-beamed decor, manacles, whips, and racks, hung suspended from the white stuccoed walls. Here the prima donna hostess speaking in German described how her clients would pay 300 marks to be active or passive, in the drama of their own fantasy of power or orgiastic impo-tence. Passing through another sojourn to the doctor's quarters, where there was all the modern paraphernalia of a surgery complete with surgical enemas, I passed a client deeply and reverently immersed in his own fantasy. He remained motion-less in impotent inertia: a kneeling position, with his head slightly bowed, encapsulated in a zipped leather hood with two slits for the eyes, as if in an act of religious worship. He was naked except for this hood, and round his neck hung slackly a small leather lead, held gently by a woman fully clad in leather.

Back on the streets of London, one middle-aged women who had had enough of prostitution, said

> I've seen too much of men. I have gone off men. I've gone off them for ages, I don't bother if I never see another man. You see all sorts of peculiar things, this and that, whipping and beating. It just drives you mad. When you are young its alright, but now, 'Oh No'. Once I had a man and he said, 'You look like my wife', you can come to my house and you can lie down and have sex with me in a coffin. 'No way', I said, he might have had the lid down on me. See, you meet all the mental cases and it just makes you mad in the end. (Interview 13)

And another explained, I do all kinds of things. But I always use a condom. Whipping, bondage and all that kind of stuff, but I insist on a condom. (Interview 2)

Yet prostitutes who offer bondage are often seen to the conventional public orthodoxy as perverse and sadistic, although, on the whole, they tend simply to want to avoid any physicality with clients. Bondage is a strategy for physical and sexual avoidance. Even North (1970:66) recognized,

> 'quite often prostitutes express themselves forcefully about rubber fetishistic clients, speaking of them with contempt, derision and dislike, although, at the same time they agree that such customers are relatively easy to handle and the least dangerous'.

In pursuit of this separation of sexuality and intimacy, prostitute women avoid sexual intercourse wherever possible, offering all kinds of other services (cf. Day's 1987 analysis of prostitutes' social distancing).

d. Sadistic clients

Prostitute women in the course of their work encountered many sadistic clients. Most referred to this issue through their endless descriptions of physical and sexual abuse. Eighty per cent of women interviewed in London have been beaten, physically assaulted with objects, thrown out of moving cars, dumped, choked, had their hair pulled, or stabbed, by male clients; some of these physical experiences were as a sequel to sex whilst other acts of violence seemed to be disconnected to the sex, but part of the way in which men, as Roberts has illustrated above, held such women in contempt. For some clients sadism and violence are part of the fantasy. And as one transsexual prostitute explained,

> 'I've had some really weird punters. One day I saw my whole life flash past. I went back with a guy. He was very rich. He owned his own company. You know like Yves Saint Laurent, something like that. He gave me champagne. I felt a bit giggly and a bit tipsy, and he said, "I've got a present for you". And I thought to myself, "Why!, he doesn't even know me, why should he have a present for me?" He went into the kitchen and said, "I'll get it." And he came out with something behind his back, and by God he had an axe in his hand and he said, "It's not going to hurt, I'll do it quick, it will be all over." I started to cry and said, "Please don't kill me." I managed to get out of the flat, but I didn't report it, the police would only say, "Well, what do you expect, I suppose he found out what you really were.". . . I also had this other punter who tried to rob me. He got a knife and he pushed it to my throat. He cut my fingers and my legs, look'. (Interview 14)

e. Hand relief

Hand relief and oral sex allow the identity of the transsexual prostitute to remain concealed from the client. One transsexual explained. 'I offer hand relief or French with a durex, and if they say they want sex I say, "I'm on."' (Interview 14). Many girls just try to do hand relief rather than any other kind of contact, none kiss nor allow their clients to touch them, all prefer hand relief. 'I give them an hour for 40 or 50 pounds I try to do hand relief if I can' (Interview 8).

'I offer French and sex with a rubber, £30 together in a car, then £10, or £15 for a play around, which is "the wank". I talk to them, give them comfort, listen to them and some men don't want any sex at all because of AIDS'. (Interview 10)

Women, whilst they have some choice in what they will offer or be prepared to do for money cannot dictate the male demand. Male desire then is just as much about hand relief, oral sex and bondage as it is about sexual intercourse.

e. Voyeurism

Voyeurism extends from watching street girls on the corner of streets, to participating in watching live sex shows. The kerb-crawling voyeur is commonly known as a 'cruiser', not to be confused with homosexual males chatting one another up. In all the red light areas in London and Birmingham, residents are plagued by men who drive round and round and round, and who watch, stare and sometimes stop. Some drive on and some, as one London police officer explained, 'drive in to the kerb and then masturbate'.

Sex clubs like the 'Moulin Rouge' in Amsterdam's red light district flourish, and for the sum of twenty-five gilders (at 1988 prices) the voyeuristic and the curious can watch a live sex show complete with vaginal and oral sex, and even be invited to participate in the 'orgy'. The scenario is typical of sex shows I watched throughout Western Europe. A man and woman dressed in scanty clothing, the male in G-string, the female in bra and underpants, take to the stage. The audience look on, neither shocked or amused. Instead the majority of the onlookers, on this occasion Japanese tourists, gaze at the drama as if scientists looking through a microscope, in clinical fashion. Women are not usually to be seen in these places and when apparent are accompanied by, or accompany a man. Fondling and kissing and gyrating to the music, the performers undress one another, whilst the man erects to order, probably facilitated by a cocaine habit. Oral and vaginal sex commence and the show is over. The actors, tired and bored, bow their way out to applause. The performers are poorly paid and are one of the lowest paid workers in the sex industry.

Whether on the street, in a bar or in a club, women hated the job. One former prostitute explained,

'I hated it. I never felt clean. Even after I had washed and washed, I could smell them on me. I would go shopping after bathing and I would think people could smell me and know what I was. I just got through each client by thinking about something else, hoping he would come quickly, get it over with. I used to make them think that they could go deep into me, I would raise my legs up and bend my knees and push them against his chest. So he couldn't really get near me at all. . . .' (Interview 40).

Conclusion

It is men that we need to study,[1] to understand their desire for power, for sexual mastery. We need to address and confront why it is that men are orgasming to visual images of womens subordination harm and abuse in pornography, and also to their use and subordination and insult in prostitution. We need to examine the social construction of male sexual arousal and the chanelling of sexual arousal into a context of abuse and harm in which women are degraded. It is men who have a responsibility to address this problem of their sexuality and arousal responses individually and collectively. We need also to recognize that the male client in all his guises is the man amongst us. As Dworkin said in interview with Elizabeth Wilson about the men who read pornography,

'Leftist writers from Abbie Hoffman to Gore Vidal to leftwing investigative journalists publish in pornography magazines and the actual producers of pornography are men, not exclusively but in shocking numbers, who were active in the anti-war movement, who are roughly my age, who were my political comrades'. (1982:28)

We need also to recognize that prostitution as an organization and as an industry is consumer-led, existing only to pander and respond to the demands of men. Theorizing throughout the decades has made paramount the pathology of male and female sexuality in an effort for explanation. The involvement of women is economic and women explicitly or implicitly are the subjects of coercion. Women are reduced, in the sale of sex or fantasy or the will to power, to the level of a commodity. This commodification sets prostitution apart from any other form of commodification, for however much the conditions for women might be improved, their enslavement remains. But there is a paradox, for the alienation which destroys the labourer is quintessential to the preservation, autonomy and survival of the prostitute. It is only through the process of alienation that she is able to do her work. Selling the body in the eyes of the public is selling one's being and soul. Prostitute women develop distancing strategies. They call themselves by different names in order to preserve their real name and real persona. They ask for the money first to indicate that the service is purely for money. They try to retain the self by offering anything but sexual intercourse; in this way bondage or sadistic services provide a distance from the client. No-one in their private lives usually knows about their work. Certain body zones, for example the mouth, are sacrosanct and actions of stroking, caressing, indicating intimacy are out of bounds for clients. The body has clear client and clear private zones, enabling prostitute women to sell parts of their bodies as commodities whilst retaining something of their soul.

Note

1 On February 19 1992, appeal against conviction and sentence of *R v Brown and ors* was heard at the court of appeal before Lord Lane. The appellants belonged to a group of sadomasochistic homosexuals who over a ten year period had willingly participated in acts of violence against each other, including whipping, genital torture involving the insertion of fish hooks through the penis and the cutting of the penis with a knife to acts of coprohilia and urination. One of the appellants had had the urethra enlarged for sexual practices. The court of appeal upheld the convictions of assault and aiding and abetting assault. The case of Brown goes to the House of Lords on a point of law of general public importance in November 1992. Meanwhile the decision of the court of appeal should in theory have implications for sadomasochism in prostitution even though the client or the prostitute consents.

References

BARRY, K. (1984) *Female Sexual Slavery*, New York, New York University Press.

BARRY, K. (1991) 'Prostitution, Sexual Violence, and Victimization: Feminist Perspectives on Women's Human Rights', in VIANO, E. (Ed.) *Victim's Rights and Legal reforms: International Perspectives*, Onait, Proceedings of the Sixth International Institute on Victimology.

CAMERON, D. and FRASER, E. (1988) *The Lust to Kill*, Cambridge, Polity.

CALDER-MARSHALL, A. (1959) *Havelock-Ellis: A Biography*, London, Rupert Hart-Davies.

DAVIS, A. (1984) *Women, Race and Class*, London, The Women's Press.

DAVIS, K. (1971) 'Prostitution', in MERTON, R.K. and NISBET, R. (Eds) *Contemporary Social Problems*, London, Hart-Davies.

DWORKIN, A. (1981) *Pornography: Men Possessing Women*, London, The Women's Press.

DWORKIN, A. (1974) *Woman Hating*, New York, E.P. Dutton.

DWORKIN, A. (1982) Interview with Elizabeth Wilson, *Feminist Review*, 11:23–9.

EDWARDS, S. (1981) *Female Sexuality and the Law*, Oxford, Martin Robertson.

ELLIS, H.H. (1936) *Studies in the Psychology of Sex*, Vol. 3, New York, Random House.

ENGELS, F. (1972) *The Origin of the Family Private Property and the State*, New York, Pathfinder.

FREUD, S. (1962) *Three Contributions to the Theory of Sex*, New York, E.P. Dutton.

FREUD, S. (1974) *New Introductory Lectures*, Oxford, Hogarth Press.

FOUCAULT, M. (1972) *The Archaeology of Knowledge*, London, Tavistock.

GIOBBE, E. (1990) *Confronting the Liberal Lies about prostitution*, in LEIDHOLDT, A. and RAYMOND, J. (Eds) *The Sexual Liberals and the Attack on Feminism*.

GRBICH, J. (1991) 'The Body in Legal Theory', in FINEMAN, M. and THOMADIEN, N. (Eds) *At the Boundaries of Law: Feminism and Legal Theory*, London, Routledge.

HEATH, A. (1982) *The Sexual Fix*, Basingstoke, Macmillan.

HUDSON, D. (1987) 'You Can't Commit Violence Against an Object: Women, Psychiatry and Psychosurgery', in HANMER, J. and MAYNARD, M. (1987) *Women, Violence and Social Control*, London, Macmillan.

IRIGARAY, L. (1986) *This Sex Which Is Not One*, Ithaca, New York, Cornell University Press.

JAGET, C. (1980) *Prostitutes: Our Life*, Bristol, Falling Wall Press.

JOSEPH, G. (1981) 'The Incompatible Ménage à Trois: Marxism, Feminism and Racism', in SARGENT, L. (Ed.) *The Unhappy Marriage of Marxism and Feminism*, London, Pluton, pp. 91–108.

KAITE, B. (1988) 'The Pornographer's Body Double: Transgression in the Law', in KROKER, A. and KROKER, M. (Eds) *Body Invaders, Sexuality and The Postmodern Condition*, London, Macmillan, pp. 150–168.

KRAFFT-EBING, (1901) *Psychopathia Sexualis*, London, Rebman Ltd.

LACAN, J. (1977) *Ecrits: A Selection*, London, Tavistock.

MARCUS, S. (1971) *My Secret Life*, London, Corgi Books.

McLEOD, E. (1982) *Working Women: Prostitution Now*, Basingstoke, Croom Helm.

MORT, F. (1987) *Dangerous Sexualities*, London, Routledge and Kegan Paul.

NORTH, M. (1970) *The Outer Fringe of Sex*, London, Odyssey Press.

PHETERSON, G. (1989) *A Vindication of the Rights of Whores*, Seattle, Seal Press.

ROBERTS, N. (1986) *The Front Line*, London, Grafton Books.

THEWELEIT, K. (1987) *Male Fantasies*, Cambridge, Polity.

Chapter 7

The Inverted Gaze

Ruth Waterhouse

Portraits from the Gallery

Eleanor Butler, Sarah Ponsonby, Colette, Gertrude Stein, Radclyffe Hall, Valentine Ackland, Vita Sackville-West. A 'pot-pourri' of women's names; a collection of images, of faces, hands and bodies, of portraits and photographs, iconographies of white, European women in this century and the last.[1] Tainted and stigmatized, set aside and marginalized or regarded as oddities and eccentrics, these women are nevertheless survivors, the visible remnants of a largely invisible tradition — lesbianism. Their 'masculinization', their habit of 'cross-dressing', the rumours of 'inversion' and the allegations of 'unnatural practices' which surrounded them, differentiated them from 'real' women and cast them into the role of deviants. What do their one-dimensional images hold for lesbians in the late twentieth century? What significance can we assign to them in the era of *Section 28* and the attack on positive imagery[2]? In what ways do their portraits influence both the construction of our personal identities and the creation of lesbian traditions, histories and mythologies?

What, too, of Jane Pirie and Mariane Woods, Scottish school teachers in the early decades of the nineteenth century? They were the subjects of much scandal, involved as they were in a protracted court case to clear their reputations of something not yet admitted to official discourses, namely female homosexuality. No portrait of them comes down to us but reconstruction work by Federman enables us to read the transcripts of the infamous trial and to put ourselves imaginatively in their places, objects of a judicial gaze which peered beyond them into the privacy of their beds (Federman, 1985).

Let us also consider Anne Lister, or 'Gentleman Jack' as she came to be known. A young woman living near Halifax in the 1820s, she committed her private thoughts, reflections and experiences to paper in the form of diaries: a conventional enough exercise for young ladies at this time, but the contents of the diary were far from conventional. Heavily coded, they contain many references to Anne Lister's lesbian desire and to the responses of other women to that desire. On Monday, the 29th of January 1821, Anne writes,

> Burnt Mr Montagu's farewell verses that no trace of any man's admiration may remain. It is not meet for me. I love and only love the fairer

sex and thus, beloved by them in return, my heart revolts from any love than theirs. (Whitbread, 1988:x)

How, in the absence of a highly visible and articulate lesbian subculture, was this 'revolt of the heart' possible? How was Anne able to know that heterosexual relationships were not 'meet' for her? If, under patriarchal relations, the gaze has become a male prerogative, what enabled Anne to gaze with desire at the 'fairer sex'? How did Anne come to recognize and experience herself as different during an era which, according to Federman, did not seriously pathologize close female friendships? Furthermore, what sense did Anne make of this difference and what does her 'revolt of the heart' tell us about the history of lesbian desire? Does it suggest, for instance, that lesbian desire is an essential but usually repressed part of female nature? Or does it cast us in the direction of a socially constructed phenomenon which emerges only within certain types of societies, at certain moments in history?

It is important not to confuse sexual desire with sexual identity, yet Anne experienced her desire for women as constitutive of an 'identity problem', a problem which she partly solved by her sartorial style. Anne's subjective recognition of difference was expressed by her refusal to wear anything but black and by the 'masculinization' of her appearance.[3] Through masculine dress, Anne Lister daily demarcated her difference and she did so consciously, deliberately. This was not unproblematic in her encounters with others but was, presumably, more fitting for her subjective sense of self than feminine attire. What did the 'objects' of her gaze, particularly her lovers, make of it and how did they, in turn, look upon her — a woman dressed as much as she was able like a man? She was not, of course, alone in her 'perversities' although she felt herself to be unique. In Llangollen, the famous and feted 'ladies', Butler and Ponsonby, dressed similarly, and in the previous century there had been scandals about female to male transvestites (Federman, 1981:47–61). What does this 'cross-dressing' signify and what are its implications for lesbian iconography and its interpretation?

Little girls have few positive role models of women and even fewer of lesbians. The lesbian images we do find, typically in obscure books, long out of print, seem to confirm the popular view that lesbians are 'masculinized' women. Lesbians who dressed according to prevailing gender conventions are largely invisible or passed over as 'pseudo lesbians'. What does their invisibility do to our understanding of lesbian culture? It is important to ask why these masculinized (and largely 'caucasian') images became the predominant iconography of lesbianism in Western Culture. Was it the case that the 'masculinized' woman became the 'folk devil' of a misogynous sexology whilst images of tribadism were feminized for the purposes of male pornography? We need also to know more about why such women adopted masculine codes of dress and body adornment. For this 'cross-dressing' was not primarily functional as in the case of the pit-brow women photographed by Munby, (Edge, 1986) or the factory women depicted in the work of Lange (Tagg, 1988:208). Perhaps, to some extent, the 'cross-dressing' enabled such women to assume some of the privileges reserved for men, the privileges of the 'male gaze', for instance. Perhaps, also, 'cross-dressing' facilitated subversion of the social conventions of gender and sexuality, providing a visible means of accentuating the subjective experience of difference.

The answers to the questions posed above are complex and largely outside the scope of this article. We can only begin to speculate on the effect that the sartorial decisions of Anne Lister (and those like her) had on the newly emerging disciplines of criminology and sexology. It is unlikely, however, that these disciplines would have been untouched by such striking imagery, an imagery in some ways reminiscent of the iconography of witchcraft.[4] It cannot be coincidence that the criminologist Lombroso and the sexologist, Havelock Ellis, focused their attention on the 'masculine traits' of their female subjects, taking them as evidence of 'delinquency' and 'inversion'. The body and its adornment was, and continues to be, taken as indicative of lesbianism. It has become the major object of the 'is she or isn't she?' game played both within and outside lesbian culture(s). In the cases of Anne, Jane and Mariane, the female body became an important site for the negotiation of sexual and gendered meanings. For Anne, it was a way of making visible her 'revolt of the heart', whilst for the teachers it was used to determine the normality or otherwise of their relationship.

As Valverde suggests, 'To think and talk about sexuality is first of all to think and talk about bodies' (Valverde, 1985:29).

Corporeal Speculations

Nineteenth century Europe witnessed the rise of numerous disciplines which gave much time to thinking, talking and, of course, writing about bodies. Indeed many of these disciplines appeared to exhibit a fascination with the human body. They included such diverse pursuits as Phrenology, Anthropometry, Demography, Forensic Science, Criminology and Sexology. In each, the gaze of the expert was given legitimacy whilst others, usually less powerful, were compelled to become objects of that gaze. Who looked and who was looked at became a crucial feature of the social relationships engendered by these enterprises. Concomitant with these new disciplines was the equally innovatory technique of photography, and many of the disciplines listed above utilized and exploited its potential. The camera and its products were employed to give visual evidence to the new theories. Thus bodies were increasingly subjected to measurement and to categorization, and checked for pathologies in a manner suggestive of the witchfinder's search for bodily stigmata. These bodies were then offered up to the photographic gaze.

John Tagg (1988:63–4) however, suggests that the 'evidence' provided by documentary photography is essentially contentious for, 'like the state, the camera is never neutral. The representations it produces are highly coded, and the power it wields is never its own.' In Tagg's view photographs can never be taken as evidence of history, and as such the search for an authentic lesbian iconography may not only be elusive but illusionary. Photographs, it seems, have to be decoded and are productive of many different, even contradictory, readings. In the early days of photography, however, the art or artifice involved in the construction of a picture was scarcely acknowledged. Many of the pioneers of the camera argued that the invention recorded what was objectively there to be seen. In a sense the camera 'never lied'. Since that time, despite many arguments to the contrary, photography is still afforded a privileged status. As Tagg (1988:160) notes the photograph is taken 'as a guaranteed witness of the actuality of the events it represents. The photograph seems to declare: "This happened". The camera was there. See for yourself!'

But the human eye that looks through the lens of the camera is neither ahistorical nor asocial, nor is the object of its vision. This is particularly so when the object before the camera is the apparently 'natural object' of the human body. There is nothing, however, natural or pre-cultural about the body. It is heavily endowed with meaning, and whilst the meanings attached to it might change, it can never escape signification. The new disciplines of the nineteenth century played an important role in encoding the body as part of a regulatory process. In this process, the gaze, its direction and command, was a crucial factor. Indeed, Tagg suggests that:

> . . . the working classes, colonised peoples, the criminal, poor, ill-housed, sick or insane were constituted as the passive — or, in this structure, feminised — objects of knowledge. Subjected to a scrutinising gaze, forced to emit signs. . . (Tagg, 1988:11)

Making a similar view, Foster (1988:18) notes that, 'Photography was harnessed as an instrument of control'. Thus, the 'experts' took control of the camera and possession of the gaze. In taking their photographs they objectified the bodies of the powerless, rendering them flat and frozen, incapable of action or change. In capturing the individual's body on paper the 'experts' effectively depersonalized their subjects.

A Subject Lacking Corporeality

Despite the nineteenth century fascination for the corporeal, the founders of Sociology were busily, for the most part, averting their eyes from the contaminating and polluting influences of real bodies. For as B.S. Turner (1984) reminds us, Sociology remained largely aloof from the corporeal concerns which obsessed the other disciplines. In Sociology, the body is largely absent except as a metaphor for society as a whole. In their flight from biological determinism, the founders of the discipline displayed a tendency to etherealize humanity. Bodies and their products were consequently neglected as a sociological problem. The disembodiment of Sociology was to have particular and unfortunate consequences for the sociological understanding of gender and sexuality. It left such matters outside of culture and vulnerable to theories dependent upon biological reductionism.

As Schiebinger (1987) argues, it was the natural rather than the social sciences of the eighteenth and nineteenth centuries which prioritized research into sexual difference and they did so in order to establish the biological bases of this difference. Schiebinger points out that this enterprise firmly excluded women who were consequently unable to adopt insider strategies to challenge the emerging 'scientific theories'. These in their turn appeared to demonstrate not only women's difference but also their inferiority. Like Tagg's passive objects of a 'scrutinizing gaze', women were effectively prevented from gazing back and becoming the authors of an oppositional theory. This, in itself, confirmed the naturalness of their passivity and the rightness of their objectification.

The Feminist Body

Whilst women have been largely excluded from the mainstream discourse of both the natural and the social sciences they have, of course, been engaged in discourses of their own, that Foucault has called 'counter discourses'. Feminist discourses have had a rich history of involvement with the body, particularly women's bodies. The primary concern of many feminists has been not only with seeking to gain control over the body (witness the various campaigns against rape, prostitution, domestic violence and those for reproductive rights) but with showing how women's bodies can be the focal point of resistance through hysteria, body-size and more collectively through practices such as *titi-ikoli*. As S. Ardener (1987) tells us, the genital area is a source of great pride amongst the Bakweri women and the collective showing of these parts is sometimes used as a means of expressing anger at the insults of men. In Western cultures, too, artists such as Judy Chicago have attempted to re-value this despised area, the labia, for instance, becoming a key emblem in her collection, '*The Dinner Party*'. Feminist writers and artists have been concerned with gaining control over the processes involved in the cultural encoding of women's bodies and with the deconstruction of patriarchal meanings. Hence the continuing and often conflict-filled debates surrounding the depiction of women in pornography, and the many critiques of the medical profession's tendency to pathologize women's bodies.

In feminism, we find, too, a rejection of the view that the body can be understood outside the realm of culture, society or politics. There is a strong feminist tradition which seeks to place the body, particularly women's bodies, within the social and the historical. T. Moi (1988) comments that de Beauvoir was an important contributor to this anti-essentialist position. De Beauvoir gives ascendancy to the social not the biological. Moi (1988:92) notes, 'Beauvoir's uncompromising refusal of any notion of a female nature or essence is succinctly summed up in her famous statement, "One is not born a woman; one becomes one".'

The theory and practice of political lesbianism has, arguably, extended this anti-essentialist stance to lesbianism, with its staunch rejection of any biological basis for love between women. From this perspective there are no 'born lesbians', no fixed lesbian essence, not even any social determinants of lesbianism. On the contrary, lesbianism can be chosen as a political strategy, thereby making identity more crucial than sexual desire and its expression.

In a different context, R. McGrath (1988) takes up the anti-essentialist position. In her discussion of photography and the body, she argues that,

> Ideologies of masculinity and femininity cannot simply be peeled back like a mask to reveal the 'naked truth' of the body. The whole point is that underneath there is quite simply nothing: no central core of identity or meaning. (McGrath, 1988:58)

Just more meanings! This pertains not only to gender but also, I would suggest, to sexual identities. From this perspective there can be no 'true' or 'authentic' depiction of lesbianism which transcends history and culture. This must be borne in mind when we come to consider the 'lesbian gaze'.

Yet there is another tradition within feminism, one which posits the notion of 'female specificity'. At times, as we shall see, this approach comes perilously close to an essentialist position. It is an approach, however, that has allowed feminists on both sides of the Atlantic to foster the concept of 'women's culture', a 'feminine' or 'feminist' aesthetics (Ecker, 1985). Analysis of the body and its role in women's creativity continues to be a central feature of this perspective. Such a position challenges the long-established view that the male body furthers masculine creativity whilst the female body, from menarche to menopause, inhibits the creativity of women. Writers such as Irigaray (1988) and Cixous have been instrumental in fostering this counter-view,[5] one that suggests that women's corporeal experiences can be the source of a rich culture. It is a view which advocates the construction of an art and a literature which arises from women's specific bodily knowledge, an approach, which in the context of writing, Cixous has called '*écriture feminine*'. Although, as Moi has indicated, it is not always clear to what extent such work is dependent upon the empirical sex of its creator. For whilst warning us not to confuse sex and gender, Moi (1989:114) suggests that, for Cixous, 'writing and voice . . . are woven together. The speaking woman is entirely her voice: she physically materialises what she's thinking; she signifies it with her body!

For Irigaray and Cixous, the specificity of women's creativity arises from their pre-oedipal relationship with the mother and the mother's body, a relationship which effectively disqualifies them from patriarchal culture, and one which eventually reinforces the fact of female absence and lack (of the phallus) and situates women outside of representation. It is a view of women's creativity which stresses and prioritizes touch and feeling rather than sight and knowing. Irigaray and Cixous are not alone in their endeavours. In cinema, Barbara Hammer[6] has attempted to develop film sequences based on a specifically female experience of the body, and many of the authors in '*Glancing Fires*' appear to be writing from a similar perspective. As Saunders suggests,

> Far from being biologically disadvantaged, women are naturally privileged; their pro-creativity is both prototype and archetype, the psychophysical ground for all creativity. In her sexuality — orgasm, menstruation, birth, menopause — a woman possesses the key to an understanding of herself as self and not other. (Saunders, 1988:22)

Thus, that which has been most objectified — our corporeality — is to become the major source of our subjectivity and agency, subject and object reunited and no longer split by the Western dualist tradition.

The dangers and difficulties of this approach arise immediately. In contrast to much feminist theory, the approach is both ahistorical and asocial. It also comes disturbingly close to its masculine counterpart in privileging the 'natural body' as determinant of culture (men are the creators of culture because they alone possess the 'phallic wonder of wonders'). It also seems to assume that the female body is one body, giving rise to essentially female experiences. Devoid of patriarchal misrepresentation the female body would be revealed in its natural, uncoded form, centring on the womb which bleeds and drips, reproduces and ceases in time with the seasons, or the phases of the moon. But as we have already suggested, the human body is never free from signification, it is always circumscribed by layers of cultural meaning, ritual and custom. The experience of having a female body is affected by the cultural practices of infibulation, clitoridectomy, mastectomy and foot-binding. Some women never menstruate and some who do remain childless or childfree. Lesbian and heterosexual women may experience so-called natural processes very differently and there will be diverse experiences within these categories. Thus women's corporeal experience cannot be reduced to the biological changes of the reproductive cycle (nor can our culture) any more than it can be reduced, in psychoanalytic terms, to the fact of lack or absence.

Yet in challenging essentialism we must be wary of etherealizing culture, of absenting the body altogether. For the work of Irigaray and Cixous, amongst others, has at least given the body a legitimate place in cultural creativity. It has also enabled us to question the primacy given to the visual senses, restoring some credit to the tactile ones, senses which arguably dominate at birth. It is interesting to note in this context the importance given to the hand in lesbian sexuality in contrast to that given to the eye in the heterosexual objectification of women.

If then the body can never be decoded to the point of naturalness, to a pre-social, pre-cultural essence, what are the implications for lesbian culture, particularly lesbian iconography? Firstly, I think, it implies that contrary to many sexological mythologies the search for the 'true lesbian' (by her bodily stigmata ye shall know her) is redundant. It implies the necessity of treating past and present iconographies to a process of decoding and the necessity of reconstruction, of a recoding that comes from the active subjectivity of lesbianism, a subjectivity which not only resists all damaging forms of objectification, all tendencies to biological reductionism, but also does not lose sight of corporeality. In reclaiming our bodies and the means to bestow meaning upon them we must also take back the power of the gaze. If this is, as Mulvey (1988) and Doane (1988a+b) would suggest, a masculine preserve, it won't be an easy task. Nevertheless, lesbian artists and writers are increasingly rendering lesbian desire visible.[7] Lesbian identities have also been the subject of visual representation. Recent writing in this area has explored the extent to which these representations are merely reinforcements of dominant heterosexist imagery or whether they are radical transformations vital to the survival and visibility of lesbian culture(s) in the era of *Section 28*. Further debates have focused on the vexed question of lesbian erotica and/or pornography, and the extent to which such representations open up women's potential for pleasure or merely exploit and fetishize women's bodies. The issue of sadomasochism, of pleasure and pain, of power, control and submission, of action, passivity and surrender, have all been the subject of debate. The problem of dichotomized 'butch-femme' roles, with their implied divisions between looker and looked at, the seeker and the sought, the subject and the object has re-surfaced. Writers such as Davis and Kennedy (1986), together with Joan Nestle (1988), have questioned the validity of these divisions as inevitable features in 'butch-femme' relationships, whilst Jeffreys has remained sceptical about their radical potential. The 'spectre' of objectification rises up on all sides! Yet Valverde has argued that objectification in itself may not be so reprehensible,

> . . . we must not react against our long experience of being treated as sexual objects by going to the other extreme and denying any and all forms of objectification, pure subjects. (Valverde, 1985:53)

Is it possible to look again at lesbian identity and desire without falling into the trap of fetishization or, alternatively, into the trap of pure subjects incapable of keeping in touch with our pleasures? This, I think, remains to be seen.

If Looks Could Kill

Glancing references have already been made to the notion of the male or masculine gaze. It is time to explore this in a little more depth. Understandably much of the work done on the gaze and on scroprophilia[8] has emanated from theories of visual representation. As Lesley Stern (1982:53) notes, 'The pleasure of looking has been much discussed in film theory, and in the process the innocence of this pleasure has been put under scrutiny.

Much of the challenge arises from radical reworkings of the psychoanalytic theories of Freud and Lacan, particularly by writers such as Mulvey, Doane and Irigaray. Noticeably, these approaches have tended to focus upon the asymmetry posited by Freud who considered the gaze to be a largely phallic property arising from a desire to master the object of the gaze. From this perspective the pleasure derived from gazing is ultimately bound up with notions of power and possession. McGrath (1988:57) has suggested that 'within the world of visual representation . . . (there is) . . . a split between those who look and those who are looked at.' Pollock (1988:134) has noted that 'Conventional feminist theorization has stressed the possessive look of the presumed masculine spectator at the objectified female form.' Though Pollock believes the situation to be more complex than this, for her, the masculine possession of the gaze is exemplified by the *Flaneur*, a character or type who moved about the urban world, voyeuristically and parasitically feasting his eyes on anything he cared to view. It was almost as though the *Flaneur*'s sense of self, his very subjectivity, depended upon his ability to devour others with his eyes. Essentially masculine, the *Flaneur* was one who,

> symbolizes the privileges or freedom to move about the public arenas of
> the city observing but never interacting, consuming the sights through
> a controlling but rarely acknowledged gaze, directed as much at other
> people than at the goods for sale. (Pollock, 1988:67)

As Pollock notes, few women (perhaps Anne Lister was one of the exceptions) could command the visual privileges taken for granted by the *Flaneur*, nor did they have the same kind of easy and unmolested access to public space. The feminine domain, particularly for the bourgeois woman in the nineteenth century, increasingly became the privatized world of domesticity. For as she argues,

> Women did not enjoy the freedom of incognito in the crowd. They were
> never positioned as the normal occupants of the public realm. They did
> not have the right to look, to stare, to scrutinize or to watch. (Pollock,
> 1988:71)

They were denied even the right to scrutinize their own bodies. As Irigaray reminds us, the speculum (a mirror, from the Latin *specere*, to look) was an instrument designed by the male medical profession to look into the very cavities that were hidden from women's own gaze. No wonder then, that Irigaray suggests that touch rather than sight should be privileged as a specifically feminine sensory experience. For women, like children, may be castigated for possessing or giving knowing looks (the evil eye of folklore) and their reputation may be at stake. The norms of nineteenth century femininity demanded that women should lower their gaze, narrow their vision and restrict their knowledge. Pollock (1988:71) notes that, 'the guarded respectability of the lady could be soiled by mere visual contact, for seeing was bound up with knowing.' There was much, too, that the bourgeois lady should not know about the masculine world, particularly the double standards of its morality. Not for her the 'roving eye' or the freedom to walk the streets. Indeed, then, as now, 'street-walking' or an 'immodest gaze' could provide a justification for harassment, rape or even murder. Thus nineteenth century bourgeois morality insisted on keeping women 'in the dark' about many things, not least about sexual knowledge. The Judges in the Pirie-Woods case were, for instance, concerned to render lesbianism invisible, imagining that the feminine world was inhabited by sleeping beauties. Yet Anne Lister seems to have found a way to see through the darkness, and since her time many women have continued to look and to take pleasure in looking. How were they able to do this in a world which denied them subjectivity and insisted upon their objectification?

At First Sight

In her initial work on the subject, Mulvey (1988) argues that the gaze is male and that women are excluded from the activity of gazing. Instead they 'can be said to connote to-be-looked-at-ness' (Mulvey, 1988:62).

In contrast, the male does not carry the heavy burden of sexual objectification. His role is an active one both on the screen and off it. He both creates and directs the action. Thus Mulvey seems to condemn us to remain for ever outside of the pleasures associated with looking. (By implication the heterosexual male is also denied the pleasures of being looked at.) In a later article, however, Mulvey (1989) revises this position in order to acknowledge that women can engage in scroprophilic activity. But that we do so wearing 'transvestite clothes'. (So that *was* what all the 'cross-dressing' was about!). She suggests (1988:78) that the female spectator accepts her masculinization in 'memory of her active phase'. Indeed, since childhood the female spectator has become accustomed to putting herself into the position of the male spectator, seeing herself and other women through his controlling and critical gaze. This has become second nature albeit rather a 'drag'! From this perspective the 'lesbian gaze' could be nothing more than a 'male gaze' in disguise.

Doane (1988a) also explores the difficulties inherent in the possibilities of an active 'female gaze'. For Doane, one of the major obstacles is that of 'over-identification' with the female object on the screen (a particular problem, perhaps for lesbians). When gazing at another woman the female spectator feels herself to be inextricably bound up with the image before her: 'For the female spectator, the image is *too* close — it cannot be projected far enough' (Doane, 1988a: 207). The female spectator is thus incapable of sustaining the necessary distance between the gaze and its object. Compelled to be the sex that is perpetually objectified, 'the simple gesture of directing a camera towards a woman has become a terrorist act'. (Doane, 1988b:216).

Reminiscent of Sontag's (1977) view that photography is subliminal murder, this statement appears to preclude the use of the camera by feminists particularly if they wish to take pictures of women. That this has ramifications for lesbian film-making or photography should be obvious. Lesbian desire and lesbian identities have already been rendered invisible, and to censor depiction because of the problems associated with objectification and the 'male gaze' leads to the disembodiment of lesbian desire, unless we can find a way of making two 'absences' into a presence.

The refusal to deal with visual representation and to argue for the primacy of touch as Irigaray does is to side-step the issue, although I am not unsympathetic to her desire to give less importance to the visual in women's culture. But as Moore suggests:

> To escape the ultimate sin of objectification (why is it in itself so terrible?) Irigaray retreats into the world of transcendent orgasmic bliss where subjects melt into object and where difference dissolves, arguing that touch is the 'true' feminine sense. In a culture where the power of visual images assumes even greater importance in our lives, this seems to me to be taking the position of the child who shuts *her* eyes believing that no one can see *her* any more. . .(Moore, S., 1988:56–7)

With the promise of 'transcendent orgasmic bliss' who can really blame her? But no, we cannot shut our eyes, especially if we are lucky enough to be able to see, and many of us would argue that we don't even want to. The question is, how do we achieve a greater measure of clarity in a world which virtually excludes us from representing ourselves? Stimpson (1988:227) notes that even 'the powerless have a culture of resistance, which works through code; through the direct statements of polemic; and through the indirection of irony and parody.' For, of course, women have been objectified, but we have not been totally petrified and turned to stone. We are not pure subjects any more than we are pure objects. Denied subjectivity (lesbians particularly so we have nevertheless found a means of resistance and re-asserted our capacity to act. Our bodies may have been exploited but our history(ies) cannot be understood from a perspective which reduces us to eternal victimization. For women have created culture and from the time of Julia Margaret Cameron (Hopkinson, 1986) they have commanded an active role both behind the camera and in front of it.

Mulvey has argued for an approach which disrupts the pleasure of the male voyeur and this is, I feel, a valid strategy. It is, however, one which fails to address the issue of women's own positive pleasures in taking control of the gaze. As Stimpson puts it,

> Should feminists picture women's bodies only as exploited, at risk, which they are, or should feminists 'put forward a politics that resists deprivation and supports pleasure'? (Stimpson, 1989:238)

The answer is probably affirmative in both cases, although what this pleasure might look like and look at is not unproblematic. For femininity has so often been bound up with the denial of women's pleasure (we give it, we don't have it) and the apparent intransigence of our exploitation. How do we, as women (particularly lesbians whose pleasures have so often been pathologized) take up our pleasures, particularly our visual ones? How do we take them with, and for, each other?

In the context of the representation of women on film, Lahire (1987:277) has suggested that we need to 'restore the integrity of the "whole body"? Whilst this borders on an essentialist position (what indeed is the 'whole body'), it nevertheless points out a direction which goes beyond a mere 'inversion' of the patriarchal 'male gaze'. We must be forthright in our visual statements and particularly so about the forbidden pleasures and experiences associated with lesbianism. Robinson (1987:13) states that, as lesbians, 'we need a new language of subversive imagery', an imagery which will free us from euphemistic depictions of lesbianism, without exploiting either the women on the screen (or photograph) or the sensibilities of the women watching or looking.

'Lesbian Looks' or 'She Must be Seeing Things'

In this final section I will briefly review a small selection of recent attempts to put lesbians in the picture.

Women in general have been denied subjectivity but this denial has been particularly profound in the case of lesbians. Alongside gay men, lesbians have been the objects of medical and criminological curiosity. As 'inverts' and 'perverts', we have rarely been granted the qualities of rationality and that ability to make choices. Gay Liberation and Political Lesbianism have returned this choice to us. We construct our sexual and social lives, they do not just happen to us out of some biological malfunction. This has had important consequences for the portrayal of lesbians and gays in photography and film. Rather than the objects of cinematic voyeurism as we were in the sixties and early seventies, lesbians and gays are making a visual culture of their own.[9] At times, this is on the cultural margins, at other times it engages with the mainstream culture. Whichever, the endeavour is fraught with many problems and if we expect to find a pure or monolithic 'lesbian gaze' we will be disappointed. For as Young argues,

> The myth of the 'real' feminist, the notion that there could possibly be a
> single feminist subjectivity, a single feminist gaze or project equally valid
> for all women, has been exploded. (Young, 1988:182)

Feminists are as much divided by class, race, age and sexuality as they are united by the complexities of gender. This is also true of lesbians, many of whom remain unconvinced or untouched by any version of feminist polemics. There is no *one* lesbian culture or political ideology to give clarity to lesbian vision. There are many looks and some of them are deeply oppositional to each other. This is particularly the case where the subject of the body and sexual expression is concerned. Hence the current debates over what has become labelled as 'vanilla sex'[10] and 'sadomasochism'. Thus we cannot expect a unified image of lesbian experience, only a constantly shifting, kaleidoscopic one.

One of the major debates both within feminism generally and lesbian feminism in particular is the extent to which we should engage with the mainstream culture or create oppositional strategies on the cultural margins. The contributors to 'The Female Gaze', for instance, appear to be united in the importance they place on mainstream culture and the possibilities of feminist incursion. After all, the vast majority of women are both exposed to, and exposed by, this culture.

Interestingly, mainstream cinema[11] has addressed both lesbian and homosexual desire and identities in recent years. We might cite here such films as 'Personal Best' and 'Desert Hearts'. The characters have been largely freed from the pathology bestowed upon them in the past and the endings have not always been tragic ones. Yet many lesbians remain deeply ambivalent about these cinematic portrayals. 'Desert Hearts', for instance, was greatly transformed from the original novel by Jane Rule.[12] Even the title was radically changed to something with less poignancy. The names of the major characters were revised and the differences in their ages eradicated. For Peter Mathews (1988), a gay man, 'Desert Hearts' failed, like so many other mainstream depictions of homosexuality, to present an authentic vision of the realities of life in a heterosexist culture. It failed, in particular, to establish a different kind of perspective from heterosexual romance movies. He argues that '. . . the price of acceptance for "Desert Hearts" is still therefore playing it straight' (Mathews, 1988:33). This is the opinion of a gay man. What about the views of women, particularly lesbians? Ambivalence seems to be the key word here. Pleasure that we were being given a glimpse of lesbian vitality albeit through the highly glamorized figures of 'Vivian' and 'Cay'; discomfiture at the compromises the novel is forced to make with the film version and a sense of unease that, yet again, women's bodies were being displayed for a male audience. I suspect that the major stumbling block for many was the 'love scene' (read 'sex scene') and not only because it exposed the women (and all women by implication) to a voyeuristic gaze, but because it was also euphemistic and mystifying. Rather than challenging masculine constructions of female sexuality it facilitated a view which allowed the men in the audience to be reassured by its sweetness, softness and reliance on seduction. But is this the 'whole picture' or the only way of seeing it? Contrary to Lord Meadowbank's view, the scene did show that 'venereal orgasm' could be accomplished without the male organ! (Federman, 1985:65). Yet this in itself poses little threat to the male gaze. The film (in contrast to the novel) ends by accentuating the uncertainties of lesbian bonding, its tentative rather than its tenacious qualities. Thus the tendency to 'humanize' lesbian texts and films (see, they are just like us really!') may have made them more acceptable to mainstream audiences, but they have also glossed over the very real differences between heterosexual and lesbian lifestyles, particularly the day-to-day oppressions which characterize lesbian existence.

Are lesbians different or are they the same? This appears to be quite a dilemma. A controversial magazine which celebrates both lesbian difference from heterosexual culture and the diversity within lesbian and gay culture has recently flourished at the cultural margins. 'Square Peg' styles itself the magazine for 'modern perverts' and is contributed to by both lesbians and gays. 'Square Peg's' deceptive ideology is that it has no ideology, 'drop your dogma', anything goes! It is a curious and often very disturbing mixture of critical reviews, particularly of visual representation and of erotic and/or pornographic texts and imagery. An analysis of its contents suggests that it both endorses lesbian and gay pornography whilst giving support to the necessity of an oppositional culture: a dangerous and often bewildering combination. It gives much space, for instance, to the work of alternative film-makers like Barbara Hammer. Hammer has a strong commitment to disrupting filmic expectations of gender and sexuality. She also celebrates lesbianism through a variety of visual strategies. Richard Dyer notes that Hammer has been concerned to challenge the visual metaphors associated with human sexualities. Rocks are freed from their phallic associations, whilst her use of natural shapes and forms challenges the unnaturalness assigned to lesbian desire. Yet whilst she bases her work on 'the idea of a different (from male) sensibility grounded in a different experience of the body (Dyer, 1987:10–13), the body, its representation and viewing are by no means unproblematic for her. Whilst making the female body and lesbian sexuality visible, she acknowledges that 'even in a woman-only audience, I think there would still be the anxiety of — can I experience pleasure at looking at a woman's body?' (Hammer, 1988:30).

Is this Doane's (1988) problem of over-identification again, or does the anxiety come not so much from the act of looking in itself, but from the lack of reciprocity involved? Perhaps lesbianism (except where it is circumscribed by the restrictions of 'butch-femme' conventions) to some extent relieves women of this anxiety. For I may be the one who is looking now, but soon the gaze will be reciprocated.

Kathy Myers (1987) has many reservations about such anxieties for she suggests that over-caution in representation, a kind of visual squeamishness, can also have its dangers. Ultimately it denies women 'the right to represent . . . their own sexuality, and . . . it side-steps the whole issue of sexual pleasure (Myers, 1987:283).

Ah, pleasure! We are right back to that thorny problem! Whilst for many '*Square Peg*' contributors, pleasure is not a problem (pleasure, however achieved, is a good in itself) many of us might find their conceptualization and depiction of pleasure deeply problematic. The work of Sheila McLaughlin is a case in point. Her film, '*She Must be Seeing Things*' is one much criticized by lesbian feminists for its apparent replication of heterosexual pornographic conventions.[13] McLaughlin herself is dismissive both of 'mainstream' and of many 'alternative' portrayals by lesbianism. She says,

> Lesbian sexuality has been represented in recent American film in a very romantic way . . . They don't deal with sex, which when you do involves differences of roles, gender and power. Lesbians, especially in the 70s, were represented as looking and being the same. I'm not interested in that idea of narcissistic extension. Sameness is very safe, you don't have to deal with the issues. (McLaughlin, 1988:34–35)

From the essentialism which sees women redolent of sweetness, goodness and mutuality, McLaughlin moves towards an essentialism which asserts the universality of sexual difference and the inherently sadomasochistic nature of sexuality in both its heterosexual and homosexual forms. It is a view which many lesbian feminists would wish to challenge. Sheila Jeffreys (1988) has questioned the liberating potential afforded by the accentuation of difference. Commenting upon the re-emergence of 'butch-femme' roles (a re-emergence that has been celebrated visually) Jeffreys suggests that 'the concept of difference is not benign — it is equated with power — sexual attraction is constructed around difference, i.e. dominance and submission' (Jeffreys, 1988:65–95).

This duality is the subject of much controversy concerning the nature of lesbian sexuality and the inevitability or otherwise of sadomasochism in sexual relationships. McLaughlin, for instance, argues that her work is intended to be an ironic comment on, or a parody of, these sexual conventions, but like many parodies it seriously backfires. So, too, I would suggest, do some of the more disturbing images contained in the pages of '*Square Peg*', an example being the images and texts created by Sophie Moorcock and Della Disgrace (1988) in their work '*The Ceremony*'.[14] It is difficult to know how to read this work without feeling that it is either a crass inversion of heterosexual pornography or a lampoon at the pornography of gay men. If it is a sexual parody, it is difficult to know what it is that is being parodied. The double women's symbol on the bare arm of one of the women appears at first sight to mock conventional expectations surrounding gender and sexuality. After a moment's thought, however, we are left wondering whether it isn't lesbian feminism itself that is being sent-up! Moi (1988) has commented upon the dangers of irony and mimicry in the work of Irigaray.[15] As she suggests, mimicry can be overdone to the point that the irony is lost on its audience and the woman speaking or writing comes to speak and write just like a man. Many of the contributors to '*Square Peg*' appear to run much the same risk. In the end there is often nothing new in their visions of homoerotic desire and identity, they are merely revisions of a rather tired and tawdry heterosexual way of seeing.

Second Sight

So what, finally, would Anne Lister have made of these diverse attempts to develop an 'authentic' and alternative visual culture? Would she have recognized herself in any of these modern depictions, thereby receiving a welcome validation for her 'revolt of the heart', or would she have found them as mystifying as some of her twentieth century sisters?

Undoubtedly more questions have been raised than answered in this article and if this is unsatisfactory perhaps it is also inevitable. Faced with such a multiplicity of perspectives it is tempting to adopt the pose of the legendary monkey who refused to see any evil. But in clapping its hands over its eyes how did it ever hope to see anything good? Thus we must attempt to be as forthright as the child in the fairy tale (was Hans Andersen mistaken in thinking it was a boy and not a girl who saw through the Emperor's New Clothes?) and remain steadfast in our vision, at the same time recognizing that the dualities of subject and object, visibility and invisibility, difference and sameness are not easily dissolved by the folk remedies of twentieth century witches. Inverting the gaze seldom transforms it and there is no crystal ball to help us whilst we look for an alternative vision.

Notes

1 This paper primarily considers the iconography of white women. The 'Gaze' is not only affected by gender but by considerations of class and race. For a discussion of the latter, see Roach, J. and Felix, P. (1988), and Sulter, M. (1987).

2 '*Section 28*' of the Local Government Act prohibits: the funding by local authorities of any organization which 'promotes' homosexuality.

3 An interesting comparison can be drawn here between Anne Lister's wearing of black with the nineteenth century poet, Emily Dickinson's, adoption of white clothing. Dickinson also experienced lesbian desire and wrote of it in coded form in her poetry.

4 Whilst there are many differences, some depictions of witchcraft present female figures which appear to be masculinized.

5 For a discussion of the work of Irigaray and Cixous, see Moi, T. (1988).

6 See Hammer, B. (1988) *Square Peg No. 19*, p. 31.

7 See, for instance, '*The Lesbian Gaze*', held at the Young Unknowns Gallery S.E.1.

8 Scroprophilia refers to the pleasure derived from looking or gazing. According to Mulvey, L. (1988:59), Freud 'associated scropophilia with taking other people as objects, subjecting them to a controlling and curious gaze'.

9 For a brief analysis of the different ways in which lesbians and gays have been portrayed in the cinema, see *Square Peg No. 19*, Film Issue.

10 'Vanilla Sex': a derogatory term used by those advocating S/M relationships to denote lesbian sexuality based on equality and mutuality. From this perspective it is viewed as infantile and not 'real' sex, as it excludes power as an element heightening sexual pleasure. There is an ongoing debate within lesbian politics over the issue of power relations within lesbian sexuality.

11 Peter Mathews suggests that there are three main criteria for ensuring the popularity of films focusing on a gay or lesbian theme. Firstly, if the film 'fulfils the compact and recognisable expectations of genre (romance, comedy, thriller), if it poses no obvious threat to dominant cultural values, and perhaps if it affords a tantalising but safely distanced glimpse of prohibited pleasures'. See Mathews, P. 'Crossing Over', (1987) *Square Peg No. 19*, pp. 32–33.

12 See Grundberg, S. (1987) 'Deserted hearts: Lesbians making it in the Movies', *Gossip No. 4*, pp. 27–39. As Grundberg reminds us, the original title by Jane Rule was '*Desert of the Heart*' (first published in 1964).

13 See, for example, *Lesbian Information Newsletter* No. 15, October 1981, p. 5.

14 *The Ceremony* is doubtless open to many different interpretations and can be read on different levels. At first sight the visual imagery appears to have all the ingredients of heterosexual pornography. It is even presented as the centre-fold of the magazine. There is the powerful, masculine protagonist and the virginal bride; there is hard leather encasing soft skin, the costume and paraphernalia of bondage, the fetishism of rubber, silk and steel. Despite first impressions, however, both the people portrayed in the photographs are women although one is 'masculinized' by her rubber uniform (black — the symbol of fascism or anarchism?) and the other is 'feminized' by her wedding veil and tight fitting bodice. The 'Butch/ Femme' dichotomy appears to be graphically illustrated here, although it is difficult to know whether these roles are being parodied or taken seriously. The women are therefore 'marked' lesbian, or rather the 'masculinized' one is — are we to gather that *real* lesbians are really pseudo-men? Is this the message being conveyed here, or is it this message, itself, which is being parodied? The 'Butch' wears a good-luck horse shoe tattooed on her arm below a tattoo of the double women's symbol. If this is a 'send-up' of both conventional wedding ceremonies and heterosexual porn, it is also equally a 'send-up' of lesbian feminism and its objection to 'butch-femme' role-playing. Through her veil the 'bride' bares her teeth like a wild animal. It she mocking the idea of the virginal and passive bride or is she merely reminding us of the pornographic convention which 'reduces' the woman to animalistic behaviour? If the visual text by Disgrace leaves us wondering about her intentions the written text by Moorcock leaves us in little

doubt that the piece is little more than a replication of heterosexual pornographic conventions. The written text is littered with references to the master (Butch) and the mastered (Femme), to sadomasochism and to the 'masculinization' of active sexuality. Even the specificity of female sexual response is subjected to 'masculine' imagery, e.g. the 'phallus of her taught (*sic*) nipples'. Confronted with both texts and photographs, the work of Moorcock and Disgrace may leave many lesbians wondering who it was intended for.

15 In her work *Sexual/Textual Politics*, Toril Moi examines and criticizes the use of irony as a rhetorical strategy. She looks particularly at Irigaray's '*Speculum*', which may be seen, at one level, as a 'parody of patriarchal modes of argument'. Moi questions whether this strategy really serves to 'undo' 'phallocentric discourse'. Moi notes that mimicry of phallocentric discourse may not always be perceived as such. It may be taken at face value, the irony lost on its audience. As Moi (1988) suggests, what Irigaray 'seems not to see is that sometimes a woman imitating male discourse is just a woman speaking like a man: Margaret Thatcher is a case in point' (p. 143).

This surely returns us to the problems of parody and mimicry revealed in the work of Moorcock and Disgrace. Their work leaves us unsure as to whether they are two women replicating aspects of the 'masculine gaze' or whether they are trying to disrupt that gaze through irony. This confusion arises because we are given no sense of the political context of their work, and as Moi stresses, 'it is the political context of such mimicry that is surely always decisive' (p. 143).

Indecision doubtless has its virtues but it may prove to be a dangerous state given the political climate surrounding *Section 28*.

References

ARDENER, S. (1987) 'A note on gender iconography: the vagina', in CAPLAN, P. (Ed.), *The Cultural Construction of Sexuality*, London, Tavistock.

CAPLAN, P. (Ed.) (1987) *The Cultural Construction of Sexuality*, London, Tavistock.

DAVIS, M. and KENNEDY, E. (1986) 'Oral history of the study of sexuality in the lesbian community: Buffalo, New York, 1930–1960', *Feminist Studies*, Vol. 12 (1).

DOANE, M.A. (1988a) 'Women's state: filming the female body', in PENLEY, (Ed.), *Feminism and Film Theory*, London, Routledge.

DOANE, M.A. (1988b) 'Caught and Rebecca: the inscription of femininity as absence', in C. PENLEY, (Ed.), op.cit.

DYER, R. (1987) 'Out from under', *Square Peg No. 17*, London, Square Peg, pp. 10–13.

ECKER, G. (1985) *Feminist Aesthetics*, London, The Women's Press.

EDGE, S. (1986) *Our Past — Our Struggle*, England, Rochdale Art Gallery.

FEDERMAN, L. (1981) *Surpassing the Love of Men*, London, Junction Books.

FEDERMAN, L. (1985) *Scotch Verdict*, London, Quartet Books.

FOSTER, A. (1988) *Beyond the Man: The Male Nude in Photography*, Edinburgh, Stills Gallery.

GALLAGHER, L. and LAQUEUR, W. (Eds) (1987) *The Making of the Modern Body*, University of California Press.

GAMMAN, L. and MARSHMENT, M. (Eds) (1988) *The Female Gaze*, London, The Women's Press.

HAMMER, B. (1988) 'The story of Hammer'. *Square Peg No. 19*, London, Square Peg, pp. 30–31.

HOPKINSON, A. (1986) *Julia Margaret Cameron*, London, Virago.

JEFFREYS, S. (1988) 'Butch and femme: now and then!', *Gossip No. 5*. Only Women Press Ltd, pp. 65–95.

LAHIRE, S. (1987) 'Lesbians in education', in ROBINSON, H. (Ed.) *Visibly Female: Feminism and Art Today*, London, Camden Press, pp. 274–283.

MATHEWS, P. (1988) 'Crossing over', *Square Peg No. 19*, London, Square Peg, pp. 32–33.

McGRATH, R. (1988) 'Looking hard: the male body under patriarchy', in FOSTER, A. (Ed.), op. cit.

McLAUGHLIN, S. (1988) 'She must be seeing things', *Square Peg No. 21*, London, Square Peg, pp. 34–35.

MOI, T. (1988) *Sexual/Textual Politics. Feminist Literary Theory*, London, Routledge Kegan Paul.

MOORCOCK, S. and DISGRACE, D. (1988) 'The ceremony', *Square Peg No. 2*, London, Square Peg. pp. 24–25.

MOORE, S. (1988) 'Here's looking at you, kid', in GAMMAN, L. and MARSHMENT, M. (Eds), op. cit., pp. 44–60.

MULVEY, L. (1988) 'Visual pleasure and narrative cinema', in PENLEY, C. (Ed.).

MULVEY, L. (1989) *Visual and Other Pleasures*, Basingstoke, Macmillan.

MYERS, K. (1987) 'Towards a feminist erotica', in ROBINSON, H. (Ed.), op. cit., pp. 283–297.

NESTLE, J. (1988) *A Restricted Country*, London, Sheba.

PENLEY, C. (Ed.) (1988) *Feminism and Film Theory*, London, Routledge.

POLLOCK, G. (1988) *Vision and Difference*, London, Routledge and Kegan Paul.

ROACH, J. and FELIX, P. (1988) 'Black looks', in GAMMAN, L. and MARSHMENT, M. (Eds), op. cit, pp. 130–143.

ROBINSON, A. (1982) 'Sex on film lesbians', in ROBINSON, H. (Ed.), *Visibly Female: Feminism and Art Today*, London, Camden Press.

ROBINSON, H. (Ed.) (1987) *Visibly Female: Feminism and Art Today*, London, Camden Press.

SAUNDERS, L. (1988) *Glancing Fires*, London, The Women's Press.

SCHIEBINGER, L. (1987) 'Skeletons in the closet: the first illustrations of the female skeleton in eighteenth-century anatomy', in GALLAGHER, L. and LAQUEUR, W. (Eds), op. cit.

SONTAG, S. (1977) *On Photography*, Harmondsworth, Penguin.

STERN, L. (1982) 'The body as evidence', *Screen*, **23** (25), p. 53.

STIMPSON, C. (1988) 'Nancy Reagan Wears a Hat', *Critical Enquiry*, **14**(2), pp. 223–238.

SULTER, M. (1987) 'Black codes: the misrepresentation of black lesbians in film', *Gossip No. 5*: London, Only Women Press, pp. 29–37.

TAGG, J. (1988) *The Burden of Representation*, Basingstoke, Macmillan Education.

TURNER, B.S. (1984) *The Body and Society*, Oxford, Basil Blackwell.

VALVERDE, M. (1985) *Sex, Power and Pleasure*, London, Women's Press Issues.

WHITBREAD, H. (1988) '*I Know My Own Heart: The Diaries of Anne Lister 1791–1840*', London, Virago.

YOUNG, S. (1988) 'Feminism and the politics of power — whose gaze is it anyway?' in GAMMAN, L. and MARSHMENT, M. (Eds), op. cit., pp. 173–188.

Chapter 8

Purity and Pollution: Body Management and the Social Place of Infancy

Anne Murcott

Introduction

'He's a sicky baby . . . even now, we have races him and me who's going to reach it first. Me to wipe it up and him to rub it in.'

'I won't give him coffee, I don't think it'd do him very much good really, because I don't have milk in it . . .
You said you don't give him pork but you do give him lamb or beef.
It's a bit rich . . . I think it's the only meat that, that will make me ill, so I suppose it makes me a bit prejudiced . . . I wouldn't give him curry, er I'd try him with just about anything really, unless it's very spicy . . . well I suppose you don't know how they're going to react'

'. . . carrot came right through . . . what, unchanged?
Hm, straight through . . . chocolate pudding and it's black'

Anyone familiar with the care of the very young will recognize the concerns and discoveries expressed in these extracts from interviews with twenty young women talking about their babies. Here, care of the infant revolves around care of its body. Such care of the body — body 'management' — is an inescapable element of human existence left, of course, neither to chance nor to instinct. It is social as well as biological. Not only is the expression of human biological functions and needs culturally shaped and socially organized, but so too is people's awareness (whether a matter of active consciousness or of culture and symbolic expression) of those functions and needs. Their conceptions, thoughts and beliefs about the matter are also cultural products — and can be investigated as such.

The sociological/social anthropological literature in this area is uneven. Unsurprisingly there is much more on beliefs and mores surrounding the great, preoccupying but perhaps intermittent events of life — birth, illness, sex, death — much less, at least in the case of industrialized societies, about apparently unremarkable daily activities necessary for biological survival — eating, excreting and so on. Eating has received some recent sociological attention (Beardsworth

and Keil, 1990; Messer, 1984; Murcott, 1988); elimination, its inevitable consequence, very little. Unsurprisingly, where the latter has been considered it is in
the study of those occasions when normal functioning breaks down, as in ulcer-
ative colitis (Reif, 1973) or rectal cancer (MacDonald, 1988). Nor is it surprising
to find that two instances of that rarity, the discussion of normal elimination, are
hedged by humour. Miner's (1956) analysis that the natural is distorted in the
relegation of excretory functions to secrecy, is part of his shrewd and delightful
spoof of Nacirema (American) body ritual. And Oring (1979) is surely playing
for laughs in titling his short article, '*From uretics to uremics: a contribution to the
ethnography of peeing*'. His data presumably derive, though he does not say, by
adding discreet observation to his unexceptionable participation in public men's
rooms in America. Like Miner, he largely draws on his own cultural knowledge,
rather than specially mounting an empirical study.

This chapter is about the body management of infants, especially of their
digestive tract. It deals in much that 'everyone knows': babies eat, or demand to
eat, apparently indiscriminately, they excrete even more indiscriminately — and
they cannot talk. Not a lot can be done about any of this except to wait until they
get older. What follows represents but one part of a larger, single-handed piece
of ethnographic research devoted to the study of cultural conceptions of food
and eating set in a South Wales valley carried out in 1979/80 (for full report
see Murcott, 1987; also Murcott, 1982, 1983a, 1983b). As such, the interpretation
presented here is culturally and historically specific. Further empirical investigation at different times and places is needed to establish the extent to which this
analysis may be generally applicable.

Four closely related aspects of the study's intention are relevant here:

1   the examination of the manner in which conceptions of food entail not
    only discriminations between food items, dishes, or meals, the suitability
    of foods for persons, occasions, the style, time, place and manner of
    eating, but also the very definition of food itself;
2   the relation these may have to the conceptualization of a range of matters
    of body management, e.g. concern for health and well-being, the recog-
    nition that the mouth is used for purposes in addition to eating, the
    normal biological (digestive) consequences of eating;
3   their relation, in turn, to the interactionally produced conceptions of self,
    identity and person;
4   treating all these as usual, routine and everyday, rather than anything
    identifiably out of the way, either socially (e.g. self-conscious devotion to
    gastronomy, veganism) or sociomedically giving cause for concern
    e.g. care of the infirm elderly, mentally or physically handicapped, or
    conditions such as diabetes, or anorexia nervosa).

The election to make infancy the substantive focus of part of the work was, then,
strategic in exploiting the greater acceptability of collecting data on elimination as
one set of routine (normal, healthy) bodily consequences of eating than might be
the case for adults. Social proprieties circumscribe the occasion on which such
things can be discussed: they are, though, allowable topics between two women
talking about an infant, its rearing and welfare.

What follows begins with mothers' cultural conceptions of feeding infants in the first six or so months of life. It shows first, how conceptions of suitable food, appropriate social occasions for feeding and so on, are intimately intertwined with those of infants as physically and socially immature. The discussion then broadens to show how conceptions of the body, its management and maintenance, especially of the whole digestive tract, shade into the related conception of babyhood as a social status, the place, in other words, of infants in the normal (adult) order.

Suitable Foods, Suitable Feeding

Ordinarily, milk is the first and only food for the human infant, from which at some later stage it is gradually weaned and other items introduced into the diet. While this much is overwhelmingly obvious, the manner in which all this is accomplished reveals in finer detail how bodily concerns are conceptualized.

For instance, while there may be no question that the newborn is to be fed milk, there is the decision whether it shall be breast- or artificially-fed. Body management for both the infant and the woman herself figured prominently in the South Walian women's explanations for their decision. The similarity between this group of women's discussion and those reported by Newson and Newson (1965), Hubert (1974), Martin (1978), Graham (1980), Martin and White (1985) is striking. No matter which method they actually used (nearly half had breast-fed at some stage) all twenty women considered breast feeding to involve physical discomfort (e.g. cracked/sore nipples, leaking breasts), excessive tiredness, risk of embarrassment, and difficulty in determining the amount of milk the baby takes; again, for all, bottle-feeding demanded scrupulousness in sterilizing equipment — precautions required to protect the infant's body from contamination and risk of disease.

Though varying from one woman to another, each had clear ideas about the appropriate stage in their babies' lives that additional foods should be introduced, with considerable agreement as to the criteria deemed relevant. These included concern for health, evidence of adequate developmental progress (largely expressed in terms of a general appraisal of the baby's apparent contentedness and with an eye on weight gain) and whether it seemed to be 'getting enough' to satisfy its appetite. As to the type of food chosen as the first food and drink other than milk, women had firm notions of what was appropriate. In deference to 'tiny tummies', food must be free of lumps, very well mashed or puréed; it must be bland in flavour, relative to the average older child's or adult's diet, and water used in its preparation must be boiled. Similarly, women shared conceptions of infants' daily timetables, and expectations that, even if too young to fit in with adult routines, the infant should (in theory) at least not be allowed to dominate the domestic schedule unduly .

Women painted a very familiar picture of the infant and its place in domestic life. Age is the overriding criterion. The terms in which mothers discussed feeding/body management did not vary between those with male/female infants; nor did these women refer to gender as a consideration in the care of so young a child. It was its immaturity and physical delicacy that dictated both its dietary needs as well as the special precautions about hygiene. Its present stage of growth and development, but also its future health and behaviour indicate the manner in which its diet is gradually to be amplified — it must not get too fat and it is to begin learning the social requirements of appropriate eating, requirements which involve among other things, adherence to other (adult) timetables. But it remains an infant, not just unable to feed itself or manage its general bodily needs, but above all, unable adequately to communicate more coherently than by crying, sleeping and smiling. If it is to survive, others not only have to undertake its body management, they must also devise means of interpreting such communication in order to discover and monitor what in adults would be self-indicated (cf. Blumer, 1962, 1969).

Adults daily monitor the progress of their own eating and drinking. Preference, satisfaction of hunger and thirst, digestive experience (indigestion, constipation, diarrhoea, vomiting, flatus, etc.), excessive or insufficient consumption of food and drink, are all regarded as within a normal adult's capacity to manage. Failure to manage this, as for instance in anorexia nervosa, risks classification as abnormal. Furthermore, they are expected to manage these in socially acceptable ways (cf. Elias, 1978).

Women talked easily of the five ways they monitor their baby's progress in feeding. Crying is an obvious indicator of something awry; women rapidly become skilled at interpreting what they regard as different types of cry. Another is an appreciation of the child's demeanour; seeming satisfied, contented and happy, smiles often and cheerfully lies in its cot 'cooing' to itself. A third is the child's weight; all women thought that keeping an eye on weight gain was important, although they varied as to how much importance should be attached to it.

The fourth and fifth indicators concern digestive discharges. Whether and how a child regurgitates is closely watched. All infants were expected to be sick a little. Some women considered their own not a 'sicky' baby, but as one observed, 'she used to guzzle herself. . . and bring it back through having too much milk.' At the other extreme is the occasional infant that initially and momentarily gives cause for concern lest a propensity for spectacular regurgitation should presage a medical condition that needs attention. One such was finally identified by the paediatrician as no more than 'a "chucker-upper" . . . just one of those sort of babies'.

As important, food and the progress of eating is evaluated in terms of faeces. Breast-fed babies are held to have less unpleasant nappies, faeces are held to be of a different consistency and colour from bottle-fed babies or those already taking foods in addition to milk. Ability and readiness to try a more varied diet is checked in terms of the digestive results: variously, orange juice caused diarrhoea, rusk made it 'a little bit more solid' and 'when we've had cabbage . . . when she fills her nappy by God the whole house knows about it, you know . . . really smelly, phew, cabbage-y'.

Of these five indicators, the last two have immediate and tangible consequences. Moreover, they simultaneously have considerable interactional significance. For these are actions which, though of course known of as facts of life, are held to be unsavoury and especially to be kept under control except in emergencies. They are not only literally, but also socially polluting.

The Social Management of an Infant's Gut

The type of food provided at any one age is not however, the only aspect of feeding that is of interest: when and where the child is fed reveals further concepts of appropriateness, reflecting the taken-for-granted nature of infants — paralleled by where and when an infant evacuates. And more widely, monitoring the digestive tract itself forms part of the continuing preoccupation with eating. For it is not only items defined as food that can get into the mouth. The very young use their mouths as well as hands for exploration.[1] And not only may the mouth be used for other activities than eating, there may also be substances emitted from the mouth, which in the normal, adult course of events, are also the subject of appropriate social management. On the grounds that they can do no other, infants can be said to be granted license to dispense with the social prescriptions surrounding management of the adult digestive tract. At the same time, other rules then come into play that govern management of the infant gut.

One of the most wearingly obvious characteristics of an infant is its frequent demand for food at unsocial (*sic*) hours. Women all discussed when they fed their infants and a composite picture of continual flux is the result. In contrast to the rest of the household who took their meals in the kitchen, living-or dining-room, most elected, for convenience and comfort, to feed the child in their living room during the day, and in a bedroom for night feeds. Where an infant would be fed however, in part depended on who else is present at the time. Breast feeding evoked the fullest discussion of the suitability of feeding a child in front of others, but anticipation that infants would take a couple of years to be able to learn some semblance of table manners was also cited. On the whole, adults eat socially, in public, but infants on balance are fed in private. Babies occupy a half-hidden, semi-sequestered position within the adult world (cf. Newson and Newson, 1965).

Parallel with the particular rules surrounding when and where an infant may be fed are those associated with when and where it may evacuate its bowels. If babies demand to be fed at unsocial hours, then too they excrete as and when the demands of the digestive processes dictate. The social enormity of behaving thus in adulthood is, incidentally, well captured by MacDonald's comment on the social plight of the person with a colostomy who 'may be defecating while cooking, eating, working, sleeping, making love . . .' (MacDonald, 1988:178). Though there is probably no direct empirical confirmation of the point, rules governing excretion ordinarily prescribe that the activity is separated in both time and place from most others, especially perhaps those to do with food/eating. Women would comment on their infants' propensity to do so while being fed, and jocularly accuse them of mischief in waiting until they had just been changed.

However distasteful the task of nappy changing, women all automatically treated it as one simply to be got on with, and some even said that they did not mind. Most accepted that it is in the nature of babies to be as yet untrainable, although a couple were seeking to persuade their infants of a few months old to use a pot, already anticipating the socialization required to teach their children the social conventions surrounding this aspect of body management.

As has already been seen, regurgitation was treated as a means of monitoring an infant's feeding progress. Vomiting and belching are in our society generally regarded as matters that by adulthood are to be contained within socially accepted bounds (cf. Elias 1978). By contrast, infants are expected (not just statistically but normatively) to belch; that is, they are encouraged to release gas from the digestive tract, and praised when they succeed.

Digestive emissions not only need monitoring, not only occur in ways that bypass or break the rules for adults, but the results need to be dealt with. Women devoted themselves to what some found seemed to be perpetual cleaning up. In addition to nappy changing, there were bibs, towels and cloths to be laundered, as well as frequent changes of the infant's clothing on which it may have been sick or wetted. Commonly the infant's clothing was laundered separately from that for other household members. Anything the child was likely to put in its mouth required special care: things that had fallen to the floor were to be avoided, dummies sterilized, spoons washed separately from utensils used by the rest of the household and so on.[2] Such monitoring extended to items themselves used for cleaning the child; they had to be reserved for the infant's use, specially clean/sterilized.

Most striking were the elaborate procedures for laundering nappies (at the time the data were collected, the use of disposable nappies was not widespread). Proprietary nappy-sterilizing products commercially available proclaim that their use is sufficient for suitable disinfection with no further laundering. Most women would, however, not only use such a product but also rinse/wash as well; one woman treated the nappies to a threefold cleansing, with a second proprietary germicidal nappy softener in the final rinse. At the same time, women acknowledged this double or triple effort was unnecessary, and recognized that they were engaging in ritual. Their conception of the need for hygiene involved this extra work to ensure achieving both literal and metaphorical cleanliness. Bodily wastes regarded as unclean must be safely and surely disposed of — although women would laughingly acknowledge that their babies were not themselves quite so particular about bodily emissions.

Women expected babies both to want to suck things and to be unable to discriminate between what was and was not thought suitable — apart from food, only safe, clean things may go into or approach the infant's mouth. It was held to be in the nature of the very young to try and put any and everything in their mouths. Their essential innocence however, does not protect them from the choice of something unsuitable.

One infant magnificently broke two rules of body management simultaneously:

Q 'Is there anything you'd want to make sure he didn't put in his mouth?'
A 'He's had mostly everything. When he's messed if you haven't caught him in time, his hand has been in it, it's been in his mouth. When he wets on his — well every night I strip him off about five o'clock, I undress him, I put him on a plastic changing mat, he's got a dry nappy and he has half-an-hour before I bath him, just kicking around. Well he wees everywhere — and usually it's on my carpet. He's found out how he can wee on the carpet and still lay in the dry. But very often he catches the edge of the nappy and of course the nappy goes in his mouth. I don't think it does him any harm and so — when he does a motion now, he passed one last night — I had stripped him off and never noticed. I'd gone to get his bath and

when I came down he's put his foot in it, he's put his hand in it, and his hand was in his mouth — but I mean, he's alright.'

Q   'What did you think when you noticed?'

A   'I felt sick. My stomach just turns, but I mean if he is sick on his bib sometimes, he'll take some of it back, but it doesn't do them any harm.'

This child did the unthinkable, making his mother feel sick. Repeatedly, however, she explained her belief it did him no harm. In time he would learn not to. In this as in other alimentary matters, women anticipated the need for their children to become accustomed to social conventions. Until such time, babies have a feeding and evacuating routine of their own, within which such rule-breaking can benignly be accommodated. Babies' whole existence in the early months is hedged about with the practicalities of hygiene and sterilization. Indeed, the sort of social position occupied by babies is enclosed by these precautions of body management. It is as if mothers placed a cordon sanitaire around their infants. Not only does this, explicitly in their view, literally ensure their safety, but also, as will be seen later in this chapter, it serves a similar purpose in metaphorical terms. But first the manner in which infancy is conceptualized requires further elaboration.

The Marginality of Infancy

In suspending usual (adult) rules and introducing new ones for infants, allowances are made available for the young in respect of body management, whether it be their timetable of feeding demands, their incapacities in respect of bodily emissions or whatever. Such indulgence is allowed for those considered not quite old enough yet to have learned. Others similarly in difficulties, the very old/incontinent, the sick, the insane, live with the ever-present risk of spoiled identity (cf. Goffman, 1963) and may be catered for in enclosed physical surroundings. Such categories of people are held to revert to babyhood, despite the obvious evidence of their years. While their affliction, in theory, absolves them of responsibility for their inabilities to behave as required, in many cases those inabilities are irreversible.

This is in direct contrast to the case of infancy. While babies too are held not to be responsible, it is their extreme youth, their innocence indeed which is the reason for their as yet unsocial behaviour. Their immaturity and innocence absolves them. Their youth testifies also to the confident prospect that in time they will learn. Their inabilities, unlike the sick and insane, are held to be normal. All babies are like this: but only some adults are incontinent etc. It is not deviant for a baby to defecate indiscriminately — babies just do this; it is deviant, although in theory not motivated deviance, for lunatics and geriatrics to do the same. Crucially, age is the key factor that distinguishes deviance from normality in this case.

Inasmuch as they are not cared for in specially designated total institutions, babies are, then, part of human (adult) society, yet they cannot participate in the same way as anyone older. Their age places them on the margins of the society of which they are a part. By definition, the newborn, although evidently human, cannot yet be social, have yet to be socialized. At the same time, non-verbally, they rapidly become competent and sophisticated interactionally (cf. Denzin, 1970; also McKay, 1973). Women talked and acted in a way that gave their infants' gestures and cries meaning that makes sense in an adult scheme of things; moreover, they also accorded them human emotions and capacities — notably in respect of indicating to the mother on the infant's behalf the manner in which bodily experiences may be interpreted, (even though infants did not always behave as if they agreed) (cf. Richards, 1974:87). Thus adults confer on infants a status as special types of person. Human beings are, among other things, held to be distinguished from other beings in displaying essential qualities of 'person-hood'. While infants obviously cannot be thought of in the same way as anyone capable of expressing themselves verbally, they are still accorded a human, albeit largely neuter, persona. And a central feature of that persona entails a paradoxical conception of infants as simultaneously polluting and pure.

The Duality of Infancy: Pollution and Purity

Women's imputation of innocence is one aspect of infants' purity. The data contain others. Women continually appealed to a notion of a 'good baby' — a being that eats as and when it should, does not cry unduly, is content and happy between meals, mostly asleep, sociable and undemanding. Welcomed (even when unplanned), much loved, infants are also forgiven: 'you'd do anything for them . . . it's all hard work . . . it's a labour of love'. Hard work it is: in addition to the constant rounds of feeding, changing, cleaning and so on, infants constitute disruption, notably of the adult order. Women talked powerfully and eloquently of the overwhelming impact of the arrival of their new baby (including those for whom this was a second or subsequent child). Pre-existing routines were overturned, pre-existing activities now out of the question, and pre-existing relationships (especially marital) temporarily out of kilter. In the early weeks one of the women's main preoccupations was striving to establish, or rather re-establish what for them was a workable domestic routine.

Embodying disruption in this way constructs infants as metaphorically polluting. If, however, others did not take care of cleaning work which babies cannot do on their own behalf, babies themselves threaten to become literally polluted: they would get into a humanly unacceptable mess. Furthermore, in so doing, they would themselves represent a source of pollution to others. Not only would a dirty baby become a threat to hygiene for those around, it would also represent a metaphorical threat to an order that relies on the observance of rules of cleanliness and hygiene. Without the cordon sanitaire infants would themselves be pollutants. The potential threat is there and has to be contained.

Analyzing the Pollution and Purity of Infancy

At this point, the analysis of the material presented so far is further developed with reference to Mary Douglas' book, *Purity and Danger* (1970), a work provid-ing an off-the-shelf theory that fits as if made-to-measure. In it Douglas presents a provocative framework for the analysis both of rituals of purification, whether sacred or secular, and of marginality. If, she says, we are interested in analyzing such rituals, we have to understand the whole system of which these are a part. Wanted and unwanted, valued and disvalued, clean and dirty cannot be defined in isolation, leaving us with 'the old definition of dirt as matter out-of-place' (Douglas, 1970:48). Dirt, and its equivalents, pose a cultural problem. It constitutes an anomaly. It stands out against a culturally prescribed pattern, and will not fit in.

It is culture which mediates individuals' experience; it is the source of tidily organized ideas and values, and provides a basic pattern. But as public matters, cultural categories are rigid; they are not amenable to rapid revision in the face of new information and events requiring classification. Inevitably this gives rise to anomalies and ambiguities such that cultural provision has to be made for dealing with them. The object of disorder is not only matter, but may also be people. Those in a marginal state constitute just such a case. Left out of culture's patterned classifications, though morally blameless, they are nonetheless placeless, of indefinable status.

Infancy, marginal in respect of human/adult society, in a position outside the routine patterning of life, creates for the newborn and very young just such a placelessness. At the very beginning, a baby's position cannot be fully human, it has yet to be formed as such. Indeed, temporally further back, Douglas herself uses the example of the unborn child to elaborate the position of the innocently marginal. In this sense, babies constitute an anomaly, but one regarded positively rather than negatively. Therefore some sort of suitable and safe place is to be found for them in society.

Safety, in the present context, can refer to the matters of hygiene, cleanliness and survival of which women talked conscientiously and for which they were responsible. But it can also refer to the metaphorical threat which marginality represents — the very point where pollution dangers threaten. And one of the various sources of power controlling fortune and misfortune that Douglas notes is precisely that represented by interstitial persons.

In terms of the analysis presented here, this neatly accounts for the social place of infancy represented in these particular data. What we have so far, is the proposal that marginality of babies threatens the routine patterning of the adult world; in this sense, babyhood is an anomalous human state. What we also have is material pertaining to routine work of cleansing and purifying in the management of those anomalous human beings. Notably, this work centres on the body in general, and the digestive system in particular. It turns on the management of bodily admissions and emissions — which brings us to the heart of the analytic argument.

For, as Douglas observes, bodily refuse symbolizes danger and power. All margins are dangerous. Structures of ideas are vulnerable at their margins. Equally, bodily orifices symbolize specially vulnerable points. Matter that issues from them is most obviously marginal. Milk, blood, spit, urine, faeces or tears cross the boundary of the body. But, she stresses, the crucial point of analytic procedure is to avoid the mistake of treating 'bodily margins in isolation from all other margins' (Douglas, 1970:145).

Thus, for the present purpose of making sense of the material about mundane and routine conceptions of food, feeding, hygiene and infant body management on the one hand, and of the material about concepts of person and identity of babies on the other, the two have to be analyzed together. Moreover, they also have to be analyzed in terms of each other along the lines Douglas proposes. In the process, contemporary concepts of babyhood will become clear and the manner in which adult society contains babies might be revealed.

The Cordon Sanitaire

An earlier section of this chapter introduced the notion of a cordon sanitaire with which women surround their infants. As Douglas' work suggests, the idea of dirt is literally linked with the body, and especially its orifices. But it is not only to do with the margins of the body, but also the margins of society. Babies must be protected from dirt both from the world beyond them and from the dirt that as living beings their bodies both create and represent. That which approaches the mouth has to be extra clean — water used in the preparation of infants' food has to be boiled, feeding equipment has to be sterilized. The waste which babies excrete has to be removed and procedures for avoiding contamination observed.

So babies have to be specially protected from both literal and metaphorical pollution. Not only are faeces unhygienic, they are also defined as unaesthetic, matter out-of-place — or at least matter which, in order to contain its polluting dangers, must be put in its place. Babies, by their nature, cannot deal with these matters for themselves.

> It seems that if a person has no place in the social system and is there-fore a marginal being, all precaution against danger must come from others. He cannot help his abnormal situation. This is roughly how we ourselves regard marginal people in a secular, not a ritual context. (Douglas, 1970:117)

Not only must these functions be performed by others on behalf of babies, the very fact that they have to be so implies a significant aspect of the manner in which those babies are conceptualized. As already noted, their inabilities are not the result of adulthood gone awry — as in the case of the sick or the very old. Their inabilities are the very essence of their nature — infants by definition can do no other, that is what being an infant is. In needing to protect and care for babies in this way, their essential nature, inability and innocence is allowed for and reaffirmed. In an important sense they are pure, their purity and innocence testifies to their inability to act for themselves, and by the same token that very inability is further evidence of their purity and innocence.

Babies are essentially innocent both in the sense that they cannot help needing so much and such intimate care, and in the sense that they can know no better. Babies' innocence can be pinpointed by reverting for a moment to the example described earlier, of the child who committed the enormity of putting his own excreta to his mouth. Not only did he commit such an act unknowingly, not only could his behaviour only be regarded as unmotivated, but he was also too young to be reproved — or for reproof to have been effective. Further, as his mother insists, it did him no harm. It did no harm literally, neither did it do so socially. He attracts no opprobrium for the act, nor is his identity at risk of being spoiled as a result. His innocence both protects him and is also thereby confirmed.

Concluding observations

What I have attempted in this chapter is an analysis of mothers' concepts of food and eating among their infants, which takes account both of the whole system of baby care and management, and the concepts of body and person which emerge from those data. Throughout this range of conceptions the watchword was ever the infant's age. Yet being so young, being so incapable, places babies on the limits of human society. Their vulnerability finds practical expression in the extra care with which feeding and cleaning is carried out; their capacity as potentially polluting and disrupting is to be contained and the success with which they keep this to a minimum approved. Babies' purity is displayed in the way they are surrounded with protective precautions.

Such precautions serve a dual function. The cordon sanitaire keeps the hazard of the adult world away from the baby, protecting it from risk. But it also contributes to containing the inevitable risk that the baby itself represents. Literally polluting emissions are suitably dealt with; metaphorically, pre-social and anti-social behaviour is circumscribed, allowed but forgiven. And within its bounds, the altered scheduling of infant eating and evacuating can be maintained without disrupting the adult order with which it contrasts.

To this extent, at least in the cultural context of South Wales in the late 1970s, babies are human beings out-of-place. They are like other human beings out-of-place, like the sick, the elderly, the insane. Like those others, they are contained; but those others may be confined separately from adult society to special institutions, and are at risk of carrying the stigma of deviant. Babies' potential for pollution, the threat of disruption that they represent, is contained differently, within the cordon sanitaire but out, as it were, in adult society. Babies may be human beings out of place, but their purity remains intact.

Notes

1 The following 'horror story' was described in one interview:

> A baby up the road, about three weeks ago it was, a lady in the shop, she was hysterical it, she'd turned round weeding the garden, she'd turned round in time to see a worm disappearing down his throat. She couldn't do anything about it, it'd gone
> *A whole worm?*
> The lot.
> *What happened after?*
> I don't know, I haven't seen her since.
> *How would you feel about that if, if it was Paul did it?*
> Well there's not a lot you can do about it is there really.
> I don't suppose it would do him any harm really

2 One gave her son his own tea towel.

> Yes, they're ordinary tea towels, but they are bright ones.
> I buy the bright ones because he'll sit and play with it and I don't mind if
> he sucks these, because I boil them. He has one or two a day, and they
> are his only, I don't use them for anything else, so it's alright . . . My
> mother-in-law thinks I'm fussy, but I think there is nothing worse, I
> mean I don't like seeing children dirty and children with runny noses,
> and I think when they are ill all over you and it's not your baby . . .

She evidently has strong, and perhaps not universally held views on the level of
hygiene and cleanliness required for babies. She does not, however, try and stop
her son sucking things, merely accepting that he will do so, providing something
that satisfies her as safe for him to use. Indeed at another stage of the interview she
explained:

> If we have chicken I take the bone out of the leg and he has that, because
> all the goodness is on that . . . bone that has no sharp edges on it . . . and
> he'll have a good old chew on that. He looks revolting when he's
> finished, but still it's good for him.

She obviously was not averse to his getting dirty in some way or other, being
quite happy in those instances where she regarded it good for him.

Acknowledgments

I am grateful to the women who gave time to participate in the study, to the SSRC
(now ESRC) for a small grant and to Tony Coxon, David Morgan, Virginia Olesen
and Phil Strong for their interest and comments at various stages of the study.

References

BEARDSWORTH, A. and KEIL, T. (1990) 'Putting the menu on the agenda', *Sociology* 24
(1):139–151.
BLUMER, H. (1962) 'Society as symbolic interaction', in ROSE A.M. (Ed.), *Human
behavior and social processes*, London: Routledge and Kegan Paul.
BLUMER, H. (1969) *Symbolic interactionism: perspective and method*, Englewood Cliffs,
N.J.: Prentice-Hall.
DENZIN, N.K. (1970) '*Developmental theories of self and childhood: some conceptions and
misconceptions*', Revised version of a paper presented to the Language and
Behavior Session of the 65th Annual Meeting of the American Sociological
Association, September 1st.
DOUGLAS, M. (1970) *Purity and danger: an analysis of concepts of pollution and taboo*,
Harmondsworth: Penguin.
ELIAS, N. (1978) *The civilizing process: the history of manners*, Oxford: Blackwell.
GOFFMAN, E. (1963) *Stigma: notes on the management of spoiled identity*, Englewood
Cliffs, N.J.: Prentice-Hall.
HUBERT, J. (1974) 'Belief and reality: social factors in pregnancy and childbirth', *in*
RICHARDS, M.P.M. (Ed.) *The integration of a child into a social world*, Cambridge:
Cambridge University Press.

MacDonald, L. (1988) 'The experience of stigma: living with rectal cancer', *in* Anderson, R. and Bury, M. (Eds) *Living with chronic illness*, London: Unwin Hyman.

McKay, R. (1973) 'Conceptions of children and models of socialization', *in* Dreitzel, H.P. (Ed.) *Childhood and socialization*, Recent Sociology No. 5. New York: Collier Macmillan, pp. 27–43.

Martin, J. (1978) *Infant feeding 1975: attitudes and practice in England and Wales*, London: OPCS Social Survey Division HMSO.

Martin, J. and White, A. (1985) *Infant feeding 1985*, London: HMSO.

Messer, E. (1984) 'Anthropological perspectives on diet', *Annual Review of Anthropology*, 13:205–49.

Miner, H. (1956) 'Body ritual among the Nacirema', *American Anthropologist*, 58: 503–7.

Murcott, A. (1982) 'On the social significance of the "cooked dinner" in South Wales', *Social Science Information* 21 (4/5):677–95.

Murcott, A. (1983a) ' "It's a pleasure to cook for him . . . ": food, mealtimes and gender in some South Wales household' *in* Garmarnikow, E. *et al.* (Eds) *The Public and the Private*, London: Heinemann, pp. 78–90.

Murcott, A. (1983b) 'Cooking and the cooked', *in* Murcott, A. (Ed.) *The sociology of food and eating*, Aldershot, Hants: Gower.

Murcott, A. (1987) '*Conceptions of food: a sociological analysis*', Unpublished PhD thesis, University of Wales.

Murcott, A. (1988) 'Sociological and social anthropological approaches to food and eating', *World Review of Nutrition and Dietetics*, 55:1–40.

Newson, J. and Newson, E. (1965) *Patterns of infant care in an urban community*, Harmondsworth: Penguin.

Oring, E. (1979) 'From uretics to uremics: a contribution toward the ethnography of peeing', *in* Klein, N. (Ed.) *Culture curers, and contagion*, California: Chandler & Sharp.

Reif, L. (1973) 'Managing a life with chronic disease', *American Journal of Nursing*, 73 (2):261–64.

Richards, M.P.M. (1974) 'First steps in becoming social', *in* Richards, M.P.M. (Ed.) *The integration of a child into a social world*, Cambridge: Cambridge University Press.

Chapter 9

Afterward: Constructing a Research Agenda

David Morgan and Sue Scott

It is clear that '*The Body*' is very much on the agenda, not only in sociology but also in history, literary and cultural studies and, of course, feminist and women's studies. To say that a particular topic or subject area is on the agenda may mean one of two things. In the first place it may mean that a new subdiscipline is in the process of developing. This may be one of a series of subdisciplines — the sociology of the body, the history of the body, the social anthropology of the body and so on — or it may be the development of a new, genuinely interdisciplinary, subject area or subdiscipline. This latter variation seems less likely at present and what we are likely to get is a series of subdisciplinary developments, each open in varying degrees to the influence of and developments within the other subdisciplines. In the second place, we may see a gradual and uneven influence through the different disciplines as wholes. In other words, rather than the development of the Sociology of the Body we may have the continuing development of Sociology but a development that comes to adopt a more embodied perspective. We have argued that we should prefer the latter although, in the nature of things, the development of a specialized Sociology of the Body is the more likely with its own course modules, text books and, eventually, journals. In practice there is no reason why those who wish to develop a new subdiscipline should not do so, the hope being that this development will not develop cult-or sect-like characteristics but will continue to be open to developments within the discipline as a whole and that there will continue to be some kind of open traffic between the more established sectors of the subject and this relatively new area.

In presenting this somewhat immodest sounding chapter '*Constructing a research agenda*', we are doing so in the hope that at least some of our colleagues, working in very different areas, will at least consider the possibilities of thinking through the implications of developments in the sociology of the body. The main argument is that the issues raised in the preceding pages and in many of the recent works and studies that have been cited here and elsewhere are 'good to think with'. To say this is not, therefore, to attempt to construct a new orthodoxy but rather to encourage the development of a variety of heterodoxies. As we have suggested, few of the key issues can be regarded as settled and there may be some doubt as to whether that might be a reasonable expectation in the first place. Our approach also allows for the possibility for practitioners to decide that a more embodied sociology is not for them after all. In that case, we hope that the search for the justifications of this position will be thought worthwhile.

At the most macrocosmic level we would see a continuing debate around the interplay between biology and culture. There are clear signs that this debate is well under way and there are reasons to hope that it will transcend some of the rigidities which characterized earlier debates around sociobiology (Benton, 1991, 1992; Sharp, 1992). Certainly some of the more assertive statements about the 'social construction of x or y' are being challenged and are being replaced by new realist or materialist models. Perhaps putting the matter another way would be to say that the label 'sociological' (as in, a 'sociological perspective') would signify more of a theoretical or methodological stance rather than an ideological claim.

As we have argued, the debates around the relationships between biology and culture will continue to weave around other debates and oppositions, such as those between nature and nurture, sex and gender, free will and determinism, agency and structure, and many others. We also argued that many, if not all, of these oppositions are unhelpful if they remain as oppositions, and that one of the main contributions of feminist and post-modern critiques has been in the direction not simply of rejecting particular dichotomies but in undermining the actual process of constructing such oppositions in the first place. We would argue, therefore, that any research agenda should begin by sifting through and scrutinizing some of the key distinctions and oppositions which might be deployed, and to see how an embodied perspective might play a part in this over-all critique. Of course, such a process of re-examination at this level of grand theorizing need not confine itself to the critique of oppositions and dichotomies: there will also be a place for the examination of other key terms such as 'self' (considered directly or indirectly in several of the preceding papers) and the traditional but by no means extinct term, 'role'.

In referring to large scale topics we should not confine ourselves to issues of macro sociological theory and the key terms and distinctions that inform such theorizing. Macro-issues also include issues of global significance, those issues which affect, albeit in different ways, every single inhabitant of this planet and which necessarily entail an erosion of traditional institutional or disciplinary boundaries. Since Howard Newby expressed his concern at the relatively meagre contributions that social sciences (and especially sociology) have made to the debates concerning the environment, there has been a slow but growing recognition that sociology has a contribution to make and that it should be making that contribution much more effectively (Newby, 1991). Here a concern might be that too much ground has already been conceded to mechanistic, determinist or biological models and that the proposed solutions to key environmental problems may oscillate between some version of a technological fix or an abstract moralizing, each relatively uninformed by a critical sociological perspective. What a consideration of any environmental issue must surely point to is the interdependence of the human and the natural sciences.

This, of course, parallels the interdependence of biological and sociological perspectives suggested by the development of a more embodied sociology. The parallels could, no doubt, be pursued in more detail. For example, it can be seen that both 'the body' and 'the environment' cannot be simply taken as givens but need to be subjected to much more detailed and critical analysis. The development of a sociology of the environment should be one which informs all branches of the discipline while, no doubt, developing its own areas of expertise and understanding. This again parallels possible developments in the sociology of the body. But it may further be suggested that the concerns with the sociology of the environment could be informed by the developments that have already taken place or which might take place in the study of the body. Environmental issues, after all, deal with bodies sometimes in the most direct and apparently obvious ways (population growth, the uses of natural resources, sources of energy, issues of health and individual versus collective responsibilities and so on). Near the top of any research agenda should be the establishment of a sense of flow or interplay between these two growing and interdependent concerns.

At a more down-to-earth level, it has been suggested that the sociology of the body might inform many, indeed all, of the traditional subareas of the discipline. To illustrate, consider some of the chapter headings in a recent, popular text (Abercrombie, Warde *et al.*, 1988):

Work
Class
Gender
Ethnicity and Racism
Family and Household
Towns, Cities and the Countryside
Education
Health
Culture and Media
Deviance, Crime and Control
Politics

With some variations, such headings might appear in almost any textbook developed in the past ten years. (The fact that this present example explicitly deals with Contemporary Britain explains the exclusion of more international, comparative or developmental issues.) Some of these headings, indeed, might have appeared in almost any textbook produced since sociology became a subject for such treatment. These categories are clearly part of the way in which the discipline is understood, taught and reproduced.

It is clear that some of these subheadings are already more embodied than others: health and gender for examples. However, it is also clear that all of these subareas have bodily dimensions even if these have not always been fully explored as yet. It might, indeed, be a useful strategy to begin to explore those areas which might appear to be the *least* embodied such as class, work and education. In term of our principal orientation that a bodily perspective is 'good to think with' there may well be sound reasons for beginning with the least promising material.

Wherever the starting point, there are two sets of questions that should be asked. In the first place, what bodily understandings are already present in these subareas even if they are not always explicitly signalled as such? For example, in the area of the sociology of education some fairly obvious contributions might be found in literature dealing with sport and physical education and with the controversies surrounding sex-education. Work on physical education and the body is already in progress (Shilling, 1993) and it is worth noting that the

Leisure Studies Association planned a conference on the theme of the body for September 1992. In the second place, the enquiry should go beyond compiling an inventory of what is already known and towards asking what new questions and issues might arise from taking a more embodied perspective. To continue with the area of education it might be asked, for example, how notions of age and maturity are constructed and understood, and what the consequences of such constructions might be for the routine ordering of school procedures. At an even more basic level, questions might be asked about the significance of physical size for social interaction and how differences in size are constructed and negotiated. Clearly, this is not the place for a more detailed examination of this or any other subarea. The concern here is more with the processes of constructing an agenda rather than the specific contents in any one particular subdiscipline. In all cases, then, the procedure would begin with mapping out what is known prior to a further mapping as to what might be explored.

However, there are limits to such an approach to the construction of a research agenda based upon existing lines of demarcation. This is not to rule out such an approach altogether — indeed, we would argue that it could well provide a provocative and useful point of departure — but to recognize that such an approach does have real limitations. In the first place, some major developments in empirical-based sociology in recent years (especially in Britain, perhaps) have been where conventional boundaries have been questioned and dissolved or redrawn. This has been especially notable in the case of the sociology of work, where feminist critiques, the impact of unemployment as a permanant feature of the industrial landscape, and discussions of many forms of hidden or unpaid labour have led to some major redrawing of the boundaries. Thus the household becomes an essential element in the understanding of economic life, rather than being located in the private sphere through being bracketted with the family. The work of Foucault has, of course, been a major stimulus to this crossing of conventional boundaries as, for example, in the development of Foucaultian, and hence more embodied, approaches to debates around the labour process (Austrin, 1992).

Secondly, some major theoretical developments have pointed in the direction of a critique of all such demarcation lines rather than simply a questioning of any one particular set of boundaries. Feminist research and theory has played a major part here, one which has been clearly acknowledged throughout the present volume. In part linked to and overlapping with this has been a post-modernist critique of some of the major grand-narratives and the apparently stable institutional structure upon which sociology, in common with other disciplines, might have traditionally been based. Thus for these, and for other reasons, there are limitations to developing a research-based sociology of the body around existing subdisciplinary units.

Thus the sociology of the body might look elsewhere, to other areas of development which are, similarly, cutting across and challenging existing subdisciplinary divisions. One such development, clearly linked to the sociology of the body, is the study of the emotions. Again, this is not the place to map out all that is or might be entailed in the development of this new area. What is clear, however, is that through a critical reappraisal of the role of emotions in social life, their social construction and social deployment, and through the wider critique of conventional notions of rationality that such a reappraisal necessarily entails, we are witnessing the development of a perspective that shows scant regard for the existing divisions enshrined in textbooks. It is also clear (again several of the papers in this volume explicitly draw attention to this fact) that the study of the emotions has a large number of points of intersection with the study of the body.

The same is true of two other developments and concerns that have come to the fore in recent years, dealing with the fundamental categories of space and time. The latter in particular has been the subject of considerable attention in recent years and is likely, like the sociology of the body, to become a lively subarea in its own right. However, it is likely that the true importance of the development of a more temporal perspective within sociology (not to mention other disciplines) is the development of an area and a set of considerations which cut across and often call into question existing demarcations. In this respect we can see the development of a sociological understanding of time as being parallel to the development of the sociology of the body. And, once again, the metaphor of parallel development is misleading since the two obviously interweave and intersect at so many points. The life course, for example, is a complexely embodied as well as a temporal trajectory. Similar observations may be made regarding more sophisticated understandings of the social dimensions of space. In all cases we are moving towards an understanding of some of the fundamental categories of understanding, a realization of the sociologies of knowledge proposed by Durkheim and, later, by Berger and Luckmann. Such approaches would not necessarily eliminate some of the more traditional institution-based categories — work, family, religion etc; — but would place these at a somewhat less general level than the more fundamental concerns dealing with emotions, time, space and the body.

References

ABERCROMBIE, N., WARDE, A. *et al.* (1988) Contemporary British Society, Cambridge, Polity.

AUSTRIN, T. (1992) '*The dispersal of power and the politics of articulation*', Unpublished Paper, Department of Sociology, University of Canterbury, Christchurch, New Zealand.

BENTON, T. (1991) 'Biology and social science: Why the return of the repressed should be given (cautious) welcome', *Sociology*, **25**(1), pp. 1–30.

BENTON, T. (1992) 'Why the welcome needs to be cautious: A reply to Keith Sharp', *Sociology*, **26**(2), pp. 225–232.

NEWBY, H. (1991) British Sociological Association Public Lecture London, (Feb 1991).

SHARP, K. (1992) 'Biology and social science: A reply to Ted Benton', *Sociology*, **26**(2), pp. 219–224.

SHILLING, C. (1993) *The Body and Social Theory*, London, Sage.

Notes on Contributors

DAVID CLARK has written widely on issues to do with marriage, families and domestic life; he has a special interest in divorce and remarriage and also in therapeutic responses to 'marital problems'. His recent books include: an edited volume, *Marriage, Domestic Life and Social Change: Writings for Jacqueline Burgoyne (1944–88)* (Routledge, 1991), and (with Jane Lewis and David Morgan) *Whom God Hath Joined Together: The Work of Marriage Guidance* (Routledge, 1992). He is a Principal Lecturer in the School of Health and Community Studies at Sheffield City Polytechnic and Senior Research Fellow at the Trent Palliative Care Centre, where his current research is concerned with death, dying and terminal care.

SUSAN S.M. EDWARDS teaches Criminology/Criminal Justice, and 'Sex and Gender in the Legal Process' at the School of Law, the University of Buckingham. She is author of *Female Sexuality and the Law* (1981), *Women on Trial* (1984), *Policing 'Domestic' Violence* (1989) and has edited *Gender, Sex and the Law* (1985) and, with J. Horder, *The Gender Politics of Homicide* (forthcoming). She is currently engaged in research into violence and pornography and the Obscene Publications Act.

Dr ALAN MANSFIELD lectures in communication studies in the School of Humanities, Murdoch University, Western Australia.

BARBARA McGINN is a tax consultant, competitive bodybuilder and sometime academic with a background in social theory. Currently interested in masculinity, transvestism, bodily transformations.

DAVID MORGAN has taught Sociology at the University of Manchester since 1964. Currently, his main interests are the sociology of marriage and family life, and the sociology of gender, with particular reference to issues of masculinities and violence. He is author of *Social Theory and the Family* (Routledge & Kegan Paul, 1975), *The Family, Politics and Social Theory* (Routledge & Kegan Paul; 1985) and *Discovering Men* (Routledge, 1992).

ANNE MURCOTT, a social anthropologist by training, taught sociology in Cardiff before moving to the London School of Hygiene and Tropical Medicine where she now holds a senior lectureship. She was Editor of *Sociology of Health and Illness* from 1983–88; her main interests are in the anthropology/sociology of food.

SUE SCOTT has been involved in health-related research for a number of years, including work with the Women, Risk and AIDS Project (WRAP). She has been a lecturer in sociology at the University of Manchester where she taught on 'The Sociology of the Body' amongst other things. She has moved to a senior lecturership at the University of Stirling, where she hopes to continue to develop her interest in questions of embodiment.

JOYCE SHERLOCK is Head of Social Science at Bedford College of Higher Education. Her research and teaching revolve around sociological aspects of physical activity and have focused on leisure, education and feminism, P.E. and sport. She is currently writing a book on dance in contemporary culture, motivated by her Ph.D. research and a recent visit to Cuba, a 'dance culture'.

RUTH WATERHOUSE is a senior lecturer in Sociology at Staffordshire University, where she has been lecturing in the Sociology of Crime and Deviance, the Sociology of Culture, Social Psychology, Introductory Sociology and Women in Society since the late 1970s. In 1990–1991, she took sabbatical leave and studied for an MA in Counselling Studies at the University of Keele.

Index